CRYPTOSCATOLOGY:
CONSPIRACY THEORY AS ART FORM

ROBERT GUFFEY

CRYPTOSCATOLOGY: CONSPIRACY THEORY AS ART FORM

Published by:
Trine Day LLC
PO Box 577
Walterville, OR 97489
1-800-556-2012
www.TrineDay.com
publisher@trineday.net

Library of Congress Control Number: 2011942527

Guffey, Robert.
Cryptoscatology: Conspiracy Theory As Art Form—1st ed.
p. cm.
Includes bibliography.
Epub (ISBN-13) 978-1-936296-41-5 (ISBN-10) 1-936296-41-1
Kindle (ISBN-13) 978-1-936296-42-2 (ISBN-10) 1-936296-42-X
Print (ISBN-13) 978-1-936296-40-8 (ISBN-10) 1-936296-40-3
1. Conspiracy theories – Social aspects. 2. Conspiracies – Case studies.
3. Popular culture – United States. I. Title

FIRST EDITION
10 9 8 7 6 5 4 3 2 1

Printed in the USA
Distribution to the Trade by:
Independent Publishers Group (IPG)
814 North Franklin Street
Chicago, Illinois 60610
312.337.0747
www.ipgbook.com

Publisher's Foreword

Nothing can now be believed which is seen in a newspaper. Truth itself becomes suspicious by being put into that polluted vehicle. The real extent of this state of misinformation is known only to those who are in situations to confront facts within their knowledge with the lies of the day.
— Thomas Jefferson

What can anyone say? Things haven't changed much, and the 21st century isn't all that it was cracked up to be – or wait a minute – did Orwell's *1984*, a world of "official deception, secret surveillance, and manipulation of the past in service to manipulative political agenda," become reality?

From my standpoint, it sure seems so. TrineDay has been publishing books with inconvenient truths in them for over ten years. We can get the word out through the Internet, and some talk radio, but newspapers and the rest of mainstream media simply ignore our books. According to Jefferson, maybe the newspaper's silence is a good thing, but alas no. When our institutions fail their civic duty, we all pay the price.

Is there something we can do? I find solace, hope and even epiphany in trying to understand our world in which we live, and working to end the corruptions, exploitations and criminalities that hold it in sway. To my thinking this is not a battle-dynamic against Evil, but a long hard slog of exposing evil schemes of men – hidden within the framework of everyday life – that appear good or bad, depending on your world view. These world views are then played against one another in the most sinister of games, psychological warfare: a cacophony of voices alienating us from our civic duties and natural environments.

I first became aware of the term "conspiracy theory" when I told friends in the 1970s about things my repentant CIA/OSS/G2 father had revealed to me. They called me a "conspiracy theorist," and I decided to take up conspiracy theory as a field of study. What a wild ride! I would go into any and every bookstore

I could find, and say, "Take me to your conspiracy section." Each had at least one volume about conspiracies. Conspiracies that blamed sundry groups for all the troubles in the world. There were books that blamed it all on the Catholics, the Hippies, the Mormons, the Freemasons, the Secular-Humanists, the Right, the Left, Feminism, Communism, the Rockefellers and of course the Jews. As a matter of fact some of the books appeared formulaic: designed to pit people against each other.

As the 1970s and '80s receded, the interest in conspiracy theory grew, and with the advent of the Internet the subject exploded, even spawning a movie – *Conspiracy Theory* in 1997.

Robert Guffey's *Cryptoscatology: Conspiracy Theory as Art Form* examines the "genre" in the emerging light of today's sophistications, taking the reader on a journey into the "conspiracy world." Guffey takes to task, with humor, many of the vexing conundrums one finds in conspiracy literature, and explores the question of religion and its role in people's world view.

Guffey does a masterful job of bringing an odd world into focus through the lens of conspiracy theory. He will introduce you to people you know, people you've only heard about, and some who you never knew existed. So enjoy yourself and take time to delve into the art form of Conspiracy Theory.

> *...that truth is great and will prevail if left to herself; that she is the proper and sufficient antagonist to error, and has nothing to fear from the conflict unless by human interposition disarmed of her natural weapons, free argument and debate; errors ceasing to be dangerous when it is permitted freely to contradict them.*
> — Thomas Jefferson

Onward to the Utmost of Futures!

Peace,
Kris Millegan
Publisher
TrineDay
March 19, 2012

To Melissa
for encouraging me to put all the pieces of the puzzle
together

ACKNOWLEDGEMENTS

I'd like to briefly thank a few individuals who have been instrumental in helping me complete this book:

First, the various editors who originally published these pieces: Joan d'Arc and Al Hidell (*The Conspiracy Reader, The New Conspiracy Reader*, and *Paranoia*), Val Stevenson and David Sutton (*Fortean Times*), Chad Tsuyuki and Joanne Kozovich (*Like Water Burning*), and David Jones (*New Dawn Magazine*).

Second, Catherine Bottolfson McCallum for reading everything first.

Third, Randy Koppang for his research assistance (particularly with regard to the chapter titled "Concentration Campus").

Fourth, Eric Blair for his invaluable editorial assistance.

CONTENTS

"The police state has now become a work of art."
–Marshall McLuhan, *Take Today: The Executive as Dropout*, 1972

"While you here do snoring lie
Open-eyed conspiracy
His time doth take.
If of life you keep a care,
Shake off slumber and beware.
Awake, awake!"
—William Shakespeare, *The Tempest*, 1610

CONSPIRACY THEORY AS ART FORM

Alis, Alas, She Broke the Glass!

On July 20, 1999, I delivered a lecture about conspiracies in the back of a late, lamented bookstore called The Midnight Special that used to be located on the 3rd Street Promenade in Santa Monica, California. One of the few independent bookstores left in Southern California, it specialized in hard-to-find, alternative sources of information. In the back of the store political researchers as scholarly as Mike Davis, author of the bestseller *Ecology of Fear,* or as infamous as Christopher Hitchens, author of *God Is Not Great: How Religion Poisons Everything,* would hold court. One memorable evening the latter individual nearly got into a fist fight with a Lyndon LaRouche supporter in the first row and the cops had to be called out to break up the scene. It was a lively crowd that attended these lectures, by no means a tepid coffee klatch book club for blue-haired octogenarians eager to dissect the latest Oprah selection.

The lecture I delivered was based on an article you'll find in this very book: "Science Fiction as Manipulation: SF's Intersection with the Intelligence Community." The lecture went on well over two hours and received a positive response from the audience. One gentleman, an elderly political activist who had once worked for Jet Propulsion Laboratories and had been partly responsible for restoring Simon Rodia's Watts Towers to their prior glory, shot up out of his seat and insisted I was lying when I said that the letters JPL actually stood for Jack Parsons Laboratories. (If you want to know why that offended him, just skip ahead and read Chapter Five.) Instead of arguing with him, as Mr. Hitchens had done with his heckler, I tried to calm him down with humor. And unlike with Mr. Hitchens' performance, the cops didn't have to be called out to break up a fistfight.

Apparently one particular member of the audience was impressed with this approach. The next day I received a phone call from a stranger who told me he'd seen my lecture the previous night. I thought the voice sounded familiar and was trying to place it when the man said, "I'm Paul Krassner. I don't know if you've heard of me or not, but I publish this newsletter called *The Realist*."

Krassner could have no way of knowing that I was *very* familiar with him and his work. *The Realist* had been for decades one of the greatest satirical magazines published in post-war America. I was a fan of his writing and considered his autobiography, *Confessions of a Raving Unconfined Nut*, to be one of the funniest books written in the past fifty years. He had been a stand-up comedian since the early '60s and had been close friends with the greatest stand-up comedian of all time, Lenny Bruce, a relationship he writes about extensively in his autobiography.

This is what Krassner told me: He was surprised to hear a lecture delivered by a "conspiracy theorist" who also had a sense of humor and could make an audience laugh in between the inevitable scattershot recitation of historical factoids. Every other conspiracy theorist he'd ever met had been as humorless as... well, as humorless as a guy who's into conspiracy theories. This isn't a surprise. If you need a good laugh, a political junkie is the last person to rely upon. Just switch on CNN and see what I mean. You'll see a bunch of heart attacks with neckties waiting to implode.

I was proud of the way I had woven humor into what I felt was a well-researched presentation, so I was pleased that someone as wise and funny as Krassner had thought so much of it that he'd actually go to the trouble of digging up my phone number and asking me to write an article for his newsletter. Unfortunately, *The Realist* finally died in the Spring of 2001 and the article I wrote for Krassner later appeared in a different magazine. It appears in this book as Chapter One, as I felt it would set the proper tone for the rest of the volume.

During that phone conversation with Krassner, he said something that has always stuck with me. He said (and I'm paraphrasing here): "For some reason a lot of the greatest stand-up comedians have also been obsessed with conspiracies." He threw out a lot of names, only some of which I can recall right now: Richard Belzer, Mort Sahl, Freddie Prinze (Senior, not Junior), Dick Gregory, Krassner himself. Even Lenny Bruce. Hell, Bruce was the *victim* of a vast political conspiracy. How could he help *not* being obsessed with conspiracies near the end of his life? Conspiracies were breathing down his neck, hounding him into an early grave.

The conversation was brief, and yet the question has always lingered in my mind: *Why* would so many comedians be obsessed with conspiracy theories? What's the connection? If any trait is consistent from conspiracy theorist to conspiracy theorist, it's the indestructible drive to make connections between disparate subjects, sometimes where there are none. In this case, however, I think a reasonable connection can be made.

Both comedians and conspiracy theorists *must* see the world through an alternate set of eyes, a warped Alice-like looking glass, in order to get their jobs done. The best comedians are modern day shamans, those who hold up a mirror to the mundane world, peer deeply into it, see the things the rest of us are not capable of seeing or are too afraid to see, and come back from their journeys with visions to share. Usually what they tell us is more than obvious. That's why we laugh. We should've seen it ourselves. It was right there in front of us all the time, wasn't it? That's why we nod while laughing, suddenly realizing that we'd thought the same thing a million times before but were too embarrassed (or repressed) to actually mention this transgressive thought out loud. Comedians break taboos in a socially acceptable forum. The most dangerous comedians could never get away with performing their routines in a room full of strangers who had not *paid* to hear them. In fact, without the presence of a microphone and a stage, the very same lines that rake in millions for some comedians would—in the right (or *wrong*) circumstances—win them several blows to the face and the groin.

Similarly, when we listen to a conspiracy theorist unweave a tale well-told we are nodding in recognition as well, but this time not because our funny bone has been tickled but because our darkest fears are now being confirmed. Conspiracy theories emerge from the twisted, upside down, nightmare version of the world our greatest comedians inhabit, a world in which our recognition turns to fear and not laughter. In our worst paranoid moments we suspected that this awful possibility, whatever it is, *might* be true… but now we've had all these fears confirmed by the inevitable scattershot recitation of historical factoids that back them up with unassailable authority and simply make them *so*.

Both are alternative visions of the world. Both are told to us by shamans returning from the places the rest of us dare not go. And both know how to tell a good story.

There are a lot of stories in this volume. I consider myself to be primarily a storyteller. That doesn't mean these articles are fictional. Nor are they jokes disguised as truth. Oliver Stone once described his film *JFK* as "an alternative myth." Historians might consider that to be waffling; I, on the other hand, find it to be the most accurate description possible, particularly in a world full of "specialists" who insist they alone know for certain where truth ends and fiction begins. The late literary scholar Joseph Campbell considered myths to be more accurate than truth. In a world where the Blue Meanies in charge can be relied upon to lie to your face every single day without even blinking, people better start praying for a lot more myths and a lot fewer lies.

Fear and laughter, by themselves, never motivated anybody to take positive action in the world, but both can be motivating factors toward a sudden behavioral change in almost anyone. Every paradigm shift comes with a little fear and a fair amount of nervous laughter. H.P. Lovecraft, the famous horror writer, once wrote, "The oldest and strongest emotion of mankind is fear, and the oldest and strongest kind of fear is fear of the unknown" (12). Robert Anton Wilson, a writer who was no stranger to conspiracy theories, once wrote these words about an ephemeral realm known in occult initiations as "Chapel Perilous":

> In traditional occult metaphor... Chapel Perilous [is] a weird place to be. Like the mysterious entity called "I," Chapel Perilous cannot be located in space-time; it is weightless, odorless, tasteless and undetectable by ordinary instruments. Even more like the Ego, it is possible to deny that Chapel Perilous is really there. And yet, once you are inside it, there doesn't seem to be any way to ever get out again, until you suddenly discover that it has been brought into existence by thought and does not exist outside thought. Everything you fear is waiting for you in Chapel Perilous, but if you are armed with the wand of intuition, the cup of sympathy, the sword of reason and pentacle of valor, you will come through it all safely.
>
> That's what the legends say, and the language of myth is poetically precise. For instance, if you go into that realm without the sword of reason, you will lose your mind, but if you take only the sword of reason without the cup of sympathy you will lose your heart. Even more remarkably, if you approach without the wand of intuition, you can stand at the door for decades never realizing you have arrived. You might even think you are just waiting for a bus, or wandering from room to room looking for something lost, or watching a TV show in which "you" are not involved. Chapel Perilous is tricky that way. (10-11)

Fear and laughter are tricky as well. They're two sides of the same coin, of course, but it turns out the coin I'm referring to has *more* than two sides, perhaps an infinite amount. You can see them if you squint your eyes, tilt your head to one side, and look just *so*. To pass through Chapel Perilous safely the initiate has to see beyond the two surfaces of the coin to another world where both fear and laughter dissolve and meld together and transform into illumination and, ultimately,—if he's kept his head—active participation in our everyday world.

The shaman comes back from this other world with a pocketful of myths. The specialist, the historian, the pundit, the journalist, the expert: They appear in your home everyday inside a little box spewing harmful, sugar-coated lies.

I give you a pocketful of myths. They're researched and footnoted and delivered with a tone of authority on the part of the narrator. The author researched this book for fourteen years. Trust me, lies don't take that long to construct. Lies are easy. These myths tell the truth, or the truth as I see it. When Alice fell through the mirror, she left the world of experts and knowable facts behind and plunged into a topsy-turvy world fraught with bizarre paradoxes. I offer you the chance to do the same.

"Though Wonderlawn's lost us for ever. Alis, alas, she broke the glass!"

—James Joyce, *Finnegans Wake*, 1939

Tightening Up the Goo

On April 8, 2010, Reuters released the results of a poll in which 23,000 adults in twenty-two different countries were asked about their belief in extraterrestrials. Most of those polled were under the age of thirty-five, and ranged across all income classes. The results were as follows: 20% of those polled said that they believe extraterrestrials are currently walking among us disguised as human beings. It's interesting to note that most of those who believed in this extraterrestrial infiltration theory lived in major urban centers; those who lived in small towns, where everyone tends to know each other, were far less likely to believe the theory.

What can we conclude from these findings? Does this poll say something profound about the alienation of the typical urban dweller in the twenty-first century? Has decades of cowering in fear behind locked doors while suckling the glass teat of television led to these rampant, paranoid delusions? Yes, of course, it *could* mean that.

It could also mean that there are aliens walking among us.

Paranoia is the great undiscovered art form of the twenty-first century. Plenty of scholars have written dissertations about the growing theme of paranoia in literature, art, film, etc. Some of the most important writers of the past century claimed paranoia as their special métier. In fact, paranoia runs rampant through the literary touchstones of my own personal pantheon: the multiple anarchist conspirators uncovered by Gabriel Syme, secret agent and poet, the protagonist of G.K. Chesterton's surreal detective novel *The Man Who Was Thursday: A Nightmare* (1908); the Gnostic mythologies hidden within even more esoteric mythologies in James Branch Cabell's beautifully complicated and highly controversial satires, *The Cream of the Jest* (1917) and *Jurgen* (1919); Charles Fort's groundbreaking non-fiction reportage of overlooked paranormal data in *The Book of the Damned* (1919); the endlessly labyrinthine novel-length narratives of Franz Kafka in the 1920s; the racialist, degenerate nightmares of H.P. Lovecraft in the 1930s; the jocular metaphysics of Flann O'Brien in his posthumously published 1940s divine comedy *The Third Policeman*; the hardboiled cries from hell that emerged from Jim Thompson's typewriter in the early 1950s; the experimental routines of early William S. Burroughs from the late 1950s; the 1960s science fiction psychedelia of Philip K. Dick; the absurd paeans to insanity in the form of Thomas Pynchon's 1970s epyllion *The Crying of Lot 49* and his Great American Novel *Gravity's Rainbow*; the revisionist histories found in Steve Erickson's *Tours of the Black Clock* and *Arc d'X* published in the late 1980s and early 1990s; the alternate universes woven into our own world within the unjustly obscure pages of Jack Womack's New York novels such as *Random Acts of Senseless Violence* (1995) and *Going, Going, Gone* (2000). I could go on and on, of course, but there's no need. I trust you can come up with even better examples of your own.

However, I'm not referring to the mere theme of paranoia found within fictional narratives. I'm saying that the state of paranoia itself is a new art form, and people—either consciously or unconsciously—are well aware of this and use paranoia as a plaything, a palliative to help guide them through the intricacies of this post-post-modern world. The dilemma that human beings must face in the twenty-first century is not that they're alienated or ignorant, but that they're not alienated or ignorant enough. Technology has granted us ersatz telepathy. We're all involved in everyone's personal business twenty-four hours a day. A girlfriend breaks up with her boyfriend in high school and the whole world knows about it fifteen seconds later via Facebook. In cyberspace we can shed our identities and become other beings. We're shape shifters, a godlike power previously attributed only to deities in ancient mythologies and extraterrestrials in 1950s science fiction movies. Therefore, the results of the aforementioned poll were indeed correct. More and more, aliens are walking among us. We see them every day in our bathroom mirrors and our reflective iPod screens. Technology has made aliens of us all.

Of course, there's nothing new in this observation. After all, Marshall McLuhan was saying the same thing several decades ago. Nor is there anything new in observing the simple fact that paranoia is simply a state of heightened awareness. As Charles Manson once said (one of his many groovy aphorisms from the 1970s), "Paranoia is just a kind of awareness, and awareness is just a form of love." Indeed, we're more aware of what's going on in the world now than ever before. News stories that used to take weeks to travel from one country to another now take seconds. If that's not a heightened form of awareness, what is?

What *is* new about these observations, I'm quietly proud to say, is the context. Like the shape of celluloid aliens, the context is always shifting. And when the context shifts, the meaning of what lies within shifts as well. New mysteries arise to replace the ones that have long since been solved.

Mysteries. Primitive cultures used myths to explain the mysteries of their own society. Nowadays most of us no longer believe that a bearded gentleman on top of Mt. Olympus is responsible for fashioning lightning bolts with gargantuan blacksmith tools. But some of us do hold beliefs that are equally strange. For example, were you aware that the only way an African-American could become President of the United States is if he were placed in that position by a centuries-old Masonic cult? After all, African-Americans don't just become President. There must be something wrong with this bizarre new reality, mustn't there? Perhaps Obama's really a Muslim terrorist in disguise. Perhaps he's a mind-controlled Manchurian Candidate of a secret pagan order. Perhaps there's something erroneous about his birth certificate. Perhaps....

Just the other day about thirty of these "Obama birthers" (as some in the media have chosen to call them), most of them seemingly enjoying an upper middle-class existence, appeared in the drug-infested park across the street from my apartment building in Long Beach, California to hold a rally against the Obama administration. Oddly enough, I'd never seen any of these people in this park before. I could only conclude that they would never bother to visit this part of town except to hold protests against Obama and the people who voted for him. They all held up signs decorated with slogans like, "BARAK OBAMA IS LEADING US INTO SOCIALISM!!!" and "NEXT TIME ELECT AN *ADULT* AS PRES!" and "BEWARE THE CONSENTRATION CAMPS!!!!" (Only about three counter-protesters were present at the rally; they held up signs of their own that read, "NEXT TIME SPELL CHECK YOUR SIGNS!") I had the urge to cross the street, step up onto the stage, and point out that their heated protest against creeping "socialism" was being held in a park paid for by tax dollars. But somehow I resisted the urge.

These protestors—most of them no doubt sincere and well-meaning in their outrage against authoritarianism—spent eight years completely unconcerned about the creation of Homeland Security and the rollback of the Freedom of Information Act in the wake of 9/11 and the wholesale torture of innocent people in American-sponsored rendition camps in foreign countries, but interpret a new health care bill as the advent of the Seventh Reich. Why worry about the "consentration camps" that haven't been built yet when there are already *real* concentration camps being operated at the expense of U.S. tax dollars in Afghanistan and Guantanamo Bay? Have these Obama birthers bothered to see Alex Gibney's disturbing 2007 documentary *Taxi to the Dark Side* in which their worst paranoid fantasies have already been documented on celluloid? Probably not.

Myths are malleable, you see. Sometimes they tell us only what we want to know. The Norse gods never died. They shaved their heads, picked up a couple of misspelled signs, and are now demonstrating in downtown Los Angeles against the Obama administration's alleged support of illegal immigrants.

The earliest myths were proto-Rorschach-blots. Those listening to the myths being told around the campfire projected their own concerns and fears into the subtext, and the same is true of conspiracy theories today. I notice this a great deal with regard to the subject of Freemasonry. You can tell a lot about the political leanings of a conspiracy theorist by who he or she thinks the Masons *are.* A liberal conspiracy theorist will interpret the Freemasons as a cabal of rightwing fascists with Nazi affiliations. A conservative conspiracy theorist will interpret the Freemasons as a cabal of left-leaning socialists—*also* with Nazi affiliations, oddly enough. LaRouche followers think the Freemasons are an exclusive cabal of British empiricists. Many Southern Baptists think they're Satan worshippers (or Baal worshippers, as if those two mythological beings are interchangeable). Some conspiracy theorists with a severe anti-Semitic bent insist that the Freemasons are a cabal of baby-eating Jews. (I'm not exaggerating about the "baby-eating Jew" part, by the way. I refer you to the work of Eustace Mullins, particularly Chapter 6 of his 1968 book *Mullins' New History of the Jews,* for more information on that special form of sociopathy.)

I myself am a 32nd Degree Scottish Rite Freemason, and I assure you I've never eaten a baby—Gentile or otherwise. The story of how I became a Freemason is so strange and absurd that it would take well over two hundred pages to do the tale justice. Suffice it to say that I can blame it all on Walter Bowart, author of the ground-breaking book, *Operation Mind Control.* In 2002 Walter and I were collaborating on a screenplay about the earliest attempts on the part of the U.S. government to criminalize LSD. At that time Walter was initiated into the first degree of Freemasonry (about five years before his death from cancer in December of 2007). Since he was aware that I already knew a great deal about the traditions of Freemasonry, he suggested I join his Lodge in Culver City, CA. I've never been much of a joiner (even the mere *notion* of joining the Boy Scouts disturbed me as a child), so I demurred; however, about a year after his suggestion, due to a series of incidents more akin to a comedy of errors than the phantasmagoria of such conspiracy films as *Eyes Wide Shut* or *The Skulls*, I decided to join the local Blue Lodge located only a few blocks from my apartment in Torrance, CA. I let the Master of the Lodge know that my interest in Freemasonry was, for the most part, scholarly in nature. I couldn't help but notice that many of my favorite authors from the late nineteenth century, as well as the early twentieth century, made subtle and frequent use of hermetic, Masonic, and alchemical symbolism in their novels, stories, poems, and plays. For that reason—literary scholarship, in essence—I now sought a deeper understanding of the ancient symbolism. The Master of the Lodge seemed intrigued by this, said my reason was a perfectly valid one for wanting to join, and within a few months I was being initiated into the first degree. I had intended on halting my ascent after the third

11

degree, but eventually made my way up to the 32nd at the Scottish Rite Temple located in Long Beach, CA.

Since then I've met a lot of Freemasons. The most nefarious crime I've seen any of them commit was, perhaps, eating too much potato salad after a Monday night meeting. (And for those who think Freemasons are a cabal of Aryan Nazis, consider the fact that almost every Mason I've ever encountered was Filipino.) Now, does this mean all those spooky tales we've heard about backroom demonic shenanigans in Masonic Lodges are fictitious? Not necessarily. Just because I'm a 32nd Degree Freemason doesn't mean I'm an expert on the subject. I'm not psychically attuned to every Mason in the world. In fact, I'm friends with one woman who claims she was ritually abused by several Freemasons throughout her childhood. I have no reason to disbelieve her tale. It's a serious logical fallacy, however, to conclude that *all* Masons are child molesters based on the actions of a few, just as it's a leap to conclude that all [fill in the blank] are [fill in the blank] because you once got [ripped off by one/mugged by one in an alley/unceremoniously groped by one in an elevator/etc.].

As for the perennial Satan-worship allegations, since becoming a Freemason in 2003 the only reference I've heard to Satan was during one of the Scottish Rite degrees, and the entirety of that reference was clearly intended as a morality tale—a parable that rather reminded me of the last few minutes of Mr. Toad's Wild Ride at Disneyland more than a chapter out of Anton LaVey's *The Satanic Bible*. The simple (and, for some, unbearable) truth is that almost all the esoteric "secrets" of Freemasonry are readily accessible in any public library in the United States and have been for generations. Yes, the Freemasons might be the most amorphous of all the ink blots in the postmodern pantheon of boogeymen delineated in this grimoire of myths.

Myths tell us a lot about ourselves: our fears, our dreams. They convey everything an extraterrestrial anthropologist would need to know about human ethics and our true sense of self and our place in the universe, perhaps even more than the various organized religions still clinging to our collective unconscious in the twenty-first century. Myths reveal our essential selves in ways that might make us very uncomfortable. How much do the numerous volumes written by Holocaust deniers, for example, tell us about the human race? Sadly, they tell us a great deal—far more than we would like to know. Just because the majority of Americans find these theories abhorrent doesn't mean we should ignore them or conclude they're not meaningful. The truth is, they're *very* meaningful. *All* conspiracy theories are meaningful… just like all myths are meaningful.

Every myth structure is composed of darkness and light. Every Olympian mountaintop has its counterpart in Hades. Every heroic whistleblower who uncovers secret documents like *The Pentagon Papers* has a doppelganger, a Jungian dark double, attempting to foist off *The Protocols of the Learned Elders of Zion* on a gullible public. The field of conspiracy theory is littered with the carcasses of sincere truth seekers who failed in their search. In the early 1990s the rightwing militia movement was at the height of its popularity, spurred by the election of Democrat Bill Clinton to the Presidency. For years these militia members, led by homegrown heroes like attorney Linda Thompson and shortwave radio host William Cooper, congregated in "covert" meeting halls in order to exchange dark tales about the swarm of U.N. black helicopters that would soon arrive to round up the last remaining patriots in this country. In the wake of this mini-Ragnarok, the Clintons were supposedly going to build concentration camps in the Midwest and Alaska to confine all these patriots, leaving the U.S. wide open for socialist rule. So spoke the prophecies.

When these same militia groups were tied to the destruction of the Oklahoma City Federal Building in 1995 their media presence waned slowly. A couple of years ago the militia movement had devolved into a forgotten joke. In March of 2010, however, a Christian militia in Michigan was indicted for plotting to assassinate police officers and Muslims with homemade bombs as a preemptive strike against the imminent takeover of the "Anti-Christ." On April 17, 2010, a neo-Nazi rally was held outside City Hall in downtown Los Angeles to protest Obama and the evil gnomes who influence his policies from their subterranean lair in Zurich. Yes, the black helicopters are emerging once again from the mists of myth... and once again, appropriately enough, they're spurred by the election of a Democrat to the presidency.

This game goes way back. During the Carter administration an eccentric attorney named Dr. Peter Beter (yes, that was his real name) claimed that President Carter had been assassinated by Soviet agents and replaced with "organic robotoids" intent on taking over the United States for Bolshevik rule. Lyndon Johnson was implicated in the murder of John F. Kennedy within days of the assassination. Kennedy was accused of being a secret agent for the Pope. Harry Truman, duped by the Scottish Rite Freemasons, allowed the atom bomb to be dropped on Hiroshima in order to fulfill a centuries-old alchemical plot hatched by the Scottish Rite Freemasons long before the Great Pyramids were first constructed. Franklin Roosevelt allowed the Japanese to bomb Pearl Harbor in order to drag the United States into World War II (that one goes without saying). We could keep going farther and farther back in time, but I think you get the picture. A similar—and even more ominous litany—could be compiled with regard to Republican Presidents.

But this time around, the fear and confusion are far worse than with any previous administration. How are lightning bolts formed? Are violent storms a curse from the Gods? How did Barack Obama *really* end up in the White House? Is he the genetically engineered spawn of the Illuminati?

Of course he is.

Joseph Campbell, in his classic study of mythology, *The Hero With a Thousand Faces*, never wrote about what happens when the Hero's quest for truth is derailed and decays into mere paranoia... into an obsessive need to explain away those shifts in society that do not accord with the Hero's limited reality tunnel.

But it's crucial to note that only a lazy thinker would dismiss all this paranoia as mere insanity. As Joseph Heller once wrote, "Just because you're paranoid doesn't mean they aren't after you." Similarly, we would be remiss if we condemned all such conspiracy theories as pure jabberwocky. After all, conspiracy theories will be with us for a long time, so we might as well become a little more intimate with them.

If, in the twenty-first century, paranoia has become an art form, then it's no wonder that conspiracy theory has become an art form in its own right as well. It's a brand new literary genre still only in its infancy (at least in relation to other, more well-established genres). Consider the parallels with other nascent art forms of the latter half of the twentieth century. Within the past few decades, for example, we have watched the music video evolve from a simple marriage of music and stage-bound visuals to that of a complicated new art form. Many of our most important film directors today began their careers directing music videos, an art form dismissed as trivial trash only two decades ago. Similarly, within the next ten years we will begin to see the field of conspiracy theories morph and evolve in surprising ways. Expect to see a slew of college courses analyzing conspiracy theories, not only from a literary perspective (as we've seen in recent years with other formerly debased genres such as detective fiction, science fiction and the graphic novel medium), but from the perspective of cultural studies as well.

I myself have been using such writings in my own courses at CSU Long Beach, where I've been teaching since 2002. When I allow my students to choose their own topics for their final argumentative essays in my composition courses, they often choose those with a conspiratorial bent. It's a popular subject among students, particularly for teenagers and people in their early twenties. I know of some colleagues who have also used conspiracy theories to teach rhetoric, composition, and even logic. From observing this trend, combined with the ubiquity of conspiracy theories in popular media (including films, television,

15

comic books, pop music, video games, and even trading cards), I concluded the time was right for an exploration of its contents.

Though this book is by no means an encyclopedia, its breadth of subject matter is intended to be as close to encyclopedic as possible. Under analysis in this volume is almost every major conspiracy theory, from the most famous to the utterly obscure. Subjects covered include (but are by no means limited to) conspiracies involving Christianity, Judaism, Islam, Freemasonry, Mormonism and Scientology, 9/11, Columbine, the Oklahoma City Bombing, the JFK and RFK assassinations, alien implants, the Illuminati, Bohemian Grove, the Heaven's Gate mass suicide, Jonestown, the L.A. Riots, O.J. Simpson, the origin of AIDS, the 1969 moon landing, all eight years of the George W. Bush administration, World War I, World War II, Vietnam, both Iraq Wars, and even some future bloody conflicts thrown in for good measure.

This doesn't mention such perennial favorites as: mind control in advertising, education, popular literature and the field of covert intelligence; the ostensible influence of secret societies on revolutions, wars and other historical events; little known political assassinations; the esoteric connections between conspiracies and the paranormal; applying conspiracy theory to the Hegelian Dialectic; the always bizarre world of UFOS, and (as they say on those late night commercials) much, much more.

Paranoia surrounds us. Instead of staving it off, let's embrace it for awhile. By growing comfortable with it, we might actually be able to become one with it. We might be able to use it creatively for our own eventual illumination, little grasshopper. As we delve deeply into the world of conspiracies, to be sure, we delve deeper into the collective unconscious of the twentieth and twenty-first centuries. Or as a wise scholar once wrote in a slightly different context....

"Let's tighten up the slack sentimentality of this goo with something gutsy and grim.

"As Zeus said to Narcissus: 'Watch yourself.'"
          –Marshall McLuhan, "Media Ad-vice," 1972

Works Cited

Lovecraft, Howard Phillips. *Supernatural Horror in Literature*. New York: Dover, 1973.

McLuhan, Marshall. Introduction. "Media Ad-vice" *Subliminal Seduction*. By Wilson Bryan Key. New York: Signet, 1974, pp. vii-xviii.

Wilson, Robert Anton. Introduction. *The Illuminoids: Secret Societies and Political Paranoia*. By Neal Wilgus. Albuquerque: Sun Publishing, 1978, pp. 8-12.

PART ONE

OVERVIEW

Mae Brussell's

First Issue

CONSPIRACY NEWSLETTER

Why Is the Senate Watergate Committee Functioning As Part of the Cover-Up?

I. Knowledge Omitted from the Campus

II. The Cover-Up
- A. Concealing the motives
- B. Witnesses not called
  1. Martha Mitchell
  2. Louis Tackwood
  3. Tom Charles Huston
  4. William Sullivan

III. Martial Law Without the Riots
- A. Institutions to dismantle
- B. The enemy list
- C. The warfare state
- D. Political prisoners of America

Introduction:

July 21, 1973 — Paul Krassner and I decided to publish *Conspiracy Newsletter* a year ago.

The arrests at the Watergate Hotel, and the magnitude of the events taking place, occupied my year.

Nine years research into past government conspiracies and previous election manipulations was the background for the newsletter.

The Watergate witnesses, and evidence about the illegal entry into the Democratic National Headquarters, was a continuation of earlier investigative work.

One year later, with almost 700 subject files assembled on the Watergate espionage operation, *Conspiracy Newsletter* is finally getting started.

For those who subscribed a year ago and waited, thank you.

Many people asked me why, after many years of research, my first published article was in *The Realist?*

The answer is simple.

I respect Paul Krassner. For ten years, I have subscribed to *The Realist.*

Only the alternative press has been faithful to the freedoms we deserve.

The Realist

At a time when *Deep Throat* is making $50-million, indicating a desire and taste of free adults to choose their own entertainment, the Supreme Court permits others to dictate what we shall see or read.

Nixon's Supreme Court is a worse danger to our liberties than sexual pleasures.

Freedom of the press, freedom to live and to love is what the struggle is all about. There are hundreds of conspiracies taking place. They are all ordered from the White House.

Political assassinations, the killing of Presidential candidates, is for the purpose of denying our maximum freedoms.

I. Knowledge Omitted from the Campus

The arrests at the Watergate Hotel in Washington D.C. took most Americans by surprise. We had been educated with a continuous series of denials that conspiracies at the White House level could exist.

The news media, a major source of information, treat high level conspiracies with platitudes, indifference, and unimaginative cover stories to conceal facts. Propaganda is an important weapon of the fascist state. TV and the media are filled with clandestine agents, some posing as liberal writers, whose purpose is to break the credibility of researchers or discredit evidence that would confirm conspiracies.[1]

Colleges and academic institutions have no courses on agent provocateurs or how to recognize espionage operations.[2] When the accurate history of the 1960's and 70's is written about violence in the U.S., facts will reveal that government provocateurs created most of the violence. A series of our own Reichstag fires was the justification later for a domestic intelligence unit to deny our liberties guaranteed by the Constitution.[3]

There is no information available on ways to protect society from sabotage. The Watergate Affair exposes how investigators and the Dept. of Justice work with their espionage agents in acts which amount to treason.[4] Top lawyers of the nation, instead of obeying the law, worked in collusion with corporate interests for purposes of power and profits.[5] G. Gordon Liddy, counsel for the White House and CREEP, helped create the famous April 7, 1972 law which concealed donations and illegal corporate financing.

Page 13

CHAPTER ONE

©ONSPIRACY INC:
ANATOMY OF A DISCIPLINE

The world of conspiracy research is fraught with bizarre paradoxes. Often the most thorough research is done by complete amateurs (groundbreaking journalist Mae Brussell being the prime example), while the most amateurish research is done by well-trained professionals (i.e., almost any *Los Angeles Times* article with the word "conspiracy" in the title).

To see what I mean, I suggest perusing Rich Cohen's article "Welcome to the Conspiracy," featured in the May 2004 issue of *Vanity Fair*. The article purports to be an objective critique of conspiracy research. However, the actual purpose of Cohen's article is not to offer genuine criticism of conspiracy research at all (such a task would be welcome). Instead, his ultimate purpose is to leave in the reader's mind the impression that conspiracy researchers are a) anti-Semites, b) right-wing fundamentalists, and c) always men. Just a quick glance at the masthead of almost any conspiracy journal would render that last proposition laughable. In fact, one of the great progenitors of this type of research was none other than Mae Brussell, a liberal Jewish woman, the daughter of one of the most prominent Rabbis in Los Angeles history, Edgar Magnin.

Brussell's skills as a political researcher were beyond reproach. Brussell wrote about Watergate before the *Washington Post*.[1] I refer interested researchers to the compilation *The Mae Brussell Reader*, released by Prevailing Winds in 1991, if you

---

1   Indeed, she did so in the pages of Paul Krassner's underground magazine *The Realist*.

wish to judge Brussell's reportage for yourself. As famed investigative journalist Seymour Hersh once said of Brussell, "She's crazy, but she's right." Alas, mainstream publications are very often neither crazy nor right.

The job of most professional journalists consists of rewriting news releases sent to them by PR Newswire or Business Wire and very little else. Sometimes, I suspect, they don't even do that much. I have a friend who works at Business Wire; he often sees news releases he himself has edited reprinted word for word in a mainstream newspaper. With such a lackadaisical atmosphere pervading the halls of newsrooms across the country, it's not surprising that amateurs are forced to fill the void with articles in conspiracy 'zines, postings on the internet, hit-and-run phone calls on radio talk shows, and graffiti on alley walls.

Loose in the conspiracy world is an anarchy of information, to which there's an upside and a downside. Most conspiracy magazines are a synthesis of both. The upside and the downside appear side by side without even a wink or a nudge from the editors to explain the difference. On one page you might find a meticulously researched, thoroughly footnoted article examining the origins of the Gulf War Disease by Dr. Alan Cantwell, and on the next you'll find someone named "Anonymous" ranting about the cabal of homosexual Communists attempting to take over the world. Few people can oscillate between these two categories and remain sane, though why this should be the case perplexes me. You don't need a degree in advanced physics to tell the difference between legitimate research and illegitimate research (or, more often than not, no research at all). Legitimate conspiracy research (Noam Chomsky, eager to remain in the good graces of academia, prefers to call it "Institutional Analysis") is footnoted and sourced, and pure speculation is clearly labeled as such. Illegitimate conspiracy research is very often based on little more than hearsay or the wild imagination of the researcher himself. That doesn't mean such goofiness doesn't have a place in the universe. Some of it is purely insane, some of it is clever disinformation manufactured by one or more intelligence agencies to muddy the waters, some of it is misinformation from sincere but sadly misled researchers, some of it is outright satire, but none of it is boring.

Since Rich Cohen was unable to offer an objective critique of the emerging discipline known as "conspiracy research," I thought it might be beneficial to correct Cohen's mistake and do his job for him. After all, in times such as these when conspiracies are conducted right in front of our faces, and murderous thugs wander the halls of the White House cooking up imaginary threats to keep us frightened, it's important not to waste our time conjuring up plots and counter-plots that don't even exist. Let's leave such fear mongering to the professionals, shall we?

What follows is an overview of the more obscure conspiracy theories floating around out there. If possible, I'll attempt to identify which of the five categories the theory falls into (i.e., Insanity, Disinformation, Misinformation, Satire or Legitimate Research). However, I'd like to point out that in even the most suspect conspiracy theory there's often a kernel of truth. As political researcher Dave Emory likes to say, "Even a blind pig can find an acorn once in awhile." I'll try to uncover that acorn in each of the following examples.

Stephen King Shot John Lennon

During the summer of 1998 various people kept coming up to me and saying, "Have you seen this weird guy who drives around Torrance in a van that has a sign on it that says STEPHEN KING SHOT JOHN LENNON?" No, I would reply, I've never seen it. In fact, I appeared to be the only one in Torrance who never did see it, though I would've liked to.

Later that year on Halloween I happened to find myself up in Monterey, CA. While walking down the street on Sunday morning, only about two blocks away from my hotel, I glanced to my right and saw a van parked alongside the curb. The van had a sign on it that read, STEPHEN KING SHOT JOHN LEN-

NON. Well, how could I pass that up? I walked on up to the van and perused the hundred little newspaper clippings taped to its side. The driver, an aging hippie named Steven Lightfoot, climbed out of the back to explain his theory, the main thrust of which was that Ronald Reagan wanted Lennon dead in order to destroy the spirit of the sixties. This I could understand. I'm still not quite clear on how this ties into Stephen King, however. After he finished telling me that Stephen King was also John Doe #2 of Oklahoma City Bombing Fame, I asked him if he'd ever been to Torrance, CA.

"Cravens Ave.?" he said. "Sure! I was there for a long time."

"Why did you leave?"

He slammed his fist into his palm and yelled, "No one there cares about *the story*, damn it!"

"Look," I said, "sometimes I write for *Paranoia* magazine. What if I try to get the story out through them?"

He replied that a copy of his "book" (in truth a stapled pamphlet) was $3. I gladly gave up the three sawbucks, at which point Lightfoot jotted down his pager number on the back of the "book" (he has no address, since he lives out of the van) and said, "Reproduce as many copies as you want. Pass 'em around. The Word needs to get out!" [Lightfoot's pager number is 408-233-4944, if you're interested in getting in contact with him.]

"I promise I'll show a copy to the editor of *Paranoia* magazine," I said as I strolled away from the van. Upon returning home I sent a copy to one of the editors of *Paranoia* in Rhode Island as well as to Jack Womack in New York. Womack, author of the novel *Random Acts of Senseless Violence*, is a connoisseur of such strangeness. He wrote back, "A friend of mine remembers seeing the S.K.S.J.L. van parked on Amsterdam at 72nd a few years ago, which is probably about as close as anyone would let him get to the Dakota, 2 blocks away." Another friend of mine remembers seeing the van at a Grateful Dead concert in Irvine, while yet another friend has heard him calling into the Stephanie Miller show on KABC (790 AM). The man's quite ubiquitous. Sometimes I wonder if he has the divine power of bi-location.

I don't think I need to point out that this particular theory falls under the Insanity Category. However, there are indeed unanswered questions surrounding the assassination of John Lennon. In 1988 Arthur O'Connor, NYPD lieutenant of detectives, suggested to a British barrister named Fenton Bresler, "It's possible Mark [David Chapman] could have been used by somebody. I saw him the night of the murder. I studied him intensely. He looked as if he could have been programmed..." (Bresler 17). Indeed, Chapman exhibited the behavior of a hypnotized subject. In 1972 Lennon himself had told Paul Krassner, the publisher of *The Realist*, "Listen, if anything happens to Yoko and me, it was *not* an accident" (Krassner 214). That was the same time when Lennon and Ono were also funding the publication of Mae Brussell's research.

A more exhaustive examination of these issues can be found in Fenton Bresler's 1989 book *Who Shot John Lennon?* Though based on little more than circumstantial evidence, the book raises some intriguing questions that need to be addressed. A good start, of course, would be for the FBI to release its files on Lennon sans all redactions that serve to reduce the pages into a mess of blacked-out rectangles with a maximum of two words visible (if you're lucky). Until the government ceases to insist on absolute secrecy in the interest of that all-purpose bugaboo known as "national security," you can look forward to more insane theories like Lightfoot's proliferating on the internet and beyond.

Real Aliens Prefer Strawberry Ice Cream

On October 14-16, 1988, a syndicated television broadcast hosted by Mike Farrell made great waves in the UFO field. Titled *UFO Cover-up? Live!*, the show purported to be a true exposé of the government's secret agreement with the alien Grays. Though the conditions of this agreement were left ambiguous, the show clearly implied that the government had given the aliens an underground base in Nevada where they were being allowed to carry out genetic experiments on human abductees. The main sources for this information were two "members of the intelligence community" who used the code names Falcon and Condor. Both claimed to be members of a secret group known as the Aviary. They were only shown behind screens and their voices were distorted in order to protect their identity. As Jacques Vallée has pointed out: "It should be fairly obvious that the people presumably charged with the security of the projects on which Falcon, Condor, and the other members of the Aviary claimed to work, would immediately find out who they were... since the projects in question are supposed to be highly classified, hence would be known to a very small group where leaks could be traced instantly" (Vallée 43-44). Though the Aviary itself may exist (or may have existed at one time) in some form or another, it's doubtful that the two gentlemen featured on the show were actually members of such an organization.

Among Falcon and Condor's stranger claims was that the aliens preferred to eat ice cream and vegetables. Over twenty years later, those who saw the show seem to remember this detail most of all. *Communion* author Whitley Strieber has said, "[The show] contained a lot of credible information about aliens and UFOs and the cover-up, but it also contained the story that the aliens liked strawberry ice cream, turning the whole thing into a laughing stock. It was very cleverly done" (Strieber Interview).

The techniques used to obfuscate the few moments of serious information were indeed clever, but simple. For example, the UFO witnesses were forced to read from teleprompters, making them sound stilted and rehearsed. While the witnesses related horrifying tales of alien abduction, the sound track consisted of an upbeat Russian polka, subtly transforming their tragedy into utter slapstick. Mike Farrell's narration was so obviously tongue-in-cheek, the viewer felt alienated from the material even more. Similarly, the painted backdrops of "a bright sunny room overlooking a garden" served as an effective anti-environment when juxtaposed with the ominous information concerning the intentions of the aliens, who were depicted as idealized Disneyesque cartoon characters (Andrews 4-5).

I think it would be safe to say that *UFO Cover-up? Live!* was a clever piece of propaganda manufactured by the intelligence community itself. By the way, this particular documentary was the first in television history to be granted the privilege of being broadcast simultaneously in both the United States and the Soviet Union. Such international cooperation seems quite suspicious, particularly during the Cold War, and only strengthens the idea that the program's main intent was one of disinformation. As Jacques Vallée has said, "If the objective of [this] particular piece of disinformation art was to destabilize the few groups that are still seriously doing UFO research, to place the few competent investigators in a ridiculous light, and to disseminate spurious data, then they have succeeded beyond their wildest dreams, as the disintegration of American UFO research over the last few years demonstrates" (Vallée 45).

NASA Mooned America!

What a title! One can't help but admire any conspiracy researcher who could cook up a title as colorful as that. Ralph René, a former member of Mensa who prefers to be known only by his last name for some reason, was forced to self-publish his book in 1992 after Victoria House Press in New York threatened to rewrite it entirely. Upon receiving *NASA Mooned America!* in the mail, I was immediately struck by the fact that it was bound in black electrical tape. Most people would interpret this as a bad sign, but not me. Anyone who's so committed to his research that he'll resort to binding his book in electrical tape is clearly of interest.

Over the course of 176 pages, René attempts to prove that NASA faked every one of its moon landings in a warehouse near Mercury, Nevada, a theory first proposed in Bill Kaysing's 1981 book *We Never Went To the Moon*. (Kaysing claims that Peter Hyams' 1978 film *Capricorn One* was based on his research. By the way, if you want to get *really* conspiratorial, consider the fact that *Capricorn One* stars none other than O.J. Simpson.) René expands on Kaysing's original proposal by analyzing original NASA photos, comparing contradictory statements by the Apollo astronauts (or "astro-nots," as René likes to say), and deconstructing the unchallenged assumptions concerning human survival in space. René raises many intriguing questions. How did the Moon Rover fit onto the Lander? Why are there no stars visible in any of the NASA photographs of the Moon? Why wasn't color footage used during the 1969 landing? How did the astronauts withstand the deadly radiation in the Van Allen belt?

Most of René's questions have simple answers, and I would refer the interested reader to Michael Bara's article "Who Mourns For Apollo?" at http://www.lunaranomalies.com/fake-moon.htm for analysis far more in-depth than any I can offer here. René's technical acuity is far from unassailable. At one point he seems incapable of distinguishing between "shadows" and "silhouettes," for example. However, that doesn't mean the entire book is worthless. Far from it. Though in my opinion René fails to prove his central thesis, he *does indeed* prove that NASA fakes photographs. His analysis of two photographs taken from Michael Collins' 1974 book *Carrying the Fire* proves that the July 1966 photograph (#66-40127) of Michael Collins' space-walk was derived from a picture of Collins in a Zero-G airplane; the original figure has clearly been flopped over, reduced in size, and superimposed onto a black background. René's analysis of NASA's 4/22/72 photo (AS16-107-17446), depicting Charles Duke and the Moon Rover during the Apollo 16 mission, is certainly intriguing. Even my most skeptical friends have been dumbfounded by the fact that the Rover's antenna clearly *overlaps* the cross-hairs on the photo. I'd like to meet the professional photographer who can explain that one away.

Because NASA fakes photographs, one can't immediately leap to the conclusion that we never went to the Moon. I can imagine a number of reasons for altering NASA photos, one of them being to remove evidence of alien artifacts that certain NASA officials would prefer to keep from profane eyes like yours and mine. Richard Hoagland, former advisor to both NASA and Walter Cronkite, insists that the famous photo of Alan Shepard hitting a golf ball on the Moon is manufactured (8/20/97 Interview). This photo depicts Shepard and Ed Mitchell standing side by side, despite the fact that there were only two cameras taken along on the Apollo 14 moon landing—*both* of them strapped to the chests of Shepard and Mitchell. This faked photo can be found in the center of Shepard's 1994 book *Moon Shot*.

Another valid point examined in René's book is the mystery surrounding the deaths of Virgil Grissom, Roger Chaffee, and Ed White. Grissom was becoming increasingly critical of NASA just prior to his "accident." According to Mike Gray in his book *Angle of Attack*, Grissom told his wife Betty, "If there is a serious accident in the space program, it's likely to be me" (218). Grissom and his two companions died on January 27, 1967 when a fire broke out in the Apollo spacecraft they were testing on Pad 34 at Cape Kennedy. As René says, "...I cannot understand why Grissom et al entered that capsule in the first place if they knew it was to be pressurized with oxygen over 14.7 psi.... Apparently not one of them complained. Didn't anyone know about Calorimeter Bombs? Didn't NASA send them copies of the fire reports? Or maybe no one told them they were jacking up the pressure!" (47-48)

Even more suspicious is the fact that government agents raided Virgil Grissom's house before anyone even knew about the fire, confiscated his personal diary, and never returned it to his widow. As if that wasn't enough, on the morning of the fire the outward opening hatch of the capsule was changed to a hatch that opened *inward*. Of course, the pressure created by the fire prevented this "new, improved" hatch from being opened from either the inside *or* the outside.

René believes Grissom was the main target of the assassination, and apparently Grissom's widow agrees. On May 14,

1997, she openly accused NASA of a cover-up in relation to her husband's death (5/16/97 Hoagland Interview). On February 11, 1999, the Associated Press reported that Grissom's son, Scott Grissom, had alleged, "My father's death was no accident. He was murdered." Furthermore, a NASA investigator, Clark MacDonald of McDonnell-Douglas, accused the agency of covering up the real cause of the fire by destroying his original report, along with numerous taped interviews, from thirty-one years before.

René strikes me as a sincere researcher attempting to find the truth. I don't believe he's Insane, a Disinformation Specialist, or a Satirist. I suspect the bulk of his book falls under the category of Misinformation. However, that doesn't mean it isn't worth studying. There's more than just one acorn worth uncovering here.

THE ELDERS OF ZION AND SHA NA NA

A typical entry in the ever-expanding genre known as "satirical" conspiracy theories is one that presents itself as a legitimate journalistic exposé attempting to counteract a small group of privileged scoundrels who are committing various forms of skullduggery against the masses. This genre could very well date back to *Dialogue in Hell between Machiavelli and Montesquieu* by Maurice Joly, a rare book published in France in 1865. *Dialogue* was plagiarized in the early twentieth century by unknown authors and refashioned into the infamous *Protocols of the Learned Elders of Zion*—which makes its first appearance as an appendix in a 1905 book bearing the unwieldy title *The Big in the Small, and Antichrist as a Near Political Possibility; Notes of an Orthodox Person* by Sergei A. Nilus (Berlet 248). This appendix was later published in a separate volume and used by the Nazis as a means of stirring up anti-Semitism in Germany, Britain, and the United States. Even though *Protocols* itself may not have been intended as a satire, its original source certainly was.

At roughly the same time that *Protocols* made its debut, Léo Taxil published *Les Mysteres de la Franc-Maconnerie* in which he wove an elaborate tall tale involving devil-worshipping Freemasons operating in secret in modern day France. It became quite popular, as popular as Dan Brown's *The Da-Vinci Code* is today, despite the fact that the contents of the book were entirely concocted by the author. Eventually, Taxil revealed the entire hoax during a public lecture at the Hall of the Geographic Society in Paris before a disappointed audience of devout Catholic priests eager to hear more horror stories about female Freemasons engaging in lewd sex acts with Baphomet. Not only did Taxil describe his twelve-year-long prank as "the most fantastic hoax of modern times," but he also commented, "It is a bit unusual indeed, that we managed to get our staggering stories swallowed in our 19th century." If he were alive today, Taxil would no doubt be surprised to learn that his hoax is still being quoted as fact by right-wing Christians even at the dawn of the twenty-first century. (Taxil's confession was originally published in a French newspaper called *Le Frondeur* on April 25, 1897. An English translation of the speech can be viewed at www.altreligion.about.com/library/texts/bl_confessiontaxil.htm.)

A more recent entry in this genre includes Leonard Lewin's *Report From Iron Mountain* (Dial Press, 1967). This book purports to be the minutes of a group called Iron Mountain 15, a high level government task force. Concluding that the world economy could only "suffer" from peace, the group decides to convene for the purpose of thinking up methods of "invisible warfare" that can stimulate the economy as sufficiently as traditional warfare. Among several possibilities, the committee suggests faking an invasion from outer space. Though the author himself admitted the book was intended to be a satire, Col. L. Fletcher Prouty (former advisor to President Kennedy) said, "But the people at the Hudson Institute, the Pentagon, and the government contractors were talking like this in those days. So it wasn't really exaggerated enough to be satire. I'd always believed it to be leaked information" (Bowart Chp. 38, p. 3).

In his 1992 book *JFK: The CIA, Vietnam and the Plot to Assassinate John F. Kennedy*, Col. Prouty wrote:

> During the Kennedy years, people within the government and their close associates in academia and industry discussed frequently and quite seriously many of the major questions phrased by Leonard Lewin in *Report From Iron Mountain*. I had been assigned to the Office of the Secretary of Defense before the Kennedy election and was there when the McNamara team of "Whiz Kids" arrived. Never before had so many brilliant young civilians with so many Ph.D.s worked in that office. It was out of the mouths of this group that I heard so frequently and precisely the ideas that Lewin recounts in his "novel." (287-88)

Which demonstrates that just because something is satirical doesn't necessarily mean it's not true.

By the way, a personal favorite among even more recent examples of this genre appeared in *Paranoia* #9. John Glenn and A.S. Hamrah co-wrote an article that begins with the provocative sentence, "Doesn't it seem, well, odd to you that so many retired counter-culturites claim to have been at Woodstock, yet a) there just wouldn't have been room there for all of them, and b) when you ask around yourself, you can't find anyone who was really there?" Glenn and Hamrah's thesis is that Woodstock was faked by the CIA. They raise some interesting questions ("Does it strike you as suspicious that although Otis Redding supposedly performed at Woodstock, he *died* in 1967?"), almost all of them complete jabberwocky. I think it's safe to assume that this article falls under the category of Satire, and comes heartily recommended to those interested in uncovering the "typically ham-fisted intelligence community conspiracy" behind the "grotesque miscalculation that was Sha Na Na" (54).

Giant Owls, Monkey Viruses, Magic Bullets, and Other Unconventional Flying Objects

I've saved the best for last. I would definitely be remiss—as remiss as Rich Cohen was in his *Vanity Fair* article—if I ended this chapter without highlighting some of the legitimate researchers of both the past and the present. I've already mentioned Dr. Alan Cantwell, for example. If one reads his book *AIDS and the Doctors of Death* in tandem with *Emerging Viruses* by Dr. Leonard Horowitz, *Dr. Mary's Monkey* by Edward Haslam, and *AIDS Inc.* by journalist Jon Rappoport, one will come away with a pretty clear picture of how the AIDS virus was created, who developed it, who released it and why. No "theory" here, just facts.

If one reads the 1978 book *The Assassination of Robert Kennedy* by William Turner and Jonn Christian, one will realize that Sirhan Sirhan could not have been responsible for any of the wounds suffered by Senator Kennedy that fateful summer night in 1968. This is a classic in its field, written by an FBI agent and a professional newsman, and deserves to be more widely known among those interested in the hidden agendas guiding American history from behind the scenes. The bullets that murdered John F. Kennedy's younger brother did not come from Sirhan Sirhan's gun; in fact, the probable identity of the real gunman can be found within the pages of this very book. No "theory" here, just facts.

In *America's Secret Establishment* by Stanford Economics professor Antony Sutton, one will learn that Yale University's elite Skull & Bones is not just a "debating society," the quaint description used in a recent *Los Angeles Times* report (published prominently on the front page of the 3-23-04 Calendar section) titled "What Binds Bush, Kerry," in which "investigative journalist" Robin Abcarian bends over backwards to leave the reader with the impression that the Yale secret society Skull & Bones is nothing more than a "debating society where members of the senior class... get together and discuss important topics of the day." In case you forgot, back in 2004 both major

Presidential candidates were members of this infamous secret society, so it would behoove every American to read Antony Sutton's book and study it closely. Hardcore facts abound in this book, and Sutton's theories are clearly labeled as such.

On a related note, check out Alex Jones' 2000 documentary *Dark Secrets Inside Bohemian Grove*, an exposé of more secret society shenanigans among the political elite. You want to know what politicians like Henry Kissinger and George Bush are up to in their off-hours? Apparently they get dressed up in crimson robes, worship a 45-foot stone owl (voiced by the previously mentioned Walter Cronkite), and sacrifice babies in "effigy" in a high-security gorge near Sacramento in Northern California. No "theory" here, for the whole ritual was covertly caught on videotape by Jones. If you can get past the "What I Did On My Summer Vacation" production values and the occasional misinterpretation of the events depicted here (i.e., the typically Christian tendency to confuse paganism with Satanism), you will come away with a number of "illuminating" sights, indeed. Forget Kubrick's tepid fantasies in *Eyes Wide Shut*; here are the real facts. (For more information, see www. infowars.com.)

Some people live for presidential campaigns, not unlike wrestling fans or soap opera addicts, waiting on the edge of their seats for the next melodramatic plot twist to unfold. As with professional wrestling and daytime soap operas, however, these plot twists may not be quite as extemporaneous as the most rabid fans would prefer to believe. Fortunately, as any reader of conspiracy 'zines knows only too well, the truth is often much stranger than such ephemeral fictions. The life of any hardcore political junkie will remain unfulfilled until he or she reads *Votescam: The Stealing of America* by James and Kenneth Collier, a pair of muckrakers (in the best sense of that word) who literally dedicated their lives to uncovering the truth behind the rampant manipulation of elections in the United States. Anyone who read this book when it was initially published in 1992 was not at all surprised when the curious debacle known as the 2000 Presidential elections came apart at the seams in Dade County, Florida. One would be hard pressed to choose a better locale for the hi-jacking of a country if one were writing the scenario as a screenplay (presupposing, of course, that the elections themselves were *not* a screenplay). Upon finishing this book, one will realize how prophetic the Collier brothers truly were. The facts, as laid out in this overlooked work of political science, are incontrovertible.

Finally, no discussion of conspiracies would be complete without some mention of UFOs. The best overview of this vast and complex subject remains *Above Top Secret* by journalist Timothy Good. However, the skeptics out there would be more thoroughly challenged by *Unconventional Flying Objects* written by Paul Hill, a well-respected NASA scientist who spent twenty-five years acting as "an unofficial clearing house at NASA, collecting and analyzing sightings' reports for physical properties, propulsion possibilities, dynamics, etc." He took special precautions to preserve this study for posthumous publication. If you have friends who think no scientific evidence for the extraterrestrial origin of UFOs exists, I suggest you show them this book. They will be hard pressed to dismiss this scientific study as mere "theory."

Conclusion: From the Sublime to the Absurd

Regretfully, I didn't get around to those special theories that mix various categories together: for example, the theory that AIDS comes from Bigfoot (Insanity & Misinformation); or Peter Moon's theory—which can be found in his 1997 book *The Black Sun*—that Mark Hamill of *Star Wars* fame is the surgically-altered progeny of Project Paperclip Nazi scientists involved with covert time travel experiments on Long Island (Insanity, Disinformation, Misinformation, and Satire).

In the end, the important point to remember is this: In the modern day digital environment truth is as malleable as viscous liquid. You can't make up anything that won't come true a few minutes later. A few years ago, during the news coverage of the JFK Jr. plane crash tragedy, a hoaxer posing as a captain in the Coast Guard called into Dan Rather's program and claimed that sections of JFK's private plane had been recovered from the ocean. When Dan Rather realized he'd been had, he grew quite indignant and apologized to the audience profusely. Fifteen minutes later, the real captain called in and reported the same information! The *phony* captain had scooped the *real* captain with an *imaginary* story! As the late comic book writer Steve Gerber once said, "The world has become parasatirical."

According to media ecologist Robert Dobbs, "...in software/wetware conditions we just have to *think* about something collectively and it's done" (Interview). If so, the more imaginative conspiracy theorists might do well to be a bit more careful with the apocalyptic scenarios they tend to promote. Though some of these may be illusory today, our collective obsession with them might evoke them into being tomorrow.

"What's coming at you is coming from you."

–Meatball Fulton

Works Cited

Abcarian, Robin. "What Binds Bush, Kerry." *Los Angeles Times* 23 March 2004: E1, E4.

Andrews, George C. *Extraterrestrial Friends and Foes*. Lilburn: IllumiNet Press, 1993.

Berlet, Chip. "Anti-Masonic Conspiracy Theories." *Heredom*. Washington, D.C.: Scottish Rite Research Society, 2002. 243-75.

Bowart, Walter. *Operation Mind Control*. Ft. Bragg: Flatland Edition, 1994.

Bresler, Fenton. *Who Killed John Lennon?* New York: St. Martin's Press, 1989.

Cohen, Rich. "Welcome to the Conspiracy." *Vanity Fair* (May 2004): 138-54.

Dobbs, Robert. Dave Porter Interview. *Genesis of a Music*. Pacifica Radio. KPFK, Los Angeles. 24 Sep. 1994.

Glenn, Josh and A.S. Hamrah. "Woodstock Never Happened!" *Paranoia* (#9, summer 1995): 54.

Gray, Mike. *Angle of Attack*. New York: Norton, 1992.

Hoagland, Richard. Art Bell Interview. *Coast to Coast AM*. KABC, Los Angeles. 16 May 1997.

---. Art Bell Interview. *Coast to Coast AM*. KABC, Los Angeles. 20 Aug. 1997

Krassner, Paul. *Confessions of a Raving, Unconfined Nut*. New York: Simon & Schuster, 1993.

René, Ralph. *NASA Mooned America!* Passaic: René Foundation, 1994.

Prouty, L. Fletcher. *JFK: The CIA, Vietnam and the Plot to Assassinate John F. Kennedy*. New York: Birch Lane Press, 1992.

Strieber, Whitley. Interview with Richard Belzer and Jim Marrs. *Coast to Coast AM*. KABC, Los Angeles. 9 July, 1999.

Vallée, Jacques. *Revelations: Alien Contact and Human Deception*. New York: Ballantine, 1991.

PART TWO

POP CULTURE AS MIND CONTROL, MIND CONTROL AS POP CULTURE

CIA Headquarters - Langley, Virginia
Is it in the shape of an owl?

CHAPTER TWO

HONEY, DID YOU LEAVE YOUR BRAIN BACK AT LANGLEY AGAIN?

A Brief History Of Modern Mind Control Technology

Since 1947 the Central Intelligence Agency has been actively researching advanced forms of mind control. A process that began with simple interrogation techniques evolved into the use of hypnosis, LSD and other mind-altering drugs, aversion therapy, psychosurgery, and intra-cerebral implants. These developments eventually led to the wireless electromagnetic variety now included in the much-touted "non-lethal weaponry" of the twenty-first century. Unfortunately, most Americans don't realize that the twenty-first century arrived in their country nearly fifty years earlier than expected.

In 1943, while working for Sandoz Pharmaceuticals in Basle, Switzerland, Albert Hofmann first synthesized ergotamine molecules in a unique mixture he called LSD-25. By now it should be well known that Sandoz's most enthusiastic purchaser of this strange new chemical was none other than Allen Dulles, the third director of the fledgling Central Intelligence Agency. By late 1950 Dulles had become thoroughly convinced that the North Koreans were using LSD as a truth serum on American POWs. Adding to this conviction was Dr. Hofmann's comment to Dulles that "he would have confessed to anything to escape from the fear unleashed in his mind" by the LSD (Thomas 95). Outraged over the very notion that the drug would be used to convert helpless Americans to Communism when it could be used much more ethically to convert helpless Communists to capitalism, Dulles arranged in 1952 for Sandoz to ship a large quantity of LSD to the CIA's Office of Technical Services Staff (TSS) under an operation named after one of his favorite vegetables: Artichoke. However, before the miracle drug could be utilized against the enemies of America, the TSS decided it should be tested thoroughly on the closest available subjects: in other words, fellow Americans.

Under the leadership of Dr. Sydney Gottlieb, infamous for being one of the first American mind control specialists, the TSS initiated a series of LSD experiments at respected research centers all across the country. Prisoners, psychiatric patients, mentally retarded children, and even fellow intelligence officers became unwitting guinea pigs for this War Against Communism. In November of 1953 Gottlieb spiked the drink of a biochemist named Dr. Frank Olson while he and other TSS operatives were holding an informal seminar at an isolated Maryland cabin. Only a few days later, Olson went flying through a *closed* window on the tenth floor of the Statler Hotel in New York (Lee and Shlain 31). Most of the researchers who speak about this incident parrot the Agency explanation released in 1975: that Olson committed suicide due to the adverse effects of the LSD. As far as I know, however, even the most distraught individual will usually take the time to open a window before he leaps through it. A more likely scenario is that an angered Olson threatened to expose the Agency's Nazi-like tactics and was disposed of accordingly. Gottlieb's assistant, Dr. Richard Lashbrook, was in Olson's hotel room that night. He claimed to have been in the next bed sleeping soundly when Olson decided to step out for a bit of fresh air.

In H.P. Albarelli's 2009 book, *A Terrible Mistake: The Murder of Frank Olson and the CIA's Secret Cold War Experiments*, the author contends that Olson was involved with a 1951 CIA-funded LSD experiment conducted in a village called Pont-St.-Esprit located in southern France:

...in late summer of that year, hundreds of villagers had suddenly fallen ill, many wildly hallucinating and behaving in bizarre ways. After a great deal of debate, scientists were called in to investigate the situation. The scientists, including at least two prominent Sandoz researchers, had concluded that the villagers had suffered ergot poisoning that originated in a shipment of contaminated baked bread they had received the same day of the outbreak. (152)

Albarelli makes a very good case that the source of the outbreak was Olson himself:

...at the time of the Pont-St.-Esprit outbreak, a group of Camp Detrick scientists just happened to be visiting France. The evidence is in Frank Olson's passport, as well as the passports of other SOD [Special Operations Division] scientists. (357)

Olson's professional expertise was in "aerosol delivery systems for chemical and biological weapons, many of them highly lethal" (702). His status as a high-ranking officer in the SOD, coupled with his presence in France at the time of the outbreak, is more than just merely suggestive. Through Albarelli's tireless research, it's clear that Olson's conscience was haunted by the mass experiments he had witnessed in southern France. His employers were concerned that Olson intended to turn whistleblower and reveal the nature of the secret operation to the media.

Regardless of Olson's intentions, the fact that the experiment at Pont-St.-Esprit was ever contemplated, planned, organized and carried out is shocking—so shocking that some hardened CIA and Army Cold Warriors at the time rightfully deemed it "un-American."

So intense was the pressure being applied to silence Frank Olson in 1953 that even he himself, in a moment of sheer desperation and fear, had begged, "Just let me go; just let me disappear." (703)

Apparently Olson's employers gave him his wish, though no doubt not in the manner he would have preferred.

Since 1975 the tragedy of Frank Olson has become somewhat of an archetype for the LSD shenanigans perpetuated by the Agency, but Olson was by no means the final victim of the cryptocracy's lust for experimentation. In 1964, at a Los Angeles symposium on biological psychiatry, doctors openly discussed the results of giving 150 micrograms of LSD to thirty mentally retarded children on a daily basis over the course of two to three months (Gregory and Rappoport). Remember, in the early sixties LSD was still legal. Across the United States, medical doctors and university professors, unhindered by our current War On Drugs, were ordering LSD from Albert Hofmann for "research purposes" at the direction of MK-ULTRA (the name given to Operation Artichoke when it was combined with MK-DELTA, a CIA program involving chemical biological warfare). In 1962 a Harvard professor named Timothy Leary published a paper titled "How to Change Behavior," which grew out of his research administering LSD to the inmates of the Concord Correctional Facility in Massachusetts. Of course, Leary later became the LSD Pied Piper leading the youth movement away from political involvement and urging them instead to "Turn on, tune in, and drop out." In the second edition of his book *Operation Mind Control*, researcher Walter Bowart writes:

> While Leary had received NIMH grants at the University of California at Berkeley from 1953-56 and while working for the U.S. Public Health Service from 1954-58, at first he denied that any of his psychedelic research projects at Harvard were funded by the government. Yet when I finally sat with him face-to-face after *Operation Mind Control* had been published (1979), and naively asked him if he was "witting" or "unwitting" of his collaboration with the CIA, Leary answered with: "Who would you work for, the Yankees or the Dodgers? I mean who was I supposed to work for, the KGB?" (Chp. 5, p. 4)

One almost wishes he had.

By the mid-sixties the CIA had concluded that LSD could not be utilized as a foolproof method for controlling the mind. LSD was too unpredictable for these cryptocrats' tastes. What they wanted was something far more reliable, something that could be used simply and quickly—at the press of a button, to be exact. Enter, stage left: Dr. José M. R. Delgado.

Dr. Delgado is a Yale University professor whose research in the 1960s revealed the fact that electrical stimulation of the brain (ESB) could be used for mind control purposes. Having been born in Spain, he was quite eager to demonstrate his manhood by hopping into a bullring and controlling a bull from afar via a transmitter hidden behind his matador's cape. As the bull charged toward the good doctor, he pressed a button that stimulated the electrode in the animal's brain, causing it to step back, then forward, then back again. He even made it walk around and around in circles. With his remote control device he was able to manipulate the bull as if it were an electronic toy (Delgado 168). In 1974, while speaking before the U.S. Congress, Delgado made the following statement:

> We need a program of psychosurgery for political control of our society. The purpose is physical control of the mind. Everyone who deviates from the given norm can be surgically mutilated.... Man does not have the right to develop his own mind....Someday armies and generals will be controlled by electronic stimulation of the brain. (Bowart Interview)

Considering Delgado's penchant for brain implants, it should be noted that a suspiciously large number of traumatic "alien" abductions occur near military bases (Strieber). On an episode of *The End of the Line*, a Santa Barbara radio show that often deals with political corruption and paranormal issues, Jeff Rense interviewed a Southern California surgeon named Dr. Roger Lier who had successfully removed three implants from two patients.[1] Though the two patients had never met before,

---

1   This show can be ordered from BioAlert Press, 475-A Linfield Place, Goleta, CA 93117.

the implants were identical. I think it's safe to assume the implants didn't just grow there on their own. *Someone* must have put them there. Personally, I consider it unlikely that advanced beings with the ability to zip through the universe at faster-than-light speed wouldn't also have access to virus-sized, nanotechnology tracking devices undetectable to the human eye. Even modern Earth science is on the verge of developing such machines.

In other words, why are little gray men from Zeti Reticuli still using twentieth century technology to track down their subjects? That would be tantamount to the U.S. military using bows and arrows to attack Kuwait. Perhaps José Delgado and friends simply need a convenient cover story for their "program of psychosurgery." Think about it: Are we being invaded from outer space or from Langley, Virginia?

The above hypothesis becomes less farfetched after one reads the following comments by the second Director of the CIA, Walter Bedell Smith, in a declassified document addressed to the Director of the Psychological Strategy Board:[2]

> 1. I am today transmitting to the National Security Board a proposal (TAB A) in which it is concluded that the problems connected with unidentified flying objects appear to have implications for psychological warfare as well as for intelligence and operations.
>
> 2. The background for this view is presented in some detail in TAB B.
>
> 3. I suggest that we discuss at an early board meeting the possible offensive or defensive utilization of these phenomena for psychological warfare purposes. (Bowart Chp. 38, p. 19)

For some mysterious reason, TABs A and B have been lost. As Walter Bowart says, "So much for the value of the Freedom of Information Act."

---

2   According to Bowart, "Declassified on 20 April, 1977 the letter is thought to have been written in 1952."

The Freedom of Information Act apparently carries as much weight in the political world as the Hippocratic oath does in the medical world. The same year Dr. Delgado was telling Congress that "We need a program of psychosurgery for political control of our society," another staunch defender of the healer's oath, Dr. Louis Jolyon West, was proposing just such a plan to the Governor of California, Ronald Reagan. West hoped to create a Center for the Study and Reduction of Violence at an abandoned missile site in the Santa Monica Mountains. He stated in print that young black males were unusually violent and required special treatment.

> Treatments discussed by West included chemical castration, psychosurgery, and the testing of experimental drugs on involuntarily incarcerated individuals. Furthermore, the activities of the Center were to have been coordinated with a California law enforcement program that maintained computer files on "pre-delinquent" children so that they could be treated *before* they made a negative mark on society. (Lee and Shlain 190)

Ronald Reagan loved this idea, of course, and was utterly perplexed when the people of California forced the State Legislature to kill the program after news of it was leaked to the press. No doubt Mr. Reagan thought to himself, *Gee, what's the problem with tracking black people through brain implants? Who on earth would object to such a wonderful thing?*

I seriously doubt that Dr. West's plans ended in frustration, however. At the exact time that West's "rehabilitation center" for African-Americans was nipped in the bud, Jim Jones began moving his predominantly black "People's Temple" to the jungles of Guyana, far from the prying eyes of the California State Legislature. Jones recruited most of his followers from the Mendocino State Mental Hospital in Ukiah, California. Strangely, every single employee of the hospital was a Temple member. When released, the patients were put into the custody of Jones, whose CIA connections are well delineated in

John Judge's essay "The Black Hole of Guyana" (available at www.ratical.org/ratville/JFK/JohnJudge/Jonestown.html).

Given the government's treatment of mental patients in the past—as victims of secret radiation tests, for example—it's really not too farfetched to consider that Jonestown may have been the perfect cover for a massive experiment. This idea is reinforced by the fact that only 408 bodies out of at least 1,100 Temple members were initially discovered at Jonestown. On 80-90% of the bodies, the Chief Medical Examiner "found fresh needle marks at the back of the left shoulder blades," while the others "had been shot or strangled" (Judge 130). Though I haven't researched this, I'm pretty certain that grape Kool-Aid is incapable of leaving puncture wounds on one's shoulder blade.

With around 400 dead in Jonestown itself, the remaining 700 must have fled into the surrounding jungle. Colonel Bo Gritz trained the Special Forces that were sent to hunt them down. According to Gritz, the extermination program became necessary after Congressman Leo Ryan was killed at the Port Kaituma airstrip. Gritz flatly states, "Jonestown I think was an extension of MK-Ultra from the CIA and there are probably other experiments going on" (Parfrey 51).

If "other experiments" are indeed being conducted, then Dr. Louis Jolyon West is no doubt at the forefront of them. Dr. West has had a very interesting career. Not only did he run a CIA-financed LSD research project at the University of Oklahoma during the 1950s and early 1960s, but out of all the doctors in the United States of America he happened to be the one chosen to examine Jack Ruby for signs of psychosis. Not surprisingly, he found them. He concluded that Ruby was "paranoid" because of his insistence that President Kennedy had been shot by a cabal of ultra-right-wingers. Perhaps the phrase "a cabal of MK-Ultra-right-wingers" would be more appropriate.

Dr. West, or "Jolly" as his friends call him, acts as a kind of dowsing rod for anyone attempting to track down government mind control experiments. Wherever one finds Jolly, the

CIA isn't too far behind. In the late sixties the doctor inserted himself into the center of what one CIA agent called a "human guinea pig farm": San Francisco's Haight-Ashbury. According to Lee and Shlain, West "rented a pad with the intention of studying the hippies in their native habitat" (189-90). In 1993 Jolly was called in as an advisor during the massacre of the Branch Dividians in Waco, which eerily resembled the events at Jonestown (Thompson). On April 19, 1995, the day of the Oklahoma City bombing, Jolly appeared on Larry King's TV show to explain the mental state of the "lone nut" responsible for the destruction, just as he'd done thirty-two years before with Jack Ruby. In light of this knowledge, Timothy McVeigh's assertion that a microchip was planted in his buttock becomes far less laughable.

Some researchers like Craig Hulet have denied the possibility of a conspiracy in the Oklahoma City bombing. During a February 1996 interview Hulet said, "All of a sudden everybody's trying to paint the picture that [McVeigh's] an Oswald. If he were an Oswald, he'd be dead." In fact, long before his 6-11-01 execution, attempts may very well have been made on McVeigh's life. On August 27, 1995 WTDY-AM (a radio station in Madison, Wisconsin) reported this intriguing bit of news:

> At the Oklahoma prison where McVeigh and Terry Nichols are being held, the Security Chief has been fired. According to the *Muskogee Daily Phoenix*, Chuck Mildner ordered that only one officer be allowed to handle food trays for the bombing suspects... after syringes and other items led him to suspect food tampering.

One wonders what those "other items" may have been. Call up the Neuropsychiatric Institute at UCLA and ask Jolly West, he'd probably know. After all, it's an interesting coincidence that the earliest mind control experiments performed by Jolly took place at Oklahoma University, where he once managed to kill an elephant with LSD (Lee and Shlain 189). I imagine the Murrah Federal Building represents even bigger game than an elephant. Given that Oklahoma is a city where 45% of people who are employed work for the government, it's no surprise that Jolly and friends would claim it as their own personal happy hunting grounds.

Unfortunately, the story of Louis Jolyon West doesn't end there. The July 1995 issue of *Los Angeles* magazine contains an article titled "The Othello Syndrome." On the cover, this diagnosis is emblazoned on the forehead of O.J. Simpson. It turns out that "The Othello Syndrome" is a term created by none other than our old friend Dr. West. Over forty years ago he wrote a paper attempting to prove that a black man will inevitably kill his spouse if she's white. Self-loathing, he said, causes them to believe that "something must be wrong with their Caucasian mates for seeking love beyond the racial pale" (Mulgannon 54). In the same *Los Angeles* article we learn that West has been friends with "famed Simpson defense counsel F. Lee Bailey" for twenty years. They met when Jolly was "a court-appointed witness at Patty Hearst's 1976 bank-robbery trial," which is fascinating since the late Mae Brussell did an excellent job of tying in the Hearst kidnapping with mind control experiments performed on inmates at Vacaville Prison (Emory, "The Terror Connection"). Much earlier F. Lee Bailey had been the defense attorney for Albert DeSalvo, the Boston Strangler, who was deprogrammed by another CIA mind control doctor named William Joseph Bryan. Bryan considered himself to be "the leading expert in the world" on hypnosis, and in 1969 was found guilty of hypnotizing four women patients into having sex with him. He once boasted to a pair of prostitutes that he "had hypnotized Sirhan Sirhan" (Turner and Christian 225-28).

There are numerous odd deaths surrounding the O.J. Simpson case that remain unreported in the mainstream media. For example, exactly two weeks after Ron Goldman and Nicole Brown Simpson were found murdered, Casimir Sucharski—an old friend of O.J.'s with definite mob connections—was "murdered in Miramar, Florida, along with two young women companions, Sharon Anderson and Marie Rogers" (Freed and

Briggs 150). Sucharski had previously gone to jail for possession of cocaine and guns recovered during a police raid on his
residence. According to the police, O.J. just barely escaped this
drug raid in the 1970s.

During his 10-12-95 interview on KPFK in Los Angeles, Dick
Gregory laid out the following information: While the Simpson
trial was still in progress Michael Nigg, a close friend of Ron
Goldman, was also murdered under mysterious circumstances.
Early in September, 1995, he was walking down the street with
a woman named Julia Long when two men held him up at gun
point, said it was a stick-up, shot him, neglected to steal anything,
didn't touch the woman, and then took off (Freed and Briggs 233).
Unless these were a special brand of surrealist muggers, I can
only conclude that something rather fishy occurred that night.
Furthermore, on that same day Judge Lance Ito broke down and
cried in court because a friend of his, a deputy sheriff involved
with the Simpson case, had been killed. According to Gregory,
three reporters investigating the Simpson/Goldman murders
were also killed under suspicious circumstances. Perhaps most
relevant to the specific focus of this chapter, however, is the fact
that juror Tracy Hampton tried to commit suicide by eating glass
after "hearing voices" in her head (Constantine 24). As if all that
weren't enough, the next door neighbor of Nicole Simpson turned
out to be Carl Colby, the son of William Colby, director of the
CIA during the Nixon administration (Emory, *One Step Beyond*).[3]
Coupled with the involvement of F. Lee Bailey and Louis Jolyon
West, these "coincidences" begin to point toward some form of
mob/intelligence involvement in the O.J. Simpson case.

In the wake of the Simpson trial and subsequent high-profile tragic farces, one often sees airhead politicians staring into

3   Not so incidentally, in 1996 William Colby gave up the ghost during a
rather mysterious boating accident near his vacation home in Maryland. The police
found the boat, but not the body. According to the 4-30-96 (Walpurgis Night) edition of the *Los Angeles Times*: "A neighbor who checked his home found his radio
and computer still on. Investigators found dinner dishes on a table and clam shells
in the kitchen sink." ("All right, buddy, put down those clam shells nice 'n easy! We're
all goin' on a little ride….") Newspaper pundits from coast to coast definitively concluded that no foul play was involved.

the TV camera with worry in their eyes, lamenting the rise of violence in society today. They would have you believe that this is due to the eradication of "family values." Meanwhile, the only values these politicians have are Manson Family values, for these are the same officials backing the research of mad scientists like José Delgado.

In the mid-seventies, Delgado abandoned his research into direct electrical stimulation of the brain in favor of electromagnetic fields (EMFs) that would affect certain areas of the brain from outside without the need of cumbersome bio-implants like the one used with the aforementioned bull so bravely subdued by Dr. Delgado. The implications of this technology are quite literally mind-blowing. These electromagnetic fields could be used to instill rage, sadness, or fear in whole cities. On the battlefield it might force even the most dedicated enemy to fall to his knees in surrender. Preston Nichols has commented on how suspicious it was when, almost before the first Gulf War had even begun, "the same Iraqis who fought a Holy War against Iran for eight years" suddenly abandoned deep bunkers equipped with "electricity, entertainment and enough food and water to last at least six months" (Nichols and Moon 133-34). It's quite possible that one of the covert reasons for the Gulf War was to test a small scale version of the U.S. military's Project HAARP.

HAARP (an acronym for High-frequency Active Auroral Research Program) is a $100,000,000 Air Force experiment located in the wilderness of Alaska. Its ostensible purpose is to study the ionosphere. However, researchers like Dr. Nick Begich believe it's actually a ground-based "Star Wars" weapon derived from the classified technology of Nikola Tesla. HAARP has the capability of creating

> ...a huge coherent controllable electromagnetic field which could be compared to a Delgado EMF, except HAARP's doesn't fill a room, it potentially fills a region the size of a large western state and, possibly, a hemisphere. Basically, the HAARP transmitter in this application will emit en-

ergy of the same level as the Earth's which is fifty times more than was needed in the wireless experiments of Dr. Delgado. What this means is that if HAARP is tuned to the right frequency, using just the right wave forms, mental disruption throughout a region could occur intentionally or as a side effect of the radio frequency transmissions. (Begich and Manning 160-61)

Though the project spokesman claims that HAARP did not become fully operational until 1998, some researchers believe it has been utilized for clandestine purposes for years and might even have operated in conjunction with the so-called "tethered" satellite lost by NASA in March of 1996 after it mysteriously broke free from the space shuttle and burnt up in the atmosphere. Richard Hoagland, co-author of the recent bestseller *Dark Mission: The Secret History of NASA*, has come to the conclusion that the tether was actually a "thirteen-mile-long tuned resonator" which, upon being irradiated by electromagnetic energy from a powerful ground-based transmitter such as HAARP, was used as a dipole in the ionosphere to perform covert experiments with the hyper-dimensional physics first described by James Clerk Maxwell in the late nineteenth century.

The power densities required for such complex experimentation are much higher than that needed to effect mass behavioral modification. If one mapped out a true line course between Project HAARP and the possible relay transmitters needed to amplify and disperse the electromagnetic energy across a densely populated area, one might very well find himself on the West Coast of the United States where such odd and wonderful events as the L.A. Riots have occurred. Could these riots have been a mere cover for secret experiments involving HAARP predecessors such as the GWEN Towers? GWEN, by the way, stands for "Ground Wave Emergency Network" (Begich and Manning 4). It's unclear whether the Towers end emergencies or help start them.

The 5-10-92 edition of the *New York Times* reported the fact that out of 18,230 people arrested during the L.A. Riots,

both the police and the city prosecutors could not account for 10,000 of them. A prosecutor was quoted as saying, "We don't know where they are. It's a mystery to many of us in the system." Did these people dissipate into nothingness or were they taken somewhere and disposed of like mad cattle? Consider this: As I write this I'm worth as much as the change in my pocket. However, if I killed myself and managed to stick around on the material plane somehow, I could sell my own body for 2.5 million dollars (Gregory and Rappoport). Healthy organs are always in demand. Now multiply 2.5 million by 10,000 and look at those zeros fly off the calculator screen. That could buy a lot of Patriot missiles, couldn't it?

In a document titled 'Mind Control Operations/Aquarius Group Activities' released by an anonymous team of intelligence officers known as Com-12, we are told the following:

> With a general ignorance through arrogance of most public population in the U.S., the erection of large cellular towers being carried out under HIGH TONE and XENO are largely going completely unnoticed.
>
> These projects are being carried out in private business capacities and therefore in Deep Black Operations cover. However, public populations would be wise to educate themselves in the construction of these seemingly innocent towers in large population areas. The cellular 800 MHZ waves are a constant wave. Due to the great proliferation of towers in key population areas, they will have a devastating effect.... (Bowart Chp. 37, p. 19)

It is very possible that these are the relay pylons being used in conjunction with HAARP. In this book, I have included a photo (page 54) of one of the possible culprits to increase your awareness and thus dispel the "general ignorance" spoken of so disdainfully by the Com-12 group.

Despite Com-12's cynicism, the information about such experiments is indeed reaching the general public, though admittedly at a slow pace. In 1995 a group of psychiatrists and mind control survivors spoke before President Clinton's Advisory Committee On Human Radiation Experiments. They revealed the fact that the radiation experiments were only a small part of a larger operation involving mind control. Though a number of journalists were indeed present during this groundbreaking testimony, none of the major newspapers reported the story. I wrote a letter to Ruth Faden, the Chair of the Committee, and asked her if she was going to investigate any further into the mind control aspects of the radiation testing. I also asked her if she could comment on why the mainstream media chose to ignore the survivors' testimony. The letter came back stamped: RETURN TO SENDER. Though Ms. Faden was obviously somewhat less than enthused by what the survivors told her, a transcript of their testimony has nevertheless been made available to the public in Jon Rappoport's book, *U.S. Government Mind Control Experiments on Children*.[4] Due to alternative publications like Rappoport's, vital information is gradually bursting free from behind the National Security curtain.

Ultimately, the only way to end the corruption and Nazi-like horror delineated in the preceding pages is to repeal the National Security Act, just as our grandfathers and grandmothers forced the government to repeal the Volstead Act in 1933. This country survived quite well for 171 years without the albatross of the National Security Act wrapped around our necks. Is it just a coincidence that Americans have grown more and more distrustful and cynical toward their government since 1947, the year this Act was rushed through Congress without any debate whatsoever? The decline of America has nothing to do with "family values," but with the black cauldron of dirty secrets hidden from the eyes of most Americans, considered by the cryptocrats to be mere "sheeple" simply because they don't have "a need to know." I think the American people should decide for themselves if they have a need to know, and the only way to do that is to organize and rip aside the façade of the military-industrial-complex for *all* to see. This can be done by resurrecting organizations like The Freedom of Thought Foundation founded by the late Wal-

4   This book can be ordered from its author at www.nomorefakenews.com.

ter Bowart. Before Bowart succumbed to a protracted illness in December of 2007, the primary goals of his organization were to "lend aid and protection to survivors of mind control, develop or discover countermeasures to electronic forms of mind control and publicize them, and conduct a tireless campaign to repeal the National Security Act." These are concerns that should be shared by every American, mind control survivor or not, for as a pastor named Martin Niemoller once wrote:

> In Germany they first came for the Communists and I didn't speak up because I wasn't a Communist.
> Then they came for the Jews, and I didn't speak up because I wasn't a Jew.
> Then they came for the trade unionists, and I didn't speak up because I wasn't a trade unionist.
> Then they came for the Catholics, and I didn't speak up because I was a Protestant. Then they came for me—and by that time no one was left to speak up.

Don't lose your voice like Pastor Niemoller did. Don't lose your voice to the politicians and the psychiatrists and the educators and the journalists who "know best," who say, "Trust us, we'll show you what reality is actually all about." If you allow yourself to trust them, you might as well pack up your brain right now, stamp it FRAGILE, and ship it over to the CIA Headquarters in scenic Langley, Virginia. They've always got room for another brain. That's why they're constantly recruiting fresh ones from college campuses.

I hear if you work at the CIA, you have to leave your brain at the door along with your hat and coat. One time an employee forgot to retrieve his brain when he left for the day, remembering it only after his commute was already halfway over. Inevitably, he entered his suburban Virginia home to the smell of pot roast and the grating sound of his wife's voice as she planted her fists on her hips (having noticed her husband's sagging head) and sighed for the fortieth night in a row: "Honey, did you leave your brain back at Langley again?"

"Yes, dear," he replied, promising to pick it up first thing Monday morning. After all, he wouldn't be needing it over the weekend. Misplacing his brain was but one of the many annoying though necessary risks of working for the Company. All in all, he couldn't complain. *At least it's a living,* he told himself doubtfully.

Yes, it's a living... but hardly a life.

Works Cited

Albarelli Jr., H.P. *A Terrible Mistake: The Murder of Frank Olson and the CIA's Secret Cold War Experiments.* Walterville, OR: Trine Day, 2009.

Begich, Dr. Nick and Jeane Manning. *Angels Don't Play This HAARP.* Anchorage: Earthpulse Press, 1995.

Bowart, Walter. Interview. *Something's Happening.* Pacifica Radio. KPFK, Los Angeles. 6 Oct. 1994.

---. *Operation Mind Control.* Ft. Bragg: Flatland Editions, 1994.

Constantine, Alex. *The Florida/Hollywood Mob Connection, the CIA and O.J. Simpson.* n.p.: The Constantine Report, 1995.

Delgado, José. *Physical Control of the Mind.* New York: Harper & Row, 1969.

Emory, Dave. *One Step Beyond.* FYI Radio. KFJC, Los Altos Hills. 12 Feb. 1995.

---"The Terror Connection—Part II: California Under Ronald Reagan." *Radio Free America.* FYI Radio. KFJC, Los Altos Hills. Sep. 1986.

Freed, Donald and Raymond P. Briggs, Ph.D. *Killing Time.* New York: Macmillan, 1996.

Gregory, Dick and Jon Rapport. Interview. *Something's Happening.* Pacifica Radio. KPFK, Los Angeles. 12 Oct. 1995.

Hoagland, Richard. Interview. *Coast To Coast AM With Art Bell.* CBC Radio. KOGO, San Diego. 7 Mar. 1996.

Hulet, Craig. Interview. *Something's Happening.* Pacifica Radio. KPFK, Los Angeles. 29 Feb. 1996.

Judge, John. "The Black Hole of Guyana." *Secret and Suppressed: Banned Ideas and Hidden History.* Ed. Jim Keith. Portland: Feral House, 1993. 127-65.

Lee, Martin and Bruce Shlain. *Acid Dreams.* New York: Grove Weidenfeld, 1992.

Mulgammon, Terry. "Not Wisely But Too Well..." *Los Angeles.* July 1995: 54.

Nichols, Preston and Peter Moon. *The Montauk Project*. Westbury: Sky Books, 1993.

Parfrey, Adam. "Bo Gritz Interrogated." *Flatland* 10 (1994): 46-51.

Strieber, Whitley. Interview. *Dreamland*. CBC Radio. KOGO, San Diego. 24 Dec. 1995.

Thomas, Gordon. *Journey Into Madness*. New York: Bantam Books, 1990.

Thomson, Linda. "Waco: The Big Lie." Granada Pavilion Lecture. Santa Monica, 11 Nov. 1993.

Turner, William and Jonn Christian. *The Assassination of Robert F. Kennedy*. New York: Thunder's Mouth Press, 1993.

HEAVEN'S GATE

As was promised – the keys to Heaven's Gate are here again in
Ti and Do (The UFO Two) as they were in Jesus and His Father 2000 yrs. ago.

CHAPTER THREE

HEAVEN'S GATE, COLUMBINE, THE UNABOMBER, AND OTHER ATROCITIES

In the Fall 1997 issue (#17) of *Paranoia* magazine I published "Honey, Did You Leave Your Brain Back At Langley Again?: A Brief History of Modern Mind Control Technology." It was subsequently reprinted in Citadel Press' 1999 anthology *The Conspiracy Reader*. Since its original publication, a number of significance events have occurred that may very well be connected to the covert world of government mind control programs. Four of them deserve special attention here.

Heaven's Gate

In Rancho Santa Fe, CA on the 26th of March, 1997, thirty-nine members of the Heaven's Gate group were found dead from an apparent mass suicide. The bodies were discovered by an ex-member who "just happened" to bring his video camera along. These grisly images were later shown all over the nightly news, something rarely allowed by normal network standards. The bodies were lying in their beds, triangular purple shrouds over their faces, their bags packed beside them. Videotaped farewell messages indicated that they committed suicide in order to advance to a "higher plane of existence" where they would rendezvous with a spaceship trailing the comet Hale-Bopp. They'd first heard of this supposed spaceship during an interview with Professor Courtney Brown on the late night radio talk show *Coast to Coast AM With Art Bell*.

Back on Feb. 23rd of 1997 the *Washington Post* had published a concise article on Courtney Brown, who wrote a 1996 book titled *Cosmic Voyage* in which he claimed to have acquired the ability to "remote view" events from afar and carry on telepathic communications with extraterrestrials. He claimed to have acquired these abilities from none other than Major Ed Dames, proprietor of Psi-Tech, a remote viewing school and research center founded by a group of "former" intelligence officers. "Major Dames is schooled in military intelligence," writes researcher Alex Constantine, "and the former commanding officer of the Army's 'Psychic Espionage Unit,' which operated under DIA and Army INSCOM charter." Constantine maintains that Dames has utilized psychic research merely as a convenient cover story for mind control experimentation (Constantine 1).

The *Washington Post* article strongly suggests that Professor Brown forged a photograph depicting a "mysterious object" trailing the comet Hale-Bopp. Brown appeared on the Art Bell radio show in November of 1996 and claimed that this object was an alien spacecraft. He contended that the photograph had been given to him by a "top ten university astronomer" who would reveal his identity during a major press conference in a week. Brown urged Bell not to make the photograph public until the secret astronomer decided to step forward. The astronomer never emerged and the photograph was proven to be a fake on January 15th when at last Art Bell released it on the internet. The photo was almost immediately recognized by University of Hawaii astronomer Oliver Hainut as an altered version of a photograph taken by his colleague David Tholen. Later a listener sent Whitley Strieber, a frequent guest on Art Bell's show, the résumé of a man named Courtney Brown who worked for the Pentagon.

Marshall H. Applewhite, the leader of Heaven's Gate, appears in Jacques Vallée's 1979 book *Messengers of Deception*. This is the first book to link government mind control experiments with the UFO phenomenon. During the course of his research Vallée speaks to a retired, high-ranking intelligence officer known as "Major Murphy." Murphy informs Vallée that a shadowy cabal is manipulating UFO cults to spread "belief in higher races and in totalitarian systems that would eliminate democracy" (219).

Applewhite's faithful companion, a woman named Bonnie Lu Nettles, had once been his nurse while he was being treated for mental instability at a Texas hospital (right in the middle of George Bush country) back in 1972. Only a few years later the pair began appearing on various college campuses, urging young and old alike to abandon their "earthly vessels" in order to take their rightful place among the friendly blonde Aryans from the stars. At this same time they began calling themselves "Guinea" and "Pig."

Not surprisingly, soon after the news of the mysterious deaths broke on national television, Dr. Louis Jolyon West appeared on ABC's *Nightline* to explain the unique mindset that would cause normal, law-abiding citizens to join a cult and commit suicide. As I mentioned in the previous chapter, Dr. West is a CIA psychiatrist who has the unusual talent of attaching himself to such stellar American icons as Jack Ruby, Patty Hearst, David Koresh, Timothy McVeigh, and O.J. Simpson... or at least he *did* until his long overdue death on the 7th of January, 1999. Appropriately enough, just before Valentine's Day (Feb. 11, 2000, to be exact) another infamous CIA mind control scientist, Dr. Martin Orne, died of cancer. (Valentine's Day also marked the death of two teenagers who might very well have been the victims of Orne's mind control milieu. More on this later.) As Walter Bowart said to me during a telephone conversation soon after their deaths, "Well, at least that's two of the monsters down!"

It should be noted that some researchers, like Richard Hoagland, have speculated that the Heaven's Gate affair was a complex intelligence operation to discredit the UFO community. This is possible, of course, though more often than not the UFO community seems to do a pretty good job of that on its own.

6-6-98

In the researcher's edition of *Operation Mind Control* Walter Bowart reported that many adult and child survivors of mind control experimentation had been programmed to "snap" on a specific date: "...some theorists report the date a multiple of 666 X 3 = 1998, which, following occult numerology, would make the exact day June 6, 1998" (Chp. 11, p. 16). I first read those words in the spring of 1994. In the weeks and days counting down to that date, the world watched in horror as violence exploded on school campuses all across the United States and beyond. In the U.S. alone there were school shootings (as well as attempts at violence that were halted just in time) in Lancaster, CA, Springfield, OR, Ft. Pierce, FL, Ft. Lauderdale, FL, Clearville, PA, Pittsburgh, PA, Pahrump, NV, and St. Charles, MO, not to mention devastating church burnings such as the one in Champagne, IL in which thirty-three people were killed. Even more bizarre was the first homicide in the Vatican (perpetuated by the head of the Pope's elite guard, Alois Estermann) in over 150 years—or at least the first we *know* about. I suspect David Yallop, author of the book *In God's Name* exposing the conspiracy behind the assassination of Pope John Paul I, would beg to differ.

Columbine

The Columbine case of 1999 is an intriguing one, to say the least. On April 18th of 1999, I was hanging out with a few skeptical friends of mine. Whenever I speak, they tend to roll their eyes. On this particular evening I said, "Hey, in a couple of days it's going to be Hitler's birthday. You just watch, there's gonna be a bunch of 'lone nut' shootings goin' off all over the place, at post offices and high schools and McDonald's fast food joints, you just watch." They rolled their eyes.

Sure enough, on the morning of April 20th, I woke up and switched on CNN to see a massacre occurring in Littleton, Colorado at Columbine High School. One of my friends called me and said, "Are you involved? How'd you know about this?" I said, "I read *Operation Mind Control!*" and hung up. I then proceeded to take fastidious notes. Within seconds the Sheriff of Littleton was telling a reporter, "Why do these kids' parents let them have automatic weapons and bombs? We need more gun legislation." As Dave Emory has pointed out, "If they had driven a truck into the high school nobody would've demanded the banning of automobiles."

One of my earliest notes reads, "3 white males, black jackets, black hats, camo fatigues." Please pay attention to the number three. *Every* single reporter on the scene described three white males entering the school. I sat there for hours and watched as the students rushed off the campus. The second they were in arm's reach reporters began sticking microphones in their tear-stricken faces and saying, "So how do you feel?" *Every* single one of the kids said they saw three white males, two of them in black trench coats, firing automatic rifles while a third man in a white t-shirt tossed bombs left and right. Hours later, however, the kids began changing their minds. One girl even said, "I thought I saw three of them, but the news said there was only two so I guess I was wrong." And they say the media has no effect on children.

By that evening, when President Clinton took to the White House podium and said, "We have to teach our children that we can't solve our disagreements with violence" (this while Clinton was bombing the hell out of Kosovo), the cover story was nailed down and the media abruptly followed in lockstep. The very same reporters who had spent the entire day fretting about the three armed men in black were suddenly fed a new batch of cue cards and maintained that the third man was only a phantom, perhaps a figment of their collective imaginations.

Eerie shades of the equally elusive "John Doe 2" of Oklahoma City Bombing fame.

At one point, while the rampage was at its height, a policeman told a CNN reporter that the gunmen tried to flee but were forced back onto campus by gunfire emanating from an *unknown source*. The policeman made it clear that they had not fired on the gunmen. So who was boxing the shooters into the trap?

And a trap it surely was. Prevented from fleeing, they were forced to take refuge in the library where most of the thirteen victims were found. After the bloodbath had played itself out, the shooters ostensibly turned their guns on themselves. At least that's what the President told us, even though an autopsy hadn't even been performed yet. Wouldn't it be more logical to assume that the missing third assailant was responsible for the death of his cohorts?

By the next morning we discovered that the dead shooters were Eric Harris (18) and Dylan Klebold (17). My initial suspicion about the Hitler tie-in was correct, of course; Harris and Klebold had purposely scheduled the attack to coincide with Hitler's birthday. We now know that Harris' father was a colonel in the Air Force, which was no surprise to me. According to mind control survivor Cathy O'Brien, her most horrendous episodes of torture occurred on Air Force Bases such as Tinker near Tulsa, Oklahoma (Bowart Chp. 9, p. 9). In Harris' room the police found a dream machine, a device invented by Brion Gysin that induces a hypnotic state via flickering, rotating lights. Harris was also an avid fan of computer video games.

According to Dr. David Grossman, author of *On Killing*, "... with the advent of computers and high-speed personal computers, [the military was] able to vastly improve the basic brainwashing techniques that had already earlier been developed. And all of it came down to desensitizing people to the idea of killing...." In a lecture delivered not long after the shootings, researcher Jeffrey Steinberg expands on Grossman's findings:

> In the 1980s and 1990s, the military spent enormous amounts of money through DARPA, the Defense Ad-

vanced Research Program office at the Pentagon, in the computer industry, to be able to develop training simulators to get people into a situation, that without even firing a gun, but using one of the "point-and-shoot" computer guns, you can go through the experience of killing an object that looks human, thousands, hundreds of thousands of times, until it becomes almost second nature.

What happened after a point, is that the very people who were hired by the military to develop these systems, went commercial. They linked up with Hollywood, they linked up with the computer industry, and they began developing the identical techniques that were used in the framework of the military to train killers, and for no other purpose. There was no other reason why tens of billions of dollars of research money went into these technologies, other than to create a desensitized human being, who kills on instinct, and therefore violates everything human. (Steinberg 5)

I don't believe that video games alone can cause anybody to kill, but when you combine them with the complex sensorium of behaviorist conditioning that was surely occurring at that school, you have a recipe for destruction.

What conditioning am I talking about? There are a number of mysterious happenings surrounding this school and these two young men in particular. For example, Eric Harris' parents were pumping him full of a drug called Luvox, as reported in the 4-29-99 edition of *The Washington Post*. Though technically an anti-depressant, it is not approved in the United States to treat depression. It "can activate mania in susceptible patients." It is contraindicated in patients with a history of "provocative, intrusive, or aggressive behavior," which clearly applies to Harris. Why would his parents force him to take this drug unless they wanted to push him over the edge?

Stranger still is the intersection between Dylan Klebold and the son of FBI agent Dwayne Fuselier, as reported in the 5-22-99 edition of the *Denver Rocky Mountain News*. Fuselier happens to be the lead investigator in the Columbine shootings.

His son helped Brooks Brown, a close friend of Klebold, produce a "1997 videotape that shows trench-coat-clad students armed with weapons moving through the school's halls and then blowing up the school. Incredibly, FBI spokesman Gary Gomes claimed there was 'no conflict of interest'" (Hidell 24).

The high school itself has been a lightning rod for controversy and death. In 1996 it was the focal point for a major censorship case involving a Bernardo Bertolucci film titled *1900*, which is about the rise of fascism in Italy. The film was shown in a Logic/Debate class in an ostensible attempt to expose the horrors of fascism. The film certainly does that. In one scene the head fascist, portrayed by Donald Sutherland, sodomizes a little boy while whirling him around in a circle and then bashing his brains against a wall. This crime is blamed on the communists, à la the German Reichstag fire, and used as an excuse for a crackdown. The teacher who showed the film, Alfred Wilder, was fired for daring to teach high school seniors the true evils of fascism. Apparently in this predominantly white, wealthy suburb this is an outright no-no. During the firestorm of controversy that followed, Bernardo Bertolucci testified on behalf of Wilder. He said in part: "The puritanical urge to divorce the sexual material in my film from its context is only a prelude to a similar desire to cut politics and history from the context in which they are embedded. How will future generations of children grapple with the present if they cannot be allowed to bear witness and debate the past?"

In early February of 1997 Alfred Wilder was vindicated and allowed to return to his job after the Colorado Court of Appeals found his dismissal to be in violation of his first Amendment rights. Ironically, the video in which Eric Harris and his buddies rehearsed the massacre-to-come was not allowed to be shown on school grounds because of the controversy surrounding Bertolucci's *1900*. If the video had indeed been shown, perhaps somebody would have realized how serious a threat it represented, and prevented the tragedy from occurring. Researcher Dave Emory has wondered "whether perhaps

Nazi elements, inside and/or outside [the] government, may have deliberately targeted Columbine High School because of the earlier case in which an attempt to remove Al Wilder from the teaching staff... was unsuccessful" (Emory 5-20-99).

Jeffrey Steinberg has a more sinister interpretation. He believes the violent Bertolucci film was shown to the children as part of a long-term program of desensitization. There seems to be some evidence that such a program was indeed underway at Columbine, and may still be occurring. Much earlier than the Al Wilder case, Columbine found itself locked into another national controversy. In 1990, around the time of that other notorious video game called the Persian Gulf War, Columbine was featured prominently in an episode of ABC's *20/20* due to a rather strange course that was considered mandatory for graduation. It was unique in the history of American high schools. Indeed, its only precedent was a fictional one and can be found in Aldous Huxley's 1932 dystopia *Brave New World*.

The name of the course was "Death Education," in which children were subjected to "experiencing" death vicariously in a number of different forms. The instructors would use films, but would also send the students on field trips to the local morgue where they were given a complete tour, shown corpses, and forced to sit in on autopsies.

In Chapter 11 of *Brave New World* Dr. Gaffney explains "the Slough Crematorium" to Huxley's protagonist Bernard Marx: "Death conditioning begins at eighteen months. Every tot spends two mornings a week in a Hospital for the Dying. All the best toys are kept there, and they get chocolate cream on death days. They learn to take dying as a matter of course" (193). Huxley, it should be noted, worked for the CIA on the MK-Ultra program and initiated Timothy Leary into their ranks (Bowart Interview).

According to Steinberg the school's argument was, "Well, death is part of everyone's experience, and therefore it's good for people to learn to come to grips with it." Steinberg goes on to state: "In reality, looking at Dr. Grossman, and other people who've studied this phenomenon in the military, this is all part of this process of desensitization.... [I]ssues that are fundamental philosophical and moral issues cease to exist, and everything is one succession of sensory experiences that all lead you to abandon that which is essentially human in yourself" (6).

Unfortunately, the milieu of death that surrounds Columbine did not end with Eric Harris and Dylan Klebold. According to the 8-18-99 edition of the *New York Times*: On the first day the school was to reopen, parents patrolling the halls before the start of classes found four swastikas carved into the walls. They covered the symbols with duct tape until school officials could remove them permanently. A parent named Tammy Theus, the mother of one of the fifteen black students at the school, said, "It's like they're laughing in our faces." Who's "they," I wonder? Harris and Klebold are dead, are they not?

Perhaps "they" are the very same individuals responsible for the threats reported in the 9-5-99 edition of the *San Jose Mercury News*: "Grappling with the aftermath of the April 20th massacre at Columbine High School in Littleton, Colorado, education officials say five other high schools in the same district have received letters threatening violence in the past month." If Harris and Klebold were the "lone nuts" the mainstream media and President Clinton claim they were, who continues to threaten Littleton?

The next fatality connected to Columbine High occurred on March 9, 2000. The following brief paragraph appeared in the 2-15-00 edition of the *Los Angeles Times*: "Two Columbine High School sweethearts were found dead early Valentine's Day at a restaurant near the Littleton, Colo. school, reopening the wounds of last year's rampage. Sophomores Stephanie Hart, 16, and Nicholas Kunselman, 15—who were reportedly dating—were found in a sandwich shop near the school where Eric Harris and Dyland Klebold killed 13 people April 20. Police said the shootings were being investigated as a double homicide and cited robbery as a possible motive."

You might assume the Columbine connection to this double homicide was a mere coincidence, if you weren't aware of the program of desensitization I've outlined in the previous pages. I suspect the fallout from this on-going experiment will continue to plague Littleton, Colorado for years to come.

I should take note of one last interesting detail... or perhaps it's just a coincidence. Early in 1997 I wrote a short story titled "Feast of Clowns" that was inspired by the life of Joseph Grimaldi, the man who turned clowning into a respected art form in Victorian England. The story was published in W.H. Horner's 2006 anthology *Modern Magic: Tales of Fantasy and Horror*. Grimaldi learned his trade from his father, who was obsessed with death and abused his son both physically and psychologically. Charles Dickens ghosted Grimaldi's autobiography, which I read for research purposes. While digging through some files in search of a *Skeptical Inquirer* article debunking the concept of government mind control programs, I accidentally came across pages 108-111 of the autobiography. I forget why I photocopied the pages, and yet there they were. One of the pages fell on the cluttered carpet. As I bent over to pick it up I spotted the word "Columbine." Since I was in the midst of writing this update, I was taken aback for a moment. Then I read the following sentences:

> The nominal pretext for the harlequinade on this December evening is, as usual, the pursuit of the lovers by Pantaloon and Clown, and the excitement of the chase lends zest to the buffoonery. But although the sympathy of the audience is officially with the runaways, and although a happy ending for Harlequin and Columbine is inevitable, the hero of the game is really the rascally Clown. Every one is on the anarchist's side. There is no end to his antics, and no particular continuity but the succession of familiar English scenes, as he races through Georgian London leaving havoc and destruction in his wake. (Dickens 109)

I hope Columbine really does have a happy ending, but I suspect the death-obsessed Clown will have the last laugh.

The Unabomber

On July 6th of 1999 investigative journalist Alexander Cockburn published a major revelation on the internet edition of the *Los Angeles Times*. Apparently, Someone On High felt the information was a tad too disturbing in its implications to print in the street edition. To correct this oversight I've decided to reprint the relevant portion of the article in these pages....

> It turns out that Theodore Kaczynski, a.k.a. the Unabomber, was a volunteer in mind-control experiments sponsored by the CIA at Harvard in the late 1950s and early 1960s.
>
> Michael Mello, author of the recently published book, *The United States of America vs. Theodore John Kaczynski*, notes that at some point in his Harvard years—1958 to 1962—Kaczynski agreed to be the subject of "a psychological experiment." Mello identifies the chief researcher for these only as a lieutenant colonel in World War II, working for the CIA's predecessor organization, the Office of Strategic Services. In fact, the man experimenting on the young Kaczynski was Dr. Henry Murray, who died in 1988.
>
> Murray became preoccupied by psychoanalysis in the 1920s, drawn to it through a fascination with Herman Melville's *Moby Dick*, which he gave to Sigmund Freud, who duly made the excited diagnosis that the whale was a father figure. After spending the 1930s developing personality theory, Murray was recruited to the OSS at the start of the war, applying his theories to the selection of agents and also presumably to interrogation.
>
> As chairman of the Department of Social Relations at Harvard, Murray zealously prosecuted the CIA's efforts to carry forward experiments in mind control conducted by Nazi doctors in the concentration camps. The overall program was under the control of the late Sidney Gottlieb, head of the CIA's technical services division. Just as Harvard students were fed doses of LSD, psilocybin and other potions, so too were prisoners and many unwitting guinea pigs.
>
> Sometimes the results were disastrous. A dram of LSD fed by Gottlieb himself to an unwitting U.S. army

officer, Frank Olson, plunged Olson into escalating psychotic episodes, which culminated in Olson's fatal descent from an upper window in the Statler-Hilton in New York. Gottlieb was the object of a lawsuit not only by Olson's children but also by the sister of another man, Stanley Milton Glickman, whose life had disintegrated into psychosis after being unwittingly given a dose of LSD by Gottlieb.

What did Murray give Kaczynski? Did the experiment's long-term effects help tilt him into the Unabomber's homicidal rampages? The CIA's mind experiment program was vast. How many other human time bombs were thus primed? How many of them have exploded?

For far more esoteric, though no less significant, information on the Unabomber I recommend Michael A. Hoffman's article "Invoking Catastrophe: The Unabom Ritual and Alchemical Process" published in the update of his fascinating book *Secret Societies and Psychological Warfare*, available from Independent History and Research, PO Box, Coeur d'Alene, Idaho 83816.

Considering the severity of the atrocities described in these pages, one might become cynical about the fate of democracy in this mind-controlled society. However, reasons for optimism persist in the words of consciousness researcher David E. Worcester: "When Pavlov went to the Russian hierarchy to report on his last findings before his death, he warned them that when you condition people... you condition them to receive something in exchange for that conditioning, and if that is not given to them they cannot be conditioned again. He warned them, 'You may develop the first cosmically aware people, people who have been taken to the point where they cannot be conditioned by mass media.'"

Ask yourselves: Are you receiving what you want in exchange for your perpetual obedience?

Are you receiving anything at all?

Works Cited

Bowart, Walter. *Operation Mind Control*. Ft. Bragg: Flatland Editions, 1994.

Bowart, Walter. Telephone interview. 14 March 2000.

Constantine, Alex. "Ed Dames & His Cover Stories for Mind Control Experimentation." n.p.: The Constantine Report, 1996. Later published in *Virtual Government*. Venice: Feral House, 1997.

Dickens, Charles. *Memoirs of Joseph Grimaldi*. New York: Stein and Day, 1968.

Emory, Dave. *Something's Happening*. Pacifica Radio. KPFK, Los Angeles. 20 May 1999.

Hidell, Al. "Columbine Update." *Paranoia* 21 (1999): 24.

Huxley, Aldous. *Brave New World*. Leicester: F.A. Thorpe, 1983.

Steinberg, Jeffrey. "The Creation of the 'Littleton' Culture." *The New Federalist* 30 Aug. 1999: American Almanac pp. 5-7.

Vallée, Jacques. *Messengers of Deception*. Berkeley: And/Or Press, 1979.

Worcester, David E. *Genesis of a Music*. Pacifica Radio. KPFK, Los Angeles. 24 July 1993.

CHAPTER FOUR:

You Name The Dwarfs: Surrealism, Advertising, and Mass Mind Control

Sigmund Freud's work had a great impact on two artistic movements of the twentieth century: surrealism and advertising. Some might suggest advertising is not an art movement. However, any poet, novelist or painter will admit that their greatest wish is to transform the way people view the world. Ultimately, this is also the wish of the advertiser, whose interest in Freud mirrored that of the surrealist.

As the twentieth century progressed, Freud's ideas began to take hold among the general populace. No longer were his interpretations of dreams solely the interest of his professional colleagues and a few strange visionaries like the founder of surrealism, André Breton. Suddenly, modern advertisers realized that the very techniques Breton glorified in his trio of manifestos—the techniques with which he hoped to shock the bourgeoisie—could be utilized to place a tight reign on the culture at large. It doesn't matter whether Freud's theory of dream significance is true or not. The fact is that the major corporations believe it to be true, just as the surrealists did, and they exploit the symbolism in their ads. The obvious difference between the two movements is this: Breton and the surrealists wished to incite riot and revolt with their art, whereas the advertisers hope to instill obedience and stupidity—and often do. I've decided to codify these two schools as "guerilla surrealism" and "corporate surrealism."

Advertisers (corporate surrealists), like Breton and his co-horts (guerilla surrealists), are fascinated by the magical and utilitarian aspects of art. Some of the guerilla surrealists saw themselves as following in the footsteps of the ancient cave-men who painted the animals they wished to kill prior to the hunt in the belief that this would ensure the animal's capture. Art as invocation, in other words. With this in mind, it's inter-esting that Marshall McLuhan once chose to define advertising in the following manner:

> Ads are the cave art of the twentieth century. While the Twenties talked about the caveman, and people thrilled to the art of the Altamira caves, they ignored (as we do now) the hidden environment of magical forms which we call "ads." Like cave paintings, ads are not intended to be looked at or seen, but rather to exert influence at a dis-tance, as though by ESP. Like cave paintings, they are not means of private but of corporate expression. They are vortices of collective power, masks of energy invented by new tribal man. (*Culture Is Our Business* 7).

McLuhan's mention of ESP is interesting in light of the fact that Sir Hubert Read, one of the most renowned art critics of the twentieth century, once edited a book about surrealism in which he postulated that "thought-transference or telepa-thy" was wholly possible, and that painters like Salvador Dali were unconsciously picking up and transmitting "messages" through their art (78, 79). Apparently Read was unaware of the fact that some artists *consciously* transmit hidden messages through their paintings. An abstract artist named John Hock once experimented with word embeds, particularly that favor-ite cultural taboo "fuck," hidden behind curved forms in the background of a painting. Strangely, he found that people who visited his house were "fascinated by the painting. Often, visi-tors could not seem to take their eyes off the canvas. The em-bedded word, he explained, 'appeared to give a magic quality to the painting'" (Key, *Subliminal Seduction* 113-14).

The simple fact of the matter is that major corporations use the very same techniques in their advertisements, as in a *New York Times Sunday Magazine* ad for Horsman Dolls where the word "fuck" was planted on the sleeve of the doll's left arm (Key, *Subliminal Seduction* 115-17). Sometimes the visual embeds are subtle, sometimes not so subtle. Either way they usually revolve around sex, the most effective Pavlovian conditioner. Not many people are aware of the fact that when the behaviorist James B. Watson ran into some trouble from the psychological community over a silly thing like "ethics," he hightailed it straight to Madison Avenue. His experiments in thought control found a welcome home among the advertising executives there. Ever wonder why the Coke bottle is shaped the way it is?

In his 1924 manifesto, Breton defined surrealism as:

> Thought dictated in the absence of all control exerted by reason and outside all aesthetic or moral preoccupations....It leads to the permanent destruction of all other psychic mechanisms and to its substitution for them in the solution of the principal problems of life. (Gaunt 8, 9)

This definition could easily be applied to advertising. The advertising man's dream is to wipe away all reason in the consumer, to force him or her to respond to the ad at a completely emotional level. Like Breton, the advertising man sees himself as occupying a space outside all aesthetic and moral considerations. Certainly, he does not create an ad with the thought that it might be hanging on the wall of a museum someday. The ad man is interested in "art" only if he can manipulate it to sell a product. Indeed, the examples of classical art appearing in modern advertisements are too numerous to mention. As for the morality question, the ad man claims that he doesn't sell anything the public doesn't already want. Like a heroin pusher on a street corner he says, "I'm not making anyone do anything. It's the customer's choice, not mine." The only difference is that the ad man isn't risking twenty years in prison. Ultimately, the ad man hopes the consumer will believe that the product (whether it's a cigarette or a computer or a new brand of hemorrhoid cream) is truly a solution to "the principle problems of life."

Of course, Breton intended his manifesto to be a blueprint for liberation. If only people could tap into the hidden wellsprings of creativity deep within themselves by exploring the intangible realm of dreams, they could cast off the shackles of irrational rationalism placed upon them by society. Freud's theory of dream significance was to be one of the tools for this revolt of the mind. However, in the early 1970s, when "members of the Woodstock Generation... were dropping out of the consumer culture that Ad Alley had taken such pains to create," Madison Avenue desperately turned to Freudian theories in order to regain control of the people, not to liberate them (Meyers 13).

Faced with a rebellious public, Ad Alley decided it needed an image overhaul. To do this, "Agency-employed psychologists and sociologists refined [an] art of emotional exploitation by using a variety of psychographic research systems" (Meyers 15). One of the most widely used systems is called VALS, an acronym for "Values and Life-styles." Developed by the Stanford Research Institute in Northern California, it divides the people of America into five distinct categories: Belongers, Emulators, Emulator-Achievers, Societally Conscious Achievers, and Need-Directed. The Belonger is an Archie Bunker conservative whose purchasing behaviors are old-fashioned and predictable. An Emulator is a young person desperately searching for an identity. An Emulator-Achiever is the successful American who has already "made it'" and needs to buy more and more objects in order to remind himself of this fact. The Societally Conscious Achiever is the most important target of the VALS system. They're the main reason it was invented in the first place. They represent the experimental section of the populace who feel dissatisfied with materialism. Because their buying habits are constrained by their "ethics," they must be made to believe that their purchases are somehow diametrically opposed to those of the Belonger-types. For example, these people might lumber into a Barnes & Noble and buy a CD from the "alternative" section, never once stopping to consider that a category labeled "alternative" can't very well be alternative in the truest—indeed, the only—sense of that word. Alternative to what, *itself*? These people are actually Belongers, but need to think that they're not. Finally, the Need-Directed are those Americans who live from paycheck to paycheck and can't afford leisure items. To the Stanford Research Institute, such people are considered invisible and irrelevant (Meyers 15-20). It should be noted that the preceding is not simply my own personal interpretation of the VALS system. This is exactly how the Stanford Research Institute describes the American population.

As stated earlier, the Institute first initiated this system in the early 1970s. Perhaps it's merely a coincidence, but in February of 1974, the novelist Philip K. Dick (author of such overtly surrealist books as *Ubik*, *Eye in the Sky*, and *Flow My Tears, the Policeman Said*) was infused by a mysterious pink beam of light that implanted the word "VALIS" into his brain. Is it just me, or is that suspiciously similar to "VALS"? Dick took the word to mean "Vast Active Living Intelligence System," though that was only a guess on his part. This ostensibly mystical experience eventually led to a series of critically acclaimed novels including *VALIS* (the original version of which was called *Valisystem A*), *The Divine Invasion*, and *The Transmigration of Timothy Archer* (Sutin 208-33). Something tells me Ad Alley was experimenting with a unique form of "product placement" in February of 1974. My advice: If you should suddenly wake up out of a deep sleep one night with a strange craving for Coca-Cola, ignore it. That was no dream—it was an advertisement.

Some people have dismissed Dick's "2-3-74 experience" (as he came to label it) as nothing but an episode of schizophrenia, which is strange since he was never diagnosed as schizophrenic. Schizophrenia is a state of mind that fascinates both the guerilla and corporate surrealists. Among the former group, Salvador Dali developed a technique intended to portray the state of schizophrenia for the all-too-sane bourgeoisie. These "paranoic" double visions were a perfect melding of two distinct images, as

79

in his 1929 painting *Invisible Man*. The corporate surrealists also utilize visual puns in order to subtly manipulate the consumer. Some "hidden" sexual images are quite obvious to anyone who cares to see them. A recent McDonald's coupon ad that ran in newspapers throughout the country was a wonderful example of this technique. On the surface it depicted a Chicken McNugget being dipped in sauce, and yet at the same time looked exactly like an ejaculating penis. The viewer need not squint his eyes or stand on his head to see this image. It's quite clear. In fact, upon an initial viewing I had to squint my eyes and stand on my head in order to see the *nugget*. It was so blatant that the *Village Voice* reprinted the ad beneath the headline, "Pecker Order" and asked, "what part of the hen is this?" (Key, *The Age of Manipulation* 47). I've reproduced the McNugget (McPenis?) ad in this book so you can peruse it for yourself. Beside it you'll find an equally suggestive Oscar Meyer ad that'll make you wonder what kind of baloney Oscar's really packing.

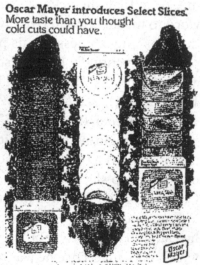

The corporate surrealists don't stop at borrowing artistic techniques from Dali. The guerilla surrealist Pablo Picasso is equally ripe for plunder. In his painting *The Mirror* Picasso uses juxtaposition and contrast in order to demonstrate the unseen connections between two aspects of a woman's life. In an ad for Berkshire stockings, the corporate surrealists utilize the same technique in order to drive home a subtle message about female sexuality. An aloof, upper class woman stands demurely against a pillar while wearing her "breath-taking... sheer... sheer... Berkshire Nylon stockings," the color for which was "borrowed from the sun-soaked gold of a stallion's satin coat." In the background a palomino is rearing up on its hind legs, in the Freudian sense suggesting out-of-control sexuality. By subtle juxtaposition, the ad man implies the "breath-taking pure sensation" lying just beneath the woman's stately, modest exterior (McLuhan, *The Mechanical Bride* 80, 81).

Whereas the guerilla surrealists wish to use their art to transmit messages of freedom, the corporate surrealists wish to transmit messages of enslavement. Artists like Breton, Dali and Picasso warp reality in order to see it more clearly. The anonymous ad men warp reality in order to obfuscate its true meaning. The former is a positive fantasy, the latter a negative one.

In Western culture "fantasy" is often used as a derogatory term. "You're living in a fantasy world!" people say, never realizing that certain fantasies might transcend truth. The scenes depicted in Hieronymus Bosch's *Garden of Earthly Delights* ostensibly never occurred in real life, and yet its subject matter is somehow more "true" than a thousand Norman Rockwell paintings. The corporate surrealists also employ fantastic elements in their work, but *their* fantasy attempts to emulate reality in a dishonest manner. The ad men show us scenes we all recognize—suburban Los Angeles, the coast of Florida, the streets of Chicago—at the same time populating them with alien beings that have eight inch waists, hairless arm pits, and teeth as white as ivory. The Belongers and the Emulators and the Emulator Achievers and the Societally Conscious Achievers and even the Need-Directed all sleepwalk through life, chasing rainbows and golden arches viewed late at night on a flickering colorful box, unaware that the personable residents of the Ad World are less real than the squid-like humanoids in a Max Ernst collage. They are dazed by a fantasy disguised as reality.

André Breton's idea of fantasy was laced with a desire for rebellion and anarchism. His political views were made explicit in the following statement:

> The only remedy... is to go back to the principles... of anarchism—not to the caricature that is made of it, nor the terror—but to... socialism, no longer conceived of as the simple resolution of political and social problems, but as the expression of the exploited masses in their desire to create a classless society where all human values and aspirations can be realized. (Lewis 171)

The corporate surrealists have no respect for human values. When they speak honestly, they reveal themselves as fascists. This shouldn't be a surprise. Mussolini himself once said that, "Fascism is corporatism." What are the ad men if not shills for the corporations that employ them? Their view of humanity is made clear enough in the following passage written by one of the most successful ad executives in America, Jerry Della Femina, who also happens to be a strident supporter of the Stanford Research Institute's special brand of psychoanalysis:

> Advertising deals in open sores.... Fear. Greed. Anger. Hostility. You name the dwarfs and we play on every one. We play on all the emotions and on all the problems, from not getting ahead...to the desire to be one of the crowd. Everyone has a button. If enough people have the same button, you have a successful ad and a successful product. (Meyers 7)

For some reason most people don't find it difficult to believe that advertising executives think this way, but claim it doesn't matter because "Aw, advertisements don't affect anyone!" Apparently they believe major corporations spend millions upon millions of dollars every year on complex ad campaigns that have absolutely no effect on anyone and bring in no revenue whatsoever. Perhaps they do it out of the kindness of their hearts in order to give otherwise useless advertising executives a much-needed source of income so they can buy Christmas presents for the kiddies. Perhaps.

However, a more rational explanation would be that corporations spend good money for these ads because they produce results. So much revenue is generated by the advertisements, it's completely illogical to think that the artists involved simply slap the images together in a couple of days without any thought at all. They spend as much time putting them together as a Max Ernst does composing a painting, perhaps more so. The truth is that the visual embeds hidden in the ads are no "coincidence," or tricks of light and shadow. They've been placed there on purpose.

In Breton's novel *Nadja* the last line reads, "Beauty will be CONVULSIVE, or will not be at all" (160). The corporate surrealists might very well agree, though for different reasons than Breton intended. After all, every advertiser depends on the convulsive, involuntary reflex to buy buy buy—to buy the manufactured "beauty" that must be instantly possessed, whether it be a pair of Berkshire Nylon stockings, a Horsman doll, an IBM computer, or a Chicken McNugget that looks like a flaccid cock dipped in honey sauce.

Beauty comes in many shapes and flavors, with attachable accessories. No batteries included.

Dissatisfaction guaranteed.

You name the dwarfs.

Works Cited

Breton, André. *Nadja*. New York: Grove Weidenfeld, 1960.

Gaunt, William. *The Surrealists*. New York: G.P. Putnam's Sons, 1972.

Key, Wilson Bryan. *The Age of Manipulation*. New York: Henry Holt, 1989.

---. *Subliminal Seduction*. New York: Signet, 1981.

Lewis, Helena. *The Politics of Surrealism*. New York: Paragon House, 1988.

McLuhan, Marshall. *Culture Is Our Business*. New York: McGraw-Hill, 1970.

---. *The Mechanical Bride*. Boston: Beacon Press, 1970.

Meyers, William. *The Image Makers*. New York: Times Books, 1984.

Read, Herbert. *Surrealism*. New York: Praeger Publishers, 1971.

Sutin, Lawrence. *Divine Invasions: A Life of Philip K. Dick*. New York: Harmony House, 1989.

0-20 (Rev. 1-26-66)

Tolson
DeLoach
Mohr
Wick
Casper
Callahan
Conrad
Felt
Gale
Rosen
Sullivan
Tavel
Trotter
Tele. Room
Holmes
Gandy

ALL INFORMATION CONTAINED
HEREIN IS UNCLASSIFIED
DATE 12/4/96 BY SW/cc/9/82

UPI-140
        (PIKE)
    WASHINGTON--THE RESIGNATION OF THE RT. REV. JAMES A. PIKE AS
EPISCOPAL BISHOP OF CALIFORNIA WAS FORMALLY ACCEPTED THURSDAY.
    THE PRESIDING BISHOP OF THE EPISCOPAL CHURCH, THE RT. REV. JOHN
E. HINES, NOTIFIED BISHOP PIKE THAT HE HAD RECEIVED THE NECESSARY
CONSENTS TO THE RESIGNATION FROM A MAJORITY OF THE CHURCH'S ACTIVE
DIOCESAN BISHOPS.
    HIS RESIGNATION IS EFFECTIVE SEPT. 15. HE WILL CONTINUE TO
BE AN EPISCOPAL BISHOP, BUT WILL NO LONGER HAVE JURISDICTION OVER THE
BIG DIOCESE OF CALIFORNIA, WHICH CENTERS AROUND SAN FRANCISCO.
    5/19--WMA12PED

good riddance!

REC. 40   100-428875-8

16 JUN 1 1966

WASHINGTON CAPITAL NEWS SERVICE

SCIENCE FICTION AS MANIPULATION: SF's INTERSECTION WITH THE INTELLIGENCE COMMUNITY

What do the CIA, science fiction, mind control, UFOs, Satanists, Charles Manson, Dianetics, JFK, the space program, Nazis and Hollywood all have in common? In order to answer that question one must be willing to follow the occultic trail of the cryptocracy. Though this trail is labyrinthine and confusing, and eventually loops in upon itself like a royal family tree, it's not impossible to navigate. Don't worry, we'll take you by the hand and lead you through this maze. But we can't dilly-dally, I'm afraid, for it truly is later than you think.

The cryptocracy has always depended on literary endeavors as a means of both secret communication as well as mass conditioning. In his 1983 book *Deadly Deceits*, retired CIA agent Ralph W. McGehee wrote:

> The [Central Intelligence] Agency was also establishing close links with both book publishing houses and media organizations in the U.S. at this time. It felt that in the

world of covert operations, book publishing had a special place. The head of its covert action staff said, "Books differ from all other propaganda media, primarily because one single book can significantly change the reader's attitude and action to an extent unmatched by the impact of any other single medium... that is, of course, not true of all books at all times and with all readers—but it is true significantly often enough to make books the most important weapon of strategic (long-range) propaganda." (40)

It should be noted that some researchers like Dave Emory have accused McGehee of being "sheep-dipped," which is spookspeak for an active intelligence agent who has been returned to civilian life under the cover of being "retired," when in fact his purpose is to spread disinformation sprinkled with a bit of truth in order to discredit valid research pertaining to the National Security State (Emory). If this is true, McGehee's quote is nevertheless still very revealing. After all, even if McGehee is spreading disinformation he's chosen to do it within a book, thus proving the veracity of the quote.

Within the literary spectrum are contained a number of different genres, some of them more valuable to the intelligence community than others—perhaps none more so than science fiction. This particular chapter will attempt to demonstrate the multitudinous intersections between the science fiction field and the various alphabet agencies of the National Security State. It's my contention that the cryptocracy has utilized science fiction as a vehicle for intelligence propaganda since before the beginning of the twentieth century.

H.G. Wells

The modern era of science fiction begins with H.G. Wells. Though well-known as the author of such classics as *The War of the Worlds*, *The Time Machine* and *The Invisible Man*, not many people are aware of the fact that he also wrote a book titled *The New World Order* published in 1940. This book was *not* science fiction – far from it. It was an overt blueprint for the gradual destruction of individual nation-states and the implementation of a one-world government.

The best summation of Wells' world view can be found in Carol White's 1980 book *The New Dark Ages Conspiracy*:

> The 1984 society of pain is H.G. Wells' "New Republic" where pain "will be administered scientifically." [...] In 1902, in his work *Anticipations of the Reaction to Mechanical and Scientific Progress upon Human Life and Thought*, Wells laid out the strategy the British have followed to reach their 1984 goal. The "Open Conspiracy," Wells began, "will appear first, I believe, as a conscious organization of intelligent and quite possibly in some cases wealthy men, as a movement having distinct social and political aims, confessedly ignoring most of the existing apparatus of political control, or using it only as an incidental implement in the attainment of these aims. It will be very loosely organized in its earlier stages, a mere movement of a number of people in a certain direction, who will presently discover with a sort of surprise the common object toward which they are all moving.... A confluent system of Trust-owned business organizations and of Universities and reorganized military and naval services may presently discover an essential unity of purpose, presently begin thinking a literature, and behaving like a State... a sort of outspoken Secret Society... an informal and open freemasonry. In all sorts of ways they will be influencing and controlling the apparatus of the ostensible governments." [...] [A]long with putting the population through alternating periods of extreme stress and "transcendental" relaxation and finally apathy as the full horrors of 1984 are unleashed. (195-96)

In his 1928 book *The Open Conspiracy*, Wells states that the "supreme duty" of this open conspiracy is "subordinating the personal life to the creation of a world directorate," which is the polite, British way of saying a "dictatorship" (Keith 18). Of course, this "open conspiracy" was open only to those willing to look for it. Despite Wells' implication that this conspiracy is out in the open for everybody to see, he insists on being rather coy in his description of its exact goals. Only in his fiction does he really cut loose and lay it all on the line.

His 1933 novel *The Shape of Things to Come* was adapted to film in 1936 with a screenplay by Wells himself. In the novel and in the film Wells lays out his vision for the twentieth century. Both film and literary scholars alike are amazed, even today, by the stunning accuracy of his "predictions." In his novel World War II begins "in 1940 in Poland, over an imagined slight taken by a Nazi over the actions of a Pole of Jewish origin" (Keith 15-16) and ends in 1949, only four years off the mark. Next comes what Wells calls "The Raid of the Germs," which sounds similar to such genetically engineered diseases as AIDS and Ebola.[1] He has World War II followed by "rebellion, a new glass-based society, and the first rocket ship to the moon" (Halliwell 1063).

How did he know all this? Wells was a member of a secret society called "The Round Table Group," an elite network of financiers, journalists and politicians who managed world affairs. The historian Carroll Quigley wrote a voluminous book called *Tragedy & Hope* in which he spoke sympathetically of their attempts to engineer the human race. He thought so highly of them, he suggested they reveal themselves to the world so everybody could thank them for their efforts.

Quigley was Bill Clinton's history professor at Georgetown University. During his acceptance speech at the 1992 Democratic National Convention, Clinton thanked only two people: JFK and Carroll Quigley. Clinton, as you may be aware, was a Rhodes scholar. According to researcher Jim Martin, "The function of the Rhodes scholarships was to identify future leaders, instill them with common values at Oxford [based on British Commonwealth rules], and send them back to their native colonies where they would spread these acquired traits" (Martin 40). The Rhodes scholarships were named after Cecil

---

1   For more information on the controversial subject of genetically engineered diseases, see Dr. Leonard Horowitz's book *Emerging Viruses: AIDS & Ebola—Nature, Accidental or Intentional?* (Tetrahedron Publishing, 1996).

Rhodes, an agent of the Rothschilds' banking conglomerate. Cecil Rhodes was the head of The Round Table Group when H.G. Wells was a member.

Could Wells' predictions have been the result of psychic intuition? Somehow I doubt it. More than likely, he received his information from those who were writing the blueprint. Mae Brussell, the late investigative journalist, always claimed that the President was chosen twenty years in advance (Vankin 100), so why wouldn't wars be planned twenty years in advance as well? The cryptocrats saw Wells' superior literary abilities as the perfect tool with which to prepare the world for this manufactured future. Wells no doubt believed he was performing his patriotic duty. As he himself once said, "The future is a race between education and catastrophe." It seems evident from his writings that he fervently believed he was helping to stamp out the catastrophe known to the rest of us as "democracy."

Intelligence work isn't always as grave a business as I've perhaps implied. Imagine the fun to be had from encoding one's devious machinations in a science fiction novel for the amusement of one's friends, then implementing the plan, standing back, and watching it unfold like a movie—a star-studded spectacle with a cast of billions. I suppose it's nice work if you can get it, and so did Wells. Throughout World War II he worked as the head of British Intelligence (Keith 12), a cushy position that enabled him to sit back in his London office and watch his novel play out on the Global Theatre constructed for him by his colleagues in The Round Table Group. In a sense, one could say that Wells was the first science fiction writer to employ the idea of "virtual reality." He didn't use the idea in a work of fiction, however—he imposed it on the world around him.

Cordwainer Smith

Undoubtedly, Wells was the first to use science fiction as a vehicle for intelligence propaganda, but not the last. One of the most interesting examples is the case of Paul Linebarger, who wrote science fiction under the name Cordwainer Smith.

He was a leading expert in psychological warfare during the 1950s and '60s, and was an advisor to President Kennedy. He wrote the book on psychological warfare—literally. Its title is *Psychological Warfare* and was published by Combat Forces Press in Washington, D.C. just after World War II. In this book Linebarger writes:

> Almost all the best propagandists of almost all modern powers have been, to a greater or less degree,literary personalities. The artistic and cultural aspect of writing is readily converted to propaganda usage…. Though literary men have converted their writing to propaganda purposes, few of them have gone on to define the characteristics of a specific conversionary literature or to compile canons of literary style applicable to the propaganda field. The contributions may lie in the future. (290)

That was in 1948. In 1950 he published his first short story "Scanners Live in Vain" in *Fantasy Book*, which was followed by at least twenty-five more stories plus two full-length novels. Linebarger admitted to his editor Frederick Pohl that there were numerous codes hidden in his stories (Smith, *The Instrumentality of Mankind* xvi). These are known in the advertising world as "phonetic embeds"—strange double-entendres, anagrams, and deliberate typos intended to plant suggestions in the reader's mind. It would probably take a computer to decipher all the codes in Linebarger's stories, but some of them can be uncovered if one is diligent enough.

I mentioned earlier that Linebarger was an advisor to President Kennedy. In light of that fact it's interesting to note the following codes. Only a few months after Kennedy's death, Linebarger published a novel called *Quest of the Three Worlds* that was chock-full of phonetic embeds. On pages 69 and 74 you'll find that the first letter of each sentence spells out "Kennedy shot," and "Oswald shot too." Perhaps this would be unremarkable in itself, but the kicker is this: The paragraph spelling out Oswald's name is entirely about hypnotism. The main character is taught to shoot a gun by hypnotism, and is then hypnotized into learning about psychological warfare with the aid of a "neuro-electric learning helmet," a phrase that sounds somewhat like "neuro-linguistic programming." Near the end of the book Linebarger writes about a secret council of "perfect ones" who "know everything" and live in a well-guarded Egyptian setting. Linebarger calls this group *The Instrumentality*. They sound very similar to The Round Table Group, or the High Cabal discussed by Col. L. Fletcher Prouty in his book *JFK*.[2] Prouty, by the way, was also an advisor to Kennedy.

This is pretty strange stuff for a Presidential advisor to be writing only a few weeks after an assassination. Three years later, in 1966, Linebarger died of a heart attack at the relatively young age of fifty-three. In that same year a dozen people tied in with the Kennedy assassination died mysteriously:

– Judge Joe B. Brown, who presided over Jack Ruby's trial, died of a heart attack.

– Earlene Roberts, Oswald's landlady, died of a heart attack.

– Hank Suydam, who was in charge of all the JFK stories at *Life* magazine, died of a heart attack.

– Albert Bogard, a car salesman who claimed Oswald had taken him on a wild car ride only two weeks before the assassination, committed suicide.

– William Pitzer, the JFK autopsy photographer, committed suicide.

– Karen Carlin, who worked at Jack Ruby's nightclub and was the last to talk to Ruby before the murder of Oswald, died of a fatal gunshot wound.

– Marilyn Walle, a woman who worked as a dancer at Ruby's nightclub, died of a fatal gunshot wound.

– Lee Bowers, Jr., the man who saw the real shooters behind the picket fence on the Grassy Knoll, died in a car accident.

---

2   See also David Ratcliffe's interview with Col. Prouty titled "JFK & the High Cabal," which can be ordered from www.ratical.org.

    – James Worrell, Jr., who saw a man running out of the back of the Texas School Book Depository, died in a car accident.

    – Capt. Frank Martin, a Dallas police captain who watched Oswald get shot, died of cancer.

    – Jimmy Levens, a nightclub owner who hired Ruby employees, died of natural causes.

    – Clarence Oliver, a D.A. investigator who worked on Ruby's case, died of "unknown" causes (Marrs 560).

In light of this litany of death, is it too farfetched to think that Linebarger was bumped off for revealing a little too much about the assassination in his fiction? In a world engineered by professional science fiction writers like H.G. Wells and Linebarger himself, one wonders if anything is too farfetched.

L. Ron Hubbard

Indeed, only in a "virtual reality" world could a character as strange as our next entry exist. Lafayette Ronald Hubbard attended George Washington University in the early 1930s at the same time as Paul Linebarger. In fact, they knew one another and wrote for the same literary journal. Alan C. Elms, a scholar of Linebarger's work, expands on this relationship in the October 1988 issue of *The New York Review of Science Fiction* (#2). During a review of Russell Miller's biography of Hubbard, *Bare-Faced Messiah*, Elms mentions the fact that:

> Hubbard had earlier engaged in modest embellishments of his personal history, but the exaggerations flowered luxuriantly during his second year at GWU. Only then did he begin to claim those years of independent travel and mystical studies in the Orient—claims based in reality upon two brief excursions with his parents to several cities in Japan and China, plus a year's residence in Guam when his father was stationed at the U.S. naval base there. No explanation is given for Hubbard's sudden explosion of autobiographical creativity at this time; one might assume he was merely try-

ing to offset his poor academic performance. But another factor was involved, not mentioned by Miller and probably unknown to him.

The editor of the literary supplement during Hubbard's final semester at GWU was Paul Linebarger, two years younger but a year ahead of him in school. Another member of the literary supplement's staff has told me that Hubbard and Linebarger soon became intensely competitive toward each other. Linebarger made good grades, wrote as fluently as Hubbard, and was equally ambitious. Linebarger held a major advantage in their bragging sessions: he really had traveled extensively by himself, not only in China but in Russia; he really had studied the classics of Oriental wisdom and sat at the feet of Chinese sages, including the great Sun Yat-sen. Linebarger had also conducted a passionate romance with an exiled White Russian woman several years his senior, had narrowly survived a suicide pact with her, and had participated directly in high-level secret negotiations between the U.S. and Chinese governments—all before he was 18. Further, Linebarger was not above adding a bit of embroidery to these genuine experiences, to make them even more colorful. Is it any wonder that Ron Hubbard might thereupon dramatically expand the scope and drama of his own exaggerations, simply in order to stay competitive? And is it any wonder that when such exaggerations appeared to gain acceptance, Hubbard would try more of the same in the future?

Perhaps it was this spirit of competition that propelled Hubbard into the welcoming arms of Naval Intelligence in the 1940s. What better way to make his previous "modest embellishments" match more closely with reality while also trying to catch up with Linebarger's already impressive experiences in the intelligence community?

During WWII Hubbard was recruited into Naval Intelligence where he studied "narcosynthesis" and hypnotic regression techniques (Nichols and Moon, *Montauk Revisited* 230). Combined with his earlier studies of magician Aleister Crowley and mathematician Alfred Korzybski, it wasn't difficult for Hubbard to create the "New Science of Mental Health," otherwise known as Dianetics. Just after World War II, in the fall of 1945, Naval Intelligence sent Hubbard on a mission to infiltrate the California branch of Crowley's organization Ordo Templi Orientis, which was located at 1003 S. Orange Grove in Pasadena in the home of John Whiteside (Jack) Parsons. In the field of chemistry Parsons is something of a legend. He's the creator of solid fuel rockets, without which we wouldn't have been able to fly to the moon. In fact, there's actually a crater on the moon named after him (Corydon 255). He was the founder of Cal Tech (perhaps a play on the word "Celtic"), which later became Jet Propulsion Laboratories. Some people claim that JPL actually stands for Jack Parsons Laboratories (Skouras) (also the 3-19-00 edition of the *Los Angeles Times*).

Though the Navy sent Hubbard to infiltrate Parsons' occult organization, I suspect Hubbard was actually playing both sides against the middle. Having learned what he could from the mind control techniques used by Naval Intelligence, he now intended on milking Parsons of whatever knowledge he had of *magickal* mind control techniques. Judging from the success of Scientology, it's evident that he succeeded. Hubbard and Parsons participated in a magickal ritual that has become famous in occult circles, the Babalon Working of 1946. According to Kenneth Grant, a former member of the OTO, the purpose of this ritual was to unseal an inter-dimensional gateway. The word "Babalon" literally means "Gateway to the Gods" (Skouras). Perhaps it's just a coincidence, but only a few months after the Working, the first flying saucers began to be seen all across America. Grant suggests that the modern era of UFOlogy begins with the Babalon Working. As Grant himself says, "Parsons opened a door and something flew in" (Andrews 117).

There were three people involved in the Babalon Working: Hubbard, Parsons, and a woman named Marjorie Cameron. According to a brief bio in the back of one of Parsons' books, Cameron "moved to Pasadena after serving in the Navy in

Washington, D.C." (Parsons 95), which means that two of the three participants in the Babalon Working may very well have been ordered to do so by none other than the U.S. Navy. Cameron married Parsons in 1946 after Hubbard stole his first wife Sara, as well as 20,000 dollars, in what Crowley called an old-fashioned "confidence trick" (Corydon 258). Six years later, on the very same day that his mother died, Parsons was killed in a mysterious explosion that destroyed his entire home. Cameron, on the other hand, lived to become a successful painter, poet, and filmmaker. To this day no one has been allowed to identify Parsons' body. The records of his death, as well as his personal papers and books, are still classified by the U.S. Department of Defense.

If you want to learn more about Parsons, a few years ago Feral House published a full-length biography titled *Sex and Rockets: The Occult World of Jack Parsons*. It's written by a man calling himself John Carter. I find this odd since that's also the name of the hero in Edgar Rice Burroughs' series of science fiction novels about Mars. The planet Mars was important to both Parsons and his second wife. According to Cameron, she and her "peculiar few" would be taken up in a flying saucer (what Crowley called a "war-engine" in *The Book of the Law*) and transported to Mars, which she believed was her true birthplace (Grant 29).

While we're on the subject of Mars, it might be worth mentioning that I attended a conference about the Monuments of Mars back on September 11, 1997, not far from JPL and Parsons' aforementioned home in Pasadena. The conference was hosted by Richard Hoagland, a persistent critic of both JPL and NASA. This conference was an exhaustive one, beginning at 7:00 P.M. and lasting until about 1:30 in the morning, during which Hoagland presented a number of JPL photographs that seemed to indicate the evidence of a past civilization on Mars, one that had been destroyed in a great cataclysm or planetary war. The final image Hoagland showed us that evening was a photograph of the Sojourner lander taken by the Mars Rover, which arrived on Mars on July 4, 1997. On the lander could clearly be seen a plaque adorned with the image of a human skull that looked eerily like the Death's Head symbol worn by the Gestapo of Nazi Germany. This seems to indicate that occult rituals at JPL didn't end with the death of Jack Parsons.

John W. Campbell

Only four years after Hubbard fleeced Parsons out of 20,000 dollars and his first wife, he published the first version of *Dianetics* in the magazine *Astounding Science Fiction* edited by John W. Campbell. Campbell's enthusiasm for Hubbard's work was instrumental in propelling *Dianetics* to an international audience. Some believe Scientology would never have gotten off the ground without Campbell's early support.

Campbell was the author of the story "Who Goes There?" which was turned into the film *The Thing* in 1951. Strangely enough, the film historian Leslie Halliwell claims that the director of *The Thing* received "mysterious help" from "either [Howard] Hawks or Orson Welles," but unfortunately doesn't elaborate any further (Halliwell 1063). In his 1997 book, *Hollywood Vs. the Aliens*, researcher Bruce Rux claims that *The Thing* was a thinly-veiled account of the Roswell Crash, its purpose to assimilate the public at large to the truth of the alien presence on Earth. Since Orson Welles was responsible for the 1938 radio broadcast of H.G. Wells' *The War of the Worlds*—which caused a panic at a time when UFOs weren't even a daily topic—it would be intriguing to know if Welles was also connected to *The Thing*. I'm still attempting to track down that information.[3] However, it is intriguing to note that the screenwriter of *The Thing*, Charles Lederer, was a close friend of Welles—so close, in fact, that he later married Welles' first wife, Virginia Nicholson. The notion, therefore, that Lederer and Welles may have collaborated unofficially on the film is not farfetched. I should also note that RKO, the studio that made *The Thing*, was a sub-

---

3   If you have information pertaining to this or related matters, please contact me in care of the publisher or at rguffey@hotmail.com.

sidiary of Time-Life and "directly connected to the CIA." This probably shouldn't be a surprise to anyone, considering the fact that RKO was owned by Howard Hughes (Rux 109), who knew Jack Parsons quite well and has even been implicated in his death. (See Appendix E to Nichols and Moon's *Montauk Revisited* for further details on the Parsons-Hughes connection.)

In less than a year John Campbell became disillusioned with Hubbard and resigned from the Dianetic Research Foundation, claiming it had turned into a cult (Corydon 280). At around that same time Aldous Huxley and his wife were receiving Dianetic auditing from Hubbard himself. This is clearly ironic since Huxley wrote *Brave New World* warning people about the very same mind control techniques used by Hubbard in *Dianetics*. Huxley himself must have realized this. Like Campbell, he too drifted away from the organization after only three or four sessions with Hubbard.

Robert A. Heinlein

Besides Hubbard, another protégé of John Campbell was Robert A. Heinlein, a famous science fiction writer with close ties to Naval Intelligence (Zubrin 28). He graduated from the U.S. Naval Academy and worked as an engineer at the Naval Base in Philadelphia during World War II along with another bestselling science fiction writer, Isaac Asimov (de Camp 44). Please keep in mind that this was the exact time and location of the alleged "Philadelphia Experiment," a Tesla-inspired time travel experiment performed by John von Neumann for the U.S. Navy (Nichols and Moon, *The Montauk Project* 14). Heinlein, himself a Naval officer, was a close personal friend of L. Ron Hubbard and Jack Parsons. According to Peter Moon, "Heinlein frequented the same haunts as Hubbard and both were made privy to the inner workings of magick and the O.T.O." (Nichols and Moon, *Montauk Revisited* 248).

In 1951, the same year that *The Thing* hit theatres, Heinlein published his novel *The Puppet Masters*, the basic plot of which has been ripped off by Hollywood about five million times. The plot involves alien parasites who invade human hosts in a covert attempt to take over the Earth. Orson Welles wrote an introduction to Judith Merrill's 1956 anthology *The Year's Greatest Science Fiction and Fantasy*, in which he stated that his favorite novel was *The Puppet Masters*. This seems unusual coming from such an erudite thespian with a background in Shakespearian drama. Having read the book myself, it's hard to imagine that Welles' interest in it was solely of a literary nature. Since it's a known fact that Welles made films like *It's All True* at the request of such influential cryptocrats as Nelson Rockefeller and John Whitney (*With Orson Welles: Stories From a Life in Film*), I don't think it's too farfetched to assume that he knew a lot more about what was going on behind the scenes than he was allowed to say in public. I once saw a documentary about Orson Welles on PBS that recounted the following story: When Harry S. Truman first met Welles, Truman said to him, "You're the second greatest actor alive today. I'm the *first*!" Truman, of course, was president during the Roswell Crash of '47, and is alleged by many researchers to have been present during the autopsy of the extraterrestrial cadavers. If Welles was aware of this, his interest in Heinlein's otherwise primitive potboiler takes on new significance indeed. Perhaps this explains why Welles was also a devoted fan of the Ray Harryhausen science fiction extravaganza *Earth vs. the Flying Saucers* (Columbia, 1956), so much so that he included footage from the film in his 1974 experimental documentary *F For Fake* (Harryhausen Interview).

Besides *The Puppet Masters*, Heinlein also wrote one of the most famous science fiction novels ever published, namely *Stranger in a Strange Land*, which is about "a human raised on Mars named Valentine Michael Smith, who tries to teach mankind to accept the peaceful Martian ways but ends up dismembered and devoured" by his worshippers à la Dionysus (Rux 187). *Stranger in a Strange Land* was based on Aleister Crowley's *Book of the Law* (*Montauk Revisited* 71). It was a favorite of none other than Charles Manson; he even named his son Valentine Michael after the main character. In the 1998 edition of *Steamshovel Press*, researcher Curt Rowlett states:

> It can be argued that the Manson murders "nailed the coffin shut" in the minds of many Americans as far as the image of the Hippies as a peace-loving, political movement was   concerned, and it should be considered that this could have been part of a CIA operation to discredit the anti-war movement in America. Manson has said in interviews that he based some of his "philosophy" on the science fiction novel *Stranger in a Strange Land* by Robert Heinlein. In a scenario perhaps reminiscent of Mark David Chapman's infatuation with *Catcher in the Rye*, could *Stranger in a Strange Land* somehow have been Manson's program-trigger mechanism? And consider that if a hippie-ex-convict-nobody like Charles Manson could program people to kill, why not the U.S. Government? (17)

If you think Rowlett's proposition is improbable, contemplate this fact: Manson wasn't the only "lone nut crazed killer" with a penchant for science fiction. In the summer of 1963 Lee Harvey Oswald checked out thirty-four books from the New Orleans public library (Groden 65). Among them were books on Russian history, biographies of John F. Kennedy, Ian Fleming's James Bond novels, and ten volumes of science fiction. Those volumes were:

1. *The Huge Winners* edited by Isaac Asimov.

2. *Nine Tomorrows* by Isaac Asimov.

3. *Big Book of Science Fiction* edited by Groff Conklin.

4. *Portals of Tomorrow* edited by August Derleth.

5. *The Sixth Galaxy Reader* edited by H.L. Gold.

6. *Mind Partner* edited by H.L. Gold, which contains a story titled "The Lady Who Sailed the Soul" by none other than Cordwainer Smith.

7. *Brave New World* by Aldous Huxley, who died on the same day that President Kennedy was assassinated.

8. *The Treasury of Science Fiction Classics* edited by Harold Kuebler.

9. *The Expert Dreamers* edited by Frederick Pohl, the man most responsible for establishing Cordwainer Smith's literary career.

10. *The Worlds of Clifford Simak* by Clifford D. Simak.

The last of these books was returned to the library on August 26, 1963, only three months before the assassination. It's intriguing that both Manson and Oswald, two of the most famous murderers in U.S. history, seemed to share an interest in books written by the only two bestselling science fiction writers present during the Philadelphia Experiment. Could the works of *both* authors have been utilized as post-hypnotic triggering mechanisms similar to the Queen of Diamonds in Richard Condon's fact-based novel *The Manchurian Candidate*? Could one of Cordwainer Smith's phonetic embeds have served a related function? Is this what Smith was subtly referring to when he planted his "Oswald code" within a scene about hypnotic programming?

None of these questions can be resolved anytime soon, because only a privileged few with a "need to know" could possibly answer them. However, many other researchers have indicated that Oswald may have been the victim of mind control, including Lincoln Lawrence in his 1968 book *Were We Controlled?*, Walter Bowart in his 1978 book *Operation Mind Control*, and G.J. Krupey in a brilliant series of articles serialized in *Steamshovel Press* #9-12 under the title "The High & the Mighty: JFK, MPM [Mary Pinchot Meyer], LSD & the CIA." These researchers prove that the unanswered questions listed above are not without foundation. In fact, Oswald was not the only science fiction fan with a connection to Black Ops mind control programs. Allow me to introduce you to yet another eccentric character in this litany of spooks....

Michael Aquino

Lt. Col. Michael Aquino, a former Green Beret, served as an intelligence officer in Special Forces, Psychological Operations, throughout his long-lasting career, despite the fact that he was also the High Priest of a Satanic Church called The Temple of Set. He founded the Temple of Set in 1975 because of his dissatisfaction with Anton LaVey's Church of Satan. When he discovered that LaVey was selling priesthoods to whoever had enough money to pay, he resigned as the editor of LaVey's newsletter. One can only imagine the shock he felt at discovering that the head of The Church of Satan could be guilty of immoral behavior. Anton LaVey, incidentally, based his religion on the one promulgated by the José-Delgado-like mad scientist in H.G. Wells' novel *The Island of Dr. Moreau* (Chapman 61).

For at least twenty-five years Aquino orchestrated psychological warfare programs in foreign countries deemed by Uncle Sam to be in need of some serious mind-fucking from the West. (That is, one *hopes* his campaigns were limited only to foreign countries.) In an article written specifically for *Paranoia* magazine Aquino states, "Within the PSYOP community, officers find that the responsibility to 'do the right thing' rests ultimately with their own sense of judgment and conscience" (29). Coming from a high priest in a Satanic Church, that's quite comforting indeed!

In 1988 Aquino's top secret security clearance was suspended while the Army conducted a criminal investigation of Aquino and his wife Lilith in connection with sixty alleged cases of sexual abuse at the day care center run by the U.S. Army at the San Francisco Presidio, the same area where the Zodiac killings occurred in the late 1960s and '70s. Some researchers like Harry Martin of the *Napa Sentinel* and Dave Emory believe that Aquino's Temple of Set was involved with the Zodiac killings. Their evidence is intriguing, but far too complicated to cover here. If you're interested, I'd refer you to Dave Emory's *One Step Beyond* report "Team Zodiac & Manson's Connections to the Zodiac Killings" available from Spitfire at P.O. Box 1179, Ben Lomond, CA 95005 or www.spitfirelist.com.

At the time of the Zodiac killings, Mae Brussell believed that the Zebra killings, the Manson killings, the Zodiac, the SLA, and similar cases were all part of a military operation to discredit the peace movement of the 1960s, and indeed each of these cases resulted in exactly that. Brussell maintained that this was part of Gov. Reagan's "strategy of terror" against California. It's a known fact that Reagan invited Aquino to the White House on numerous occasions during his presidency. He often requested that Aquino wear his black ritual robes in order to freak out diplomats from South and Central America (Bowart Chp. 30, p. 9).

At first all of this might seem like a tangent to the subject at hand, but in truth it isn't. Aquino's intense interest in mind control is evident in his trilogy of science fiction novels, which can be ordered from The Temple of Set for a "$15 donation... to cover copying and mailing costs" (Aquino 31). Aquino claims the novels are "future sequels to the film *Star Wars*." According to Walter Bowart:

> [Aquino] has been reported as having been identified standing outside the gate at Sky Walker Ranch forcing copies of these manuscripts upon people employed by George Lucas. Since Lucas does not receive "unsolicited manuscripts" the manuscripts have been returned unopened upon several occasions. One was subsequently published in a monster magazine. (Chp. 10, p. 19)

This "monster magazine" was Forrest J Ackerman's *Famous Monsters of Filmland* (#148, October 1978), or as Aquino calls it the "classic *Famous Monsters of Filmland*" (Aquino 31), a publication aimed toward eight-to-thirteen year-olds fascinated by such pressing issues as what type of jelly was used to make *The Blob*. Aquino's story is called "The Secret of Sith: A Darth Vader Fantasy." Throughout the story Darth Vader mouths a weird B.F. Skinner/José Delgado kind of philosophy about the psychocivilization of the galaxy. What follows is an example of Aquino's crystalline prose.

Princess Leia (To Darth Vader): "Who are you to pursue selfish policies of regional prosperity in callous disregard for the damage they may cause throughout [sic] the rest of the galaxy?"

Darth Vader: "…It would be far more efficient than the Senate, but neither my attention nor my reasoning processes are optimum for the task. Nor is any other organic mind capable of such performance, particularly over an extended period of time on a continuous basis. No, the only solution is to place imperial sovereignty in the hands of a positronicomputer…. No individual—or group of individuals—should have the power to make decisions completely beyond their competence."

(It's very clear that Aquino's sympathies are with Vader's fascistic pronouncements.)

Near the end of the story Aquino writes, "Amidst the wreckage Darth Vader staggered to his feet, then stiffened in shock as a laser-bolt from Leia's blaster struck him full in the back. The force of its impact tore the mask from his head and the protective plates from his chest and Leia and Solo saw with a *thrill of horror* that the humanoid features beneath were hideously decomposed and disfigured. Exposed to the air, they began to dissolve and gradually Darth Vader's entire body boiled away to nothingness…." (Bowart Chp. 30, p. 9-10)

One wonders how many magazine editors saw Aquino's manuscript before Ackerman decided to publish it. In the fourth season of *The X-Files* Glen Morgan and James Wong wrote an episode titled "Musings of a Cigarette Smoking Man" in which they revealed that the mysterious "Cancer Man" who controls world events from behind the scenes is, in his spare time, nothing more than a frustrated science fiction writer who finally manages to sell a story to a cheap porno magazine when he's in his 50s. I've always wondered if Morgan and Wong were satirizing Aquino himself.

Philip K. Dick

I've also wondered if Aquino had anything to do with the victimization of the legendary science fiction writer Philip K.

103

Dick, author of numerous novels in which mind control plays a significant role (i.e., *Valis, A Scanner Darkly, Radio Free Albemuth* and dozens of others). The subjects Dick chose to tackle in his fiction were controversial, to say the least. Throughout the 1950s, '60s and '70s he was the only science fiction author writing novels that were openly Marxist. As early as 1955 he wrote the novel *Eye in the Sky*, which was very critical of McCarthyism. Many of his novels were anti-fascist, such as *Now Wait for Last Year* (1966), *The Penultimate Truth* (1964), and the Hugo-Award-winning *Man in the High Castle* (1962). He criticized and satirized the CIA in *Clans of the Alphane Moon* (1964). He dared to expose totalitarian German pharmaceutical companies (which sound very much like I.G. Farben) in *The Simulacra*, also published in '64. He was uncommonly open about his experimentation with psychedelics, such as in his afterword to the story "Faith of Our Fathers" in Harlan Ellison's 1967 anthology *Dangerous Visions*. In that same year "he signed (along with five hundred others) a 'Writers and Editors War Tax Protest' petition that appeared in the February 1968 *Ramparts* magazine" (Sutin 160). In opposition to the Vietnam War, the signatories refused to pay the 23% of their income tax that was being used to finance the war.

I suspect that all of this brought Dick under the scrutiny of Psyops officers like Aquino, if not Aquino himself. On November 17, 1971, Dick's San Venetia home was burglarized. From the description of the break-in, it was definitely done by professionals. His fireproof file cabinet had been blown open by plastic explosives. All his business papers, cancelled checks, letters, and documents were stolen. The floor was littered with debris, including wet asbestos in which the prints of combat boots could be clearly seen. There were also broken drill bits and "rugs and towels soaked in water which had been thrown over the files to muffle the explosions" (Sutin 181). As if all that weren't enough, at the same time as the burglary, Dick's car stalled due to sabotage, stranding him miles away.

Dick reported the break-in to the local police, at which point a police sergeant warned him that if he didn't leave, "You'll probably get a bullet in your back some night or worse. This county doesn't need a crusader." The next day when he went to the County Sheriff's Dept. with a list of what had been stolen, "they had no report of a robbery having occurred" (Sutin 182-83). Soon afterwards Dick fled Marin County and moved to Canada where he checked himself into a drug rehab clinic. While in the hospital he met a man who had been a member of Special Forces and had worked with the CIA. Dick described the break-in to the man, who replied, "I would say that your house was hit because you wrote something that was true and you didn't realize it" (Williams 50).

Bishop James A. Pike

Philip Dick believed the burglary was a result of his friendship with Bishop James A. Pike. In the 1960s Pike was the Episcopal Bishop of California, a strong supporter of civil rights, and an outspoken critic of the Vietnam War. His rather liberal views on Scriptural doctrine were considered heretical by many in the Episcopal Church. In February of 1966 Pike's son Jim committed suicide after prolonged use of LSD given to him by a psychiatrist in San Francisco. In October of '66 Dick began helping Pike in his attempts to contact his dead son "through séances and other psychic means" (Sutin 149). In 1968 Pike published an account of these attempts in a book titled *The Other Side*; Pike thanked Dick and his wife Nancy in the foreword to that book. In 1970 Dick published a novel titled *A Maze of Death*, which was dedicated to Pike. In other words, their friendship was no secret.

Pike fervently believed that his attempts to contact Jim on "the other side" were successful. Dick was a bit more skeptical and feared that Pike's published account of his psychic experiences would discredit his political work in the arena of free speech and civil rights. In Jon Rappoport's book *U.S. Government Mind Control Experiments on Children*, mind control survivor Chris De Nicola provides a list of 99 experiment names and code numbers retrieved from the Radiation & Mind Control files of Dr. L. Wilson Greene between 1972 and 1976 (57). The penultimate experiment name was "Poltergeist Obsession" (62). Though it's unlikely that this is connected to Pike directly, it does demonstrate that PsyOps mind control experts like Aquino and Greene are fervently interested in the *psychological* effects of poltergeist phenomenon. I've often wondered if the supernatural events that Pike and Dick experienced were intended to push them over the brink. It seems as if Pike himself was bothered by the suspicion that his ostensibly "supernatural" experiences had been engineered by a human source. In chapter eleven of *The Other Side* Pike writes:

> As has already been suggested, the remote and private nature of some of the [psychic] data would suggest the necessity of a team of investigators who are no ordinary gumshoes, but who operate on the level of successful sophistication we used to attribute to the CIA. (316)

Pike would be well aware of such operations, since he himself had been a member of Naval Intelligence during World War II.

Three years after his first séance with Dick, Pike died alone while lost in the middle of the Dead Sea desert in Israel, his search for the true origins of Jesus effectively terminated. His death is surrounded with mystery, and Dick himself suspected that the same people responsible for the deaths of Martin Luther King and Robert Kennedy had assassinated Pike (Sutin 220). With this in mind, I decided to initiate a Freedom of Information Act search on Bishop Pike in the Fall of 1996. I didn't receive the documents until May 24th of 1999. Though it certainly took a long time, the results were fascinating. According to the FBI, "Pursuant to your request, 47 pages were reviewed and 45 pages are being released." The files begin in July of 1958 and end in September of 1968. The June 1st, 1966 document simply states:

> The resignation of the Rt. Rev. James A. Pike as Episcopal Bishop of California was formally accepted Thursday.
> The presiding Bishop of the Episcopal Church, the Rt.

Rev. John E. Hines, notified Bishop Pike that he had received the necessary consents to the resignation from a
majority of the Church's active Diocesan Bishops.

His resignation is effective Sept. 15. He will continue to
be an Episcopal Bishop, but will no longer have jurisdiction
over the big Diocese of California, which centers around
San Francisco.

At the bottom of the page an FBI agent wrote, "Good riddance!"

The very next page is deleted. It falls between June of 1966
and April of 1967, the exact time period that Dick and Pike
were conducting their séances. The "Deleted Page Information
Sheet" reads: "1 page withheld entirely at this location in the
file. One or more of the following statements, where indicated,
explain this deletion." Under Section 552, category (b) (1) is
checked off. According to the "Explanations of Exemptions"
that the FBI includes with the documents, category (b) (1)
means: "(A) specifically authorized under criteria established
by an Executive order to be kept secret in the interest of national defense or foreign policy and (B) are in fact properly
classified pursuant to such Executive order."

The cover letter, dated May 19th of 1999, indicates that the
deleted documents also fall under the category of (b) (7) (D),
which means they "could reasonably be expected to disclose
the identity of a confidential source, including a State, local,
or foreign agency or authority or any private institution which
furnished information on a confidential basis, and, in the case
of record or information compiled by a criminal law enforcement authority in the course of a criminal investigation, or by
an agency conducting a lawful national security intelligence
investigation, information furnished by a confidential source."

For over sixty years the phrase "in the interest of national security" has been tantamount to that most medieval of excuses,
"God told me to." Need I point out that Pike has been dead for
thirty years? Ask yourself: How could anything they have on
him be relevant to national defense *today*?

P.K.D. and the Pink Beam

Five years after Pike's death, Dick had some rather strange "supernatural" experiences of his own. During the months of February and March of 1974 he experienced mystical visions. What he described as pink beams of blinding light entered his home and fed information directly into his brain, granting him brief moments of telepathic insights into the people around him, even enabling him to diagnose a life-threatening hernia in his son Christopher. In a July 1974 letter Dick writes, "In the following days I felt that I must have been the involuntary recipient of an ESP experiment" (Sutin 213).

He began to hear voices in his head, which he referred to as the "AI" voice. In a March 20, 1974 journal entry he writes:

> [The pink beam] seized me entirely, lifting me from the limitations of the space-time matrix; it mastered me as, at the same instant, I knew that the world around me was cardboard, a fake. Through its power I saw suddenly the universe as it was; through its power of perception I saw what really existed, and through its power of no-thought decision, I acted to *free myself.* (Sutin 214-15).

On March 20th of 1974 Dick called the Fullerton police and told the officer who picked up the phone, "I am a machine," then asked to be locked up. The police ignored him. Dick believed "a thought-control implant by U.S. Army Intelligence" was guiding him to do these things (Sutin 216).

There was, no doubt, an unusual amount of electromagnetic energy in Dick's home at this time, a common element in both mind control and alien abduction scenarios. For example, his radio continued to play even after it had been unplugged. According to Dick's fifth wife Tessa:

> The thing about that was we *both* heard the music, and it was always between two and six A.M., and the radio wasn't even *plugged in.* [...] But we still got Easy Listening music, only Phil kept hearing it tell him that he was no

good, that he should die. And I didn't hear that. We gave up and plugged the radio back in again, because it was easier to sleep with music on. (Sutin 218)

It seems clear that Dick was being monitored long before the events of 2-3-74. His former residence in Marin County, a place famous for being the home of George Lucas, was a hotbed of intelligence community activity at the same exact time as the '71 break-in. According to Mark Phillips, co-author of *Trance Formation of America*:

I noticed how Rev. Jim Jones' former lawyer, Tim Stone, was apparently running "containment" for the CIA in Marin County, California. And I personally knew of this U.S. Army Major promoted to Lt. Col., attached to the Psychological Warfare Division and the Defense Intelligence Agency, who had ingeniously organized a "church," legal under the First Amendment of the Constitution. I learned that this Lt. Colonel, Michael Aquino, had, like Jim Jones, been supported by politicians and the CIA. (Bowart Chp. 11, p. 5).

Had Aquino been aware of Dick through his interest in science fiction? Did Aquino eventually target Dick with his black Ops mind control technology? Why would Aquino do this? Perhaps Dick's anti-fascist, anti-Nazi stance offended Aquino in some way. Perhaps he was just jealous of Dick's superior writing abilities. Who knows? The idea that Aquino was at least aware of Dick seems likely. According to Cathy O'Brien, co-author of *Trance Formation of America* and self-professed mind control survivor, the cryptocracy's network of satellites that monitored her every move were specifically referred to by her handlers, including Aquino, as the "Eye in the Sky," which was the title of Phil Dick's breakthrough novel published back in 1957 (Bowart Chp. 9, p. 10). It could very well be that the "holy" visions that so haunted Dick in the latter days of his life represented nothing more than psychological games beamed into his head by the "positronicomputer" alluded to in Aquino's dreadful fiction.

The SF Movie Industry

So far we've only focused on the intelligence community's intersection with the literary science fiction community, but the fact is the boom in science fiction films that began in the 1950s couldn't have existed without the influence of the cryptocracy. The number of military and intelligence agents involved in science fiction movies is quite staggering. William Joseph Bryan, a hypnosis expert who worked for the CIA's MK-ULTRA mind control program, a man strongly implicated in the assassination of Robert Kennedy, served as a consultant for a number of movies including *The Manchurian Candidate* (JFK's favorite film, which was taken off the market by Frank Sinatra soon after the assassination and remained unavailable until the late 1990s), numerous Roger Corman pictures, as well as Francis Ford Coppola's first film *Dementia 13*.[4]

Gene Roddenberry, creator of *Star Trek*, once worked as "LAPD historian" under Daryl Gates and Chief William H. Parker, who had definite CIA connections according to Mike Rothmiller, co-author of *L.A. Secret Police*. Ib Melchior, the writer/director of *Angry Red Planet*, was once a member of the Office of Strategic Services (OSS), the immediate predecessor to the CIA. Leslie Stevens, the executive producer of *The Outer Limits*, worked for Army Air Corps Intelligence and *Time* magazine (which was owned by CIA-connected Henry Luce). Ray Harryhausen directed military propaganda films during the Second World War before creating special effects for films like the previously mentioned *Earth vs. the Flying Saucers*, which was based on a non-fiction book by Major Donald Keyhoe titled *The Flying Saucers Are Real*.

In his 1997 memoir *The Day After Roswell*, Col. Philip J. Corso claims that his military team influenced from behind the scenes the production of such films as *The Man From Planet X* (United Artists, 1951). "This was called camouflage through limited disclosure," Corso writes, "and it worked. If

4   Please read *The Assassination of Robert F. Kennedy* by William Turner and Jonn Christian for more information on Bryan.

people could enjoy it as entertainment, get duly frightened, and follow trails to nowhere that the working group had planted, then they'd be less likely to stumble over what we were really doing" (Corso 85).

Incidentally, *The Man From Planet X* was the earliest UFO movie ever made. Perhaps the most significant section of the film is the exchange that occurs between the two main characters in the final scene. The scientist's daughter, referring to the landing of an extraterrestrial spacecraft in Scotland, asks, "Is it true that no one will ever know what happened here?" To which the dashing journalist replies, "Knowledge would only bring more fear in a world already filled with it." The scientist's daughter then asks, "Can such a thing be kept secret?" The journalist concludes, "No, but it can be reduced to gossip." Or, as Gen. Nathan Twining is quoted as saying in *The Day After Roswell*, "The cover-up is the disclosure and the disclosure is the cover-up" (Corso 81).

The list of military personnel involved in science fiction goes on and on. A more comprehensive examination can be found in Bruce Rux's 1997 book *Hollywood Vs. the Aliens: The Motion Picture Industry's Participation in UFO Disinformation*. As Rux states in Chapter 3 of his book:

> Certainly the entertainment realm was of... interest to the CIA as a potential molder of public opinion and thought. "CIA scientists understood that television and motion picture media are especially conducive to subliminal manipulation," write Lee and Solomon [in *Unreliable Sources*], "which bypasses rational defense mechanisms through split-second imagery. A once-secret document dated November 21, 1955, noted how 'psychologically the general lowering of consciousness during the picture facilitates the phenomenon of identification and suggestion as in hypnosis.'" [T]he willing "suspension of disbelief" that an audience puts itself through for the sake of enjoyment of the story... makes them automatically susceptible to mass hypnotic conditioning for the duration of the show. (167)

111

Some researchers believe that the main purpose of this conditioning, at least as it pertains to science fiction films, could either be to instill a belief in non-existent "space aliens" or, conversely, to ready the population at large for the eventual disclosure of the aliens' existence.[5] The former possibility is examined in Jacque Vallée's books *Messengers of Deception* and *Revelations*, while Rux seems to support the latter theory. The truth could very well lie somewhere in between.

In the final analysis all fiction is propaganda, whether the author realizes it or not. Some of it enlightens. Some of it deceives. The cryptocrats specialize in the latter. A good number of these specialists land lucrative positions as presidential speech writers. On the other hand, an author like Philip K. Dick accomplishes the exact opposite through his fiction. His novels represent a slight ray of hope in the world of the Black Iron Prison (Dick's term for the manufactured reality that enchains us), where Scientologists order their followers to buy multiple copies of L. Ron Hubbard's books in order to create false bestsellers (Corydon 228), and where pro-cryptocracy bestselling novelists like Tom Clancy laud the Jerry Pournelles of the world to high Heaven.

In his book *Operation Mind Control*, Walter Bowart has suggested that bestselling science fiction novelist Jerry Pournelle is the complete antithesis of writers like Dick. Bowart reports the following revealing incident: While acting as the systems operator of a forum on GENIE (General Electric Network for Information Exchange, an online service that ran from 1985 to 1999), Pournelle had a heated argument with a man named Chuck Zeps. After Zeps posted an article detailing the link between psychiatry and mind-controlled assassins, Pournelle (a trained psychologist) demanded that the net overseer throw Zeps off and "banish him to America Online" (Ch. 41, p. 16). One can often detect a cryptocrat by his hair trigger temper and addictive reliance on authoritarian behavior in order to si-

---

5   This conditioning may very well have begun with H.G. Wells' 1898 classic *The War of the Worlds*, which Wells himself admitted was inspired by newspaper accounts of anomalous aircraft seen in the sky (Rux 14).

lence the opposition. The cryptocrats' debating methods can best be summed up by the following quote from George Orwell: "If you want a picture of the future, imagine a boot stamping on a human face—forever" (220).

I recently saw Pournelle on a PBS special in which he claimed that "science fiction won the Cold War" because he and his collaborator Larry Niven had developed integral aspects of Ronald Reagan's infamous "Star Wars" technology while plotting out yet another of their voluminous space operas. The narrator commented dryly that while mainstream historians had many conflicting theories as to what led to the downfall of the Soviet Union, science fiction certainly wasn't one of them.

Another cryptocrat worth mentioning is Janet Morris. Not only has Morris authored hordes of turgid sword & sorcery and science fiction novels, she also developed a theory in response to M.A.D. (Mutually Assured Destruction). Her response took the form of a similar anagram: M.A.S. (Mutually Assured Survival), indicating that a limited nuclear war was not only survivable but even desirable in some cases (Alexander 104). However, she doesn't bother to answer the question: survivable by whom? Somehow, I doubt that you or I are included on the guest list, which is probably a good thing. The idea of being trapped in an underground bunker with a colony of cryptocrats is a fate worse than nuclear death.

Perhaps these writers are allowed to continue their work because the purpose of their fiction furthers the cryptocracy's goals. The morals of their stories are always the same; they echo the words of John B. Watson, the behaviorist so revered by the cryptocrats: "Men are built, not born." Simply put, their work helps lay the groundwork for the eventual acceptance of a police state, one in which every Good Citizen follows the orders of the voices planted within their heads by Those Who Know Best, otherwise known as The Experts, the cabal of absent-minded professors and mad scientists H.G. Wells was no doubt referring to when he wrote, on November 30, 1936, "The Universities and the associated intellectual organizations

113

throughout the world should function as a police of the mind" (Keith 307).

For those still skeptical about the very notion that the cryptocracy has an active interest in the publishing world, why not confer with the members of the closed Congressional hearing who uncovered the existence of the CIA's Project Mockingbird in 1973? They discovered that under Project Mockingbird

> ...deals were struck with a host of writers, commercial publishers and distributors. The CIA, in collaboration with the USIA, financed the publication of well over a thousand books of anti-Soviet propaganda by 1967.... Langley also financed the worldwide distribution of an animated version of George Orwell's *Animal Farm*. (Constantine 19)

This was a film shown to my English class in high school during the late 1980s. I wonder what Orwell would think about Big Brother using his fiction to brainwash school children? Only the Bad Brains in the cryptocracy would have the balls to utilize fascist techniques in order to promote a novel with an overt anti-totalitarian message.

But then again, why should I be surprised? According to another bestselling book for which the cryptocracy seems to hold an unhealthy fascination, the Devil has always quoted Scripture to get his way.

Works Cited

Alexander, Col. John B. and Major Richard Groller and Janet Morris. *The Warrior's Edge*. New York: Avon Books, 1992.

Andrews, George. *Extraterrestrial Friends and Foes*. Lilburn, GA: Illumi-Net Press, 1993.

Aquino, Michael. "Paranoia: Virtue Under Seige." *Paranoia* 18 (winter 97/98): 28-31.

Bowart, Walter. *Operation Mind Control*. Ft. Bragg: Flatland Editions, 1994.

Chapman, Douglas. "To a New World of Gods and Monsters." *Strange Magazine* 2 (1988): 16-19, 60-62.

Constantine, Alex. "Operation Mockingbird: The CIA and the Media." *Prevailing Winds* 3 (1996): 17-23.

Corso, Philip J. *The Day After Roswell.* New York: Pocket Books, 1997.

Corydon, Bent. *L. Ron Hubbard: Messiah or Madman?* Secaucus: Lyle Stuart Inc., 1987.

DeCamp, L. Sprague and Catherine Crook de Camp. *Science Fiction Handbook, Revised.* New York: McGraw-Hill, 1977.

Elms, Alan C. Review of *Bare-Faced Messiah*, by Russell Miller. *New York Review of Science Fiction* #2 (Oct. 1988).

Emory, Dave. "The Political & Sociological Implications of the UFO Phenomenon and the ET Myth." Foothills College Lecture. Los Altos Hills, Oct. 1992.

Grant, Kenneth. *Hecate's Fountain.* London: Skoob Books, 1992.

Grodin, Robert J. *The Search For Lee Harvey Oswald.* New York: Penguin Studio Books, 1995.

Halliwell, Leslie. *Halliwell's Film Guide.* New York: Charles Scribner's Sons, 1983.

Harryhausen, Ray. Interview. *"Earth vs. the Flying Saucers* Featurette." *The Golden Voyage of Sinbad.* Dir. Gordon Hessler. Perf. John Philip Law, Caroline Munro, and Tom Baker. Columbia, 1973. DVD. Columbia TriStar Home Video, 2000.

Keith, Jim. *Mind Control, World Control.* Kempton, Illinois: Adventures Unlimited Press, 1997.

Linebarger, Paul. *Psychological Warfare.* Washington, D.C.: Combat Forces Press, 1948.

Marrs, Jim. *Crossfire.* New York: Carroll & Graf, 1990.

Martin, Jim. "Quigley, Clinton, Straight & Reich." *Steamshovel Press* 8 (1993): 40-5.

McGehee, Ralph W. *Deadly Deceits.* New York: Sheridan Square Publications, 1983.

Nichols, Preston and Peter Moon. *The Montauk Project.* Westbury, NY: Sky Books, 1993.

---. *Montauk Revisited.* Westbury, NY: Sky Books, 1993.

Orwell, George. *1984.* New York: Signet, 1963.

Parsons, John Whiteside. *Freedom is a Two-Edged Sword.* Las Vegas: Falcon Press, 1989.

Pike, James A. and Diane Kennedy. *The Other Side.* Garden City, NY: Doubleday, 1968.

Prouty, Col. L. Fletcher. *JFK: The CIA, Vietnam and the Plot to Assassinate John F. Kennedy.* New York: Birch Lane Press, 1992.

Rappoport, Jon. *U.S. Government Mind Control Experiments on Children.* n.p., 1996. Available from the author at <www.nomorefakenews.com>.

Rowlett, Curt. "Project Mind Kontrol." *Steamshovel Press* 16 (1998): 13-23.

Rux, Bruce. *Hollywood Vs. the Aliens: The Motion Picture Industry's Participation in UFO Disinformation.* Berkley: Frog Ltd., 1997.

Skouras, Nick. A paper presented during Richard Hoagland's conference "The Monuments of Mars: The Pathfinder/Phoenix Connection" at The Pasadena Double Tree Hotel on 11 Sept. 1997. A complete audio recording of the conference can be ordered from She Who Remembers at (626) 287-8254.

Smith, Cordwainer. *The Instrumentality of Mankind.* New York: Del Rey, 1979.

---. *Quest of the Three Worlds.* New York: Del Rey, 1978.

Sutin, Lawrence. *Divine Invasions: A Life of Philip K. Dick.* New York: Harmony House, 1989.

Vankin, Jonathan. *Conspiracies, Cover-ups & Crimes.* New York: Paragon House, 1991.

Williams, Paul. "The True Stories of Philip K. Dick." *Rolling Stone* (November 6, 1975): 45-94.

White, Carol. *The New Dark Ages Conspiracy.* Leesburg: The New Benjamin Franklin House, 1980.

With Orson Welles: Stories From a Life in Film. Dir. Leslie Megahey. BBC TV Productions, 1979.

Zubrin, Robert. "There's No Science In Science Fiction." *The Campaigner* (April 1981): 24-30.

CHAPTER SIX

CONCENTRATION CAMPUS: THOUGHT CONTROL IN AMERICAN EDUCATION

H oles are forming in the brains of your children. Big Bird is hawking Prozac from inside a colorful box sitting in the center of your living room. Ronald McDonald has become a doctor.

It all began on the battlefield.

In 1995 Lt. Col. Dave Grossman published a revelatory book titled *On Killing: The Psychological Cost of Learning to Kill in War and Society*. The main point of the book is simple: Left to their natural instincts, soldiers in combat are unlikely to kill. During World War II, for example, only 15 to 25 percent of combat infantry were willing to fire their rifles. By the Persian Gulf War, however, the shooting rate had increased to 95%. How did the military manage to raise the firing rate so dramatically within only 45 years?

In his 1978 book, *War on the Mind: The Military Uses and Abuses of Psychology*, Peter Watson revealed the Mengele-like conditioning techniques used by the U.S. Navy to train assassins. A Naval psychiatrist, Commander Narut, explained his method as follows:

> He first exposed his subjects to "symbolic modeling" involving films specially designed to show people being killed or injured in violent ways. By being acclimated

> through these films, the men were supposed to eventu-
> ally become able to disassociate their emotions from such
> a situation.... The men were taught to shoot but also giv-
> en a special type of "Clockwork Orange" training to quell
> any qualms they may have about killing. Men are shown
> a series of gruesome films, which get progressively more
> horrific. The trainee is forced to watch by having his head
> bolted in a clamp so he cannot turn away, and a special
> device keeps his eyelids open. (Grossman 306-07)

As you can see, Stanley Kubrick's version of these techniques
is ass-backwards. In Kubrick's film the onslaught of violent images sensitized Malcolm McDowell to violence, whereas in the
real world these images actually served to *desensitize* Narut's
military subjects. Grossman expands on this point:

> In *Clockwork Orange* such conditioning was used to de-
> velop an aversion to violence by administering a drug that
> caused revulsion while the violent films were shown, un-
> til the revulsion became associated with acts of violence.
> In Commander Narut's real-world training the nausea-
> creating drugs were left out, and those who were able to
> overcome their natural revulsion were rewarded, thereby
> obtaining the opposite effect of that depicted in Stanley
> Kubrick's movie.
>
> The U.S. government denies Commander Narut's
> claims, but Watson claims that he was able to obtain
> some outside corroboration from an individual who
> stated that Commander Narut had ordered violent films
> from him, and Narut's tale was subsequently published in
> the London *Times*. (307)

So what does all this have to do with Ronald McDonald and
Big Bird and the holes in your kid's brain? Very simple....

Compulsory schooling, as with military entrainment, was
born on the battlefield. In 1806 Prussia's army was defeated by
Napoleon at the battle of Jena. Prussia believed that their defeat
was caused by soldiers *thinking for themselves* in the midst of

combat. Far too many soldiers were refusing to fire their weapons. The Prussian government wanted to know how to prevent such pesky inconveniences like "free will" in future generations, so they approached the brilliant psychologist Wilhelm Wundt of the University of Leipzig and asked him for advice. Wundt, the true father of experimental psychology, suggested they abolish voluntary schooling. Wundt recognized that the best way to control a population was to begin with the children.

Fragmentation was the order of the day.

Wundt began by dividing traditional school subjects up into sub-sets. He shattered them into divisions,—not unlike military divisions—precise regiments of lifeless facts marching through the children's porous little minds six hours a day, five days a week: History, English, Mathematics, Biology, Physical Education, etc. It was very important that no connections be made among these disparate subjects. Each was to stand alone, islands of isolated facts with no ties to the future or the past. The best way to ensure this fragmentation was to create *specialties*. Each instructor would be licensed to teach a specific subject, nothing more. If they tried to overstep their bounds they would be severely punished, ostracized from the academic world.[1]

The origins of "licensing" and academic "degrees" grew out of this authoritarian structure. The Ph.D. itself, based on the ideas of Francis Bacon in *The New Atlantis*, was created by Prussia in the early 1800s. The concept of "licensing" was later expanded upon by Andrew Carnegie in the 1890s. The purpose, according to John Taylor Gatto, author of *Dumbing Us Down*, was to "tie the entire economy to schooling and hence to place the minds of all the children [in the hands] of a few social engineers" (Gatto Interview 15).

These social engineers, led by Wundt, knew that fragmentation was the key. Once they had divided the subjects, they then set about dividing the children by segregating them according

---

1   This process continues in modern times. Witness the harassment suffered by Dr. Wilhelm Reich, a psychologist, when he dared to enter the field of biology; or the similar treatment showered upon Dr. Immanuel Velikovsky, a physician, when he dared to propose a new theory of planetary evolution.

to age groups. As Gatto has pointed out, this kind of segregation exists nowhere else, certainly not in the adult world. In what office setting do you find all the fifty-five-year-olds working in one room? Before compulsory schooling, in the era of the one-room schoolhouse, the older children were encouraged to teach the younger children. This system is known to work much better than ordering children to sit back passively and accept like a drone what their "superior" tells them.

Or like a soldier on the battlefield.

Just as a drill sergeant enjoys rattling a broomstick inside a garbage can at four in the morning in order to torture his recruits, the school system has a similar—though far more systematic—instrument of control.

> How the danger sinks and swells,
> By the sinking or the swelling in the anger of the bells—
> > —Edgar Allan Poe, "The Bells"

Bells are the most basic tool of Pavlovian conditioning. As any Freshman psychology student is well aware, Ivan Pavlov was a Russian physiologist known for his breakthrough work with the conditioned reflex. This work consisted of ringing a bell prior to feeding his dogs; he did this regularly over an extended period of time. Eventually the dogs would salivate upon hearing the bell, even when there was no food around.

In the vast laboratory known as public education, however, the experimental subjects—children in this case rather than dogs—are conditioned not to do something as trivial as salivate. No, the goal is far more sinister.

Let John Gatto, "New York State Teacher of the Year" for 1991, tell you in his own words:

> I teach children not to care too much about anything, even though they want to make it appear that they do. How I do this is very subtle. I do it by demanding that they become totally involved in my lessons, jumping up and down

in their seats with anticipation, competing vigorously with each other for my favor. It's heartwarming when they do that; it impresses everyone, even me. When I'm at my best I plan lessons very carefully in order to produce this show of enthusiasm. But when the bell rings I insist they drop whatever it is we have been doing and proceed quickly to the next work station. They must turn on and off like a light switch. Nothing important is ever finished in my class nor in any class I know of. Students never have a complete experience except on the installment plan.

Indeed, the lesson of bells is that no work is worth finishing, so why care too deeply about anything? Years of bells will condition all but the strongest to a world that can no longer offer important work to do. Bells are the secret logic of schooltime; their logic is inexorable. Bells destroy the past and the future, rendering every interval the same as any other, as the abstraction of a map renders every living mountain and river the same, even though they are not. Bells inoculate each undertaking with indifference. (Gatto, *Dumbing Us Down* 6)

There is an historical precedent for the use of bells as a Pavlovian conditioner. Bear with me as we launch into another extended quote, this one from none other than Dr. Timothy Leary, whose research into psychedelics as a behavior modification tool was supported and funded by Dr. Henry Murray, chairman of the Department of Social Relations at Harvard and the head of the CIA's Psychology Department. As I mentioned in an earlier chapter, Murray was also the man who oversaw the mind-control experiments performed from the years 1958 to 1962 on a young student-volunteer at Harvard named Theodore Kaczynski, whom the FBI would later dub "the Unabomber" (Cockburn). To be fair, it's quite possible Leary's intentions were honorable, but at this late date I'm afraid it's clear that the motives of his financial backers were far from benevolent. Either way, Leary's knowledge of the history of behavioral control is extensive, which makes the following insight that much more impressive....

> Over a thousand years ago [there existed] an organization
> of light-wizards that controlled and programmed minds
> from Istanbul, Constantinople, and Greece, through
> Southern Europe and Northern Europe, all the way up to
> the British Isles. We're talking, of course, about the hy-
> perdelic, cyberdelic, shamanic brain-fuckers centered in
> the Vatican. Those guys knew how to program minds.
>
> How'd they do it? Well, first of all, they developed the
> notion of a bell. If you were a peasant in Constantinople
> or Romania or France or wherever, the loudest sound you
> ever heard in your life was that bell five times a day. And
> where was that bell? On top of the church steeple. And
> the only sound you ever heard louder and stronger than
> that was lightning, and you know who's in charge of the
> lightning bolts. (Leary Lecture)

What Leary neglects to mention is the fact that the center for behavior modification shifted in the early 1800s from
the Vatican to the arena of public education, which is why Dr.
Henry Murray was a chairman at Harvard and not the Vatican.
If a researcher like Leary had existed a thousand years ago he
would have been forced to solicit funds from the Pope rather
than the CIA.

A few weeks ago I was having an argument with a friend. I
maintained that I had learned absolutely nothing worthwhile
from high school. My friend countered with a non sequitur, in-
sisting that kids *need* to graduate from high school in order to
get a good job. Despite being a patently false comment (employers tend not to care about your grades in high school or college),
it did inspire me to ask the following question: Since when did
education devolve into a glorified trade school? It wasn't that
way in Plato's day, nor was it that way before Wilhelm Wundt
and the implementation of compulsory schooling.

Only while researching this article a couple of days ago did
I come across the answer. During a brilliant 1994 interview
conducted by Jim Martin, the publisher of *Flatland* magazine,
John Taylor Gatto lays out the following information: Between
the years 1807 and 1819 a stream of American dignitaries trav-

elled to Prussia to consult with Dr. Wundt. They were so impressed by his work that they immediately began advocating his system of behavioral control for American education. The sons of the American elite were shipped overseas to study at Wundt's feet, and by 1900 *all* the Ph.D.s in the U.S. were being trained in Prussia. Between 1880 and 1910 the American successors to Wundt became the heads of the Psychological Departments at all the major universities. Henry Murray was no doubt among them. Wundt's main protégé, James McKeen Cattel, trained 322 Ph.D.s who in turn set up the new discipline of educational psychology; this discipline quickly grew in influence with the help of the Rockefeller and Carnegie Foundations. (Ultimately, Wundtian experimental psychology gave rise to infamous behavioral scientists such as James B. Watson and B.F. Skinner, whose work was used for the specific purpose of raising the firing rate in the U.S. military and training assassins to kill more effectively.)

> The next step came... when Andrew Carnegie [realized] that capitalism—free enterprise—was stone cold dead in the United States. [...] That men like himself, Mr. Morgan, and Mr. Rockefeller now owned everything. They owned the government. Competition was impossible unless they allowed it. Which, human nature being what it is, was a problematical thing.
>
> Carnegie said that this was a very dangerous situation, because eventually young people [would] become aware of this and form clandestine organizations to work against it. [...] Carnegie proposed that men of wealth reestablish a synthetic free enterprise system (since the real one was no longer possible) based on cradle-to-grave schooling. The people who advanced most successfully in the schooling that was available to everyone would be given licenses to lead profitable lives [...]. [Y]ou need to look at what occurred in the two decades following Carnegie's original proposal (1890-1910). You're talking about the realization of Carnegie's design. These licenses, which now extend to bus drivers and all sorts of unlikely people

who never had to be licensed, are then tied to forms of
schooling. So they've reserved that part of the work market. Through the cooperation of the government, many
of the government positions have very precise schooling
requirements. You can in fact control all of the economy
by tying jobs to schooling, and therefore you have a motivation for people to learn what you want them to learn.
(Gatto Interview 14)

Control.

Today, as the twentieth century collides with the twenty-
first, a single bell atop a church steeple would no longer be effective as an instrument of control. The population is too large,
too spread-out. The instrument of fragmentation has become
more sophisticated. The church bell has morphed into Hollywood. Why waste valuable time and money surreptitiously
planting electrodes in people's brains when you can sell them
television sets instead? The CIA's MK-Ultra program has long
been obsolete, which explains the recent explosion of books
and movies and magazine articles and even comic books concerning the subject. As Marshall McLuhan liked to say, quoting James Joyce, "pastimes are past times" (McLuhan 99). Anything that's popular is twenty to thirty years out of date.

Thought control has morphed into mind control, mind control into soul control. No implants required. Just sit back and
relax. Take a toke, dude, and trip out on those pointillist dots
on your TV screen. Go with the flow. Accept the fragmentation.

How is it possible to develop a logical train of thought with a
bell clattering in your head every forty-five minutes, as in Kurt
Vonnegut's classic science fiction story "Harrison Bergeron"?
Or, for that matter, every *seven* minutes if you're a hardcore
television addict? You must recognize the fact that a commercial interruption carries with it as much of a fragmentary effect
as any church bell in the Middle Ages.

All is not lost, however. Wundt was right; the best way to
control a population is to begin with the children. But the opposite is true, as well. What was once fragmented can be made

whole again. The primary reason kids hate school is obvious: They know, at least subconsciously, that they're being lied to. If you begin respecting them, teaching them real history, they'll *want* to learn. But that would require a radical alteration, a veritable paradigm shift, in the present system. It would first require the decertification of teaching and the destabilization of institutional schools.

"Oh, no!" cries the voice from the audience, "but how will Little Johnny learn to read and write?!"

I'm glad you asked me that, ma'am.

You're living under a false assumption if you think the school system teaches reading and writing. As Gatto has pointed out:

> ...the truth is that reading, writing, and arithmetic only take about one hundred hours to transmit as long as the audience is eager and willing to learn. The trick is to wait until someone asks and then move fast while the mood is on. Millions of people teach themselves these things, it really isn't very hard. Pick up a fifth-grade math or rhetoric textbook from 1850 and you'll see that the texts were pitched then on what would today be considered college level. The continuing cry for "basic skills" practice is a smoke screen behind which schools preempt the time of children for twelve years.... (Gatto, *Dumbing Us Down* 13-14).

This same point—the relative ease with which children can learn given the right set and setting—was proven over seventy years ago by A.S. Neill, creator of an experimental live-in school called Summerhill. Influenced by the psychoanalytic work of Wilhelm Reich, Neill decided to create a school geared toward helping the "rejects" of the British school system. In the words of investigative journalist Jon Rappoport:

> Neill operated on the idea that if you allowed students and faculty to participate, by vote, in the running of their own school, they would be more real, more alive.
>
> And then if you gave students, with no tricks, the license never to come to classes until they were ready to

learn, they would live out their childhood fantasies to the hilt. A child might play in the fields and the mud with his companions until he was fifteen—every day—and then finally school would begin to interest him. At that point he would come to class to stay.... At that juncture, twelve years of education might be telescoped into two or three years, without stinting. The classrooms at Summerhill were not remarkable.

There was no effort made to "interest" the child in a subject through special aids. Neill forbade this. He saw that when a child wanted to learn, the teaching became easy, and when he didn't the introduction of seduction was a cruel thing. (Rappoport 229)

A.S. Neill proved beyond a shadow of a doubt that kids learn much more efficiently when you leave them alone. Forget this "concept mapping" (otherwise known as "brain-storming" or "webbing") nonsense so prevalent in education today. That's the big thing in high schools now: forcing complete strangers to bounce ideas off each other until the "gestalt" inevitably reduces the very worst of these ideas into a form acceptable to the status quo. Teachers claim it encourages cooperation, but in reality it just instills conformity. Its sole purpose is to merge our children into a single hive mind consisting of brainless organic robotoids who drink alike, eat alike, sleep alike, and think alike. A regiment of tiny toy soldiers marching into oblivion to the same dissonant tune.

The purpose of school is *not* to teach.

If you don't believe me, study an average Scan-Tron sheet—or as I like to refer to them, "Scam-Trons." In case you're not aware, a Scan-Tron is a rectangular blue-and-white slip of paper that consists of a series of multiple choice questions, each question having four possible answers. For each question the student is expected to fill in one of the available bubbles with a No. 2 lead pencil. When the student is finished, the teacher feeds these little slips into a machine that reads the answers with a laser. With such back-breaking work, one wonders why teachers aren't paid more.

(Anecdotal Interlude: In high school I knew a guy named Bill who would coat the edge of the sheet with Vaseline. Somehow the Vaseline had a kind of mirror-like effect and would screw up the laser, causing the machine to interpret all of his answers as correct. Eventually he grew more clever and dabbed the Vaseline on only *some* of the answers, so the results would be more believable. Word to the unwise.)

The Scam-Tron is one of the most basic examples of behavioral programming one can find in the school system. Its intent is to instill in the student the idea that there exists only a limited number of answers for any given question—a closed universe of possibilities. I have a close friend who works as a teacher in Seattle, WA. She tells me, and I know this is true from my own experiences at Torrance High in the late 1980s, that all the kids *prefer* taking the multiple choice Scan-Trons. This is, statistically speaking, crazy. It should be obvious that an open-ended, subjective, non-linear written test in which you have to actually *think* of your own answer provides you with a much better chance of receiving a good grade. But this doesn't matter to the majority of high school students because they've simply forgotten *how* to think.

My teacher-friend in Seattle recently wrote a question for her students in which she asked them to do nothing more than give their *opinion*. Anything at all, written even semi-coherently, would have earned them at least a passing grade. Many of the students chose to leave the question blank. When she asked them why they had done this, they replied matter-of-factly that they couldn't think of their own opinion.

Fragmentation.

This is where neuro-linguistic programming comes into the picture. NLP was created by Jim Grinder and Richard Bandler in the 1970s, though the basic techniques are related to the work performed from the 1940s to the 1980s by the psychologist Dr. Milton W. Erickson under the close supervision of the

CIA (Bowart Chp. 4, p. 6). Essentially, NLP is the art of mastering the "language of the unconscious" to influence not only yourself but others as well. A baseball player might want to use it to improve his batting average—"creative visualization" could be used for this purpose—while a CIA agent might want to use it to coax vital information from a reluctant source. In the latter case, our hypothetical agent would try to "mirror and match" the source's physiology—sit the way he sits, gesture the way he gestures, breathe the way he breathes. In this way he could win the source's confidence within a surprisingly short period of time. But NLP doesn't rely only on gestures and body language; it also relies a great deal on words—words written or spoken with such precise tonality and timing that they slip into the subconscious as embedded commands.

If you think this is just a bunch of hocus-pocus, keep in mind that in 1983 Major General Albert Stubblebine formed an inter-agency team called The Jedi Project to disseminate NLP skills throughout the U.S. Army. According to John B. Alexander, a U.S. Army Psyops Colonel, even soldiers with *no* prior experience firing a .45 pistol learned better and more quickly when neuro-linguistic programming was used on them (Mandelbaum 46). If NLP could enable complete amateurs to fire a standard service sidearm with even middling accuracy, what other effects could it have on human potential—or inhuman potential, for that matter?

Walter Bowart, author of *Operation Mind Control* and a NLP practitioner himself, calls neuro-linguistic programming the 20th century's most important technology of empowerment *or* enslavement. It can be used to help people,—to "influence with integrity"—as with curing a serious phobia within minutes, for example; or it can be used to harm people, to persuade them to purchase your oh-so-unique brand of cigarettes or alcohol or coffee or ketchup or 36" television set.

My associate in Seattle has sent me numerous examples of high school exams that were purposely embedded with neuro-linguistic programming techniques. Once you're familiar with it, once you know the "taste" of it so to speak, you can detect it right off the bat. Negative programming abounds in these exams. To site a basic example, a test might consist of a whole series of sentences and paragraphs that have been spelled incorrectly or have incorrect grammar, the ostensible purpose of which is for the student to correct the mistakes. Anyone familiar with NLP will tell you that this is exactly the wrong way to teach anybody anything. Visualization, suggestion, and *positive* reinforcement are the main tools of learning. Humans don't react well to negative programming—unless, of course, your goal is to teach them negative behavior.

No matter how much money you throw at your local schools, they will not improve, because they're failing on purpose, just like that other ignoble experiment we call the "War On Drugs." As Bowart notes:

> Most students of NLP know that negative phrases can be used as effective embedded commands to produce the opposite effect. Most parents know, when dealing with a young child, to try a little reverse psychology. The "Just Say No [to Drugs]" slogan, and the billboards with a photo of a man with a gun up his nose and the slogan "Say No to Cocaine" under it, were just part of the successful psyop campaign which got Americans to take more drugs. It's well-known by now that the "war on drugs" is a complete failure. The extent to which the cryptocracy's black funds depends upon the drug trade is also widely noted.
>
> George Bush gave the game away, many believe, during one of his televised debates with Clinton when he wiped his nose in an involuntary response after he said the word "cocaine." (Bowart Chp. 10, p. 8)

I would add that George Walker Bush demonstrated the same involuntary "sniffing" reactions all throughout his debates with Al Gore. Under the new, improved Bush administration an unprecedented amount of money was spent on the War On Drugs and the results were just as effective as the War On Cancer and the War On Domestic Violence and the War

On Guns and the War On Illiteracy and the War On Terrorism. There hasn't been a more strategically fought conflict since *The Mouse That Roared*.

Yes, the Strategy of Tension is about to get a lot more tense.

Of course, such tension serves the cryptocracy well. Mae Brussell, the late political researcher and talk show host, recognized this fact back in the 1960s while investigating the Kennedy assassination, realizing that most of the crazed "lone nuts" of that tumultuous decade arose from the same intelligence milieu: Lee Harvey Oswald, Jack Ruby, Albert DeSalvo, Sirhan Sirhan, the SLA, Charles Manson, the Zodiac Killer, Jim Jones, as well as (we now know) Ted Kaczynski. Authoritarian regimes thrive amidst chaos such as this. The populace just rolls over and allows any dingbat with a wealthy father, a charming smile, and a balled-up fist to waltz into a position of power and protect them from the creeping chaos. "Only a return to the values of the past can save us!" Unfortunately, the values of the past are the values of now. The modern day equivalent of the MK-ULTRA chaos investigated by Brussell has been the rash of school shootings sweeping the country in the past few years, Columbine being the most destructive of all.

Which leads me to a revealing comment made by Dr. John Hagelin, a University professor and quantum physicist who ran for President on an independent ticket in 2000. At the State of the World Forum, held in San Francisco in October of 1999, Hagelin delivered a speech in which he discussed the school shootings. He identified a disturbing, common denominator that tied the shootings together. According to Hagelin, many of the "lone nut" teenagers responsible for these shootings were suffering from a brain dysfunction that tends to resemble a "hole" in the brain when seen in CAT Scans. These children don't have literal "holes" in their heads, of course, merely dark spots where the neurons have ceased firing. The brain centers most affected are those in charge of emotional control and decision making; they've literally atrophied due to lack of use. Doctors who have studied this phenomenon refer to it as "cortical fragmentation." Hagelin believes that this dysfunction is directly caused by the process of *education* itself.

Do you begin to see the connections now? Has it become clear to you yet?

Fragmentation is the key.

Pause a moment and wrap your mind around this: The process we are currently engaged in is known as in-depth pattern recognition. Skeptics would call it "conspiracy theory." But what is conspiracy theory if not the ability to pick out patterns, like Edgar Allan Poe's resourceful fisherman who is able to free himself from a whirlpool by noticing which pieces of wreckage are ejected from the maelstrom and attaching himself to one of them? The point of Poe's classic story "A Descent into the Maelstrom" is clear. You *must* study the debris. Don't turn your eyes away from it just because it isn't pretty, or because it doesn't seem "relevant" to you at the moment. What doesn't seem relevant now may just save your life in the future. But most people have no ability to even *begin* to comprehend the complicated process of in-depth pattern recognition. You can't blame them. They've been systematically conditioned *not* to see the patterns affecting their lives due to twelve years of constant fragmentation. They're caught in a maelstrom they don't even know exists, a maelstrom imposed upon them by a vast array of authority figures beginning with their parents and continuing on up to their elected officials and clergymen and bosses and doctors and drill sergeants and teachers. And advertisers. Lately, however, it's been very difficult to tell the difference between those last two....

Instruments of operant conditioning are being introduced day by day into the school environment on an ever-increasing basis. These instruments include surreptitious advertisements, pharmaceuticals, and toxic junk food smuggled onto the campuses by corporate underwriters. In September of 2000 the U.S. General Accounting Office released a significant report titled "Commercial Activities in Schools." The report states, "In-school marketing has become a growing industry. Some

131

marketing professionals are increasingly targeting children in school, companies are becoming known for their success in negotiating contracts between school districts and beverage companies, and both educators and corporate managers are attending conferences on how to increase revenue from in-school marketing for their schools and companies."

In the past few years high schools have become nothing more than laboratories for corporate-backed market research-ers. Pfizer hands out highly addictive stimulants like candy, causing six million normal children to become speed freaks for the express purpose of reinforcing our belief in a non-existent disease some social engineer decided to call "Attention Deficit Disorder." Microsoft and Toshiba "graciously" donate computers outfitted with the appropriately-named "ZAP ME" internet portal that bombards students with a constant stream of advertisements for its own products while also collecting data on the web-browsing habits of children. Recently, market researchers went so far as to pass out disposable cameras and 20-page booklets to elementary school students and request-ed they document their lives in both photographs and words so the researchers could better understand "what sparks kids these days." The booklets were titled *My All About Me Journal*. An "educational cable TV channel" named Noggin paid one school in New Jersey $7,500 for the privilege of butting into the students' lives.

According to Amy Goodman of Pacifica Radio's *Democracy Now*, even *Sesame Street* has gotten into the act. The show that brought us Big Bird and Kermit the Frog now hawks pharmaceuticals to kids. Traditionally, *Sesame Street* would end with an announcement that the episode had been sponsored by, for example, the letter P and the number 2. These days, however, you might hear instead, "Eli Lilly brings parents the letter P for 'Prozac'" over the images of a parrot and children playing with a big toy letter block, essentially a 15-second commercial for an anti-depressant manufactured by Eli Lilly. PBS chooses to call these segments "Enhanced

Underwrited Account Announcements" rather than "commercials" (*Democracy Now* 9-18-00).

PBS, like the Democratic Party, is nothing more than controlled opposition—a pseudo-alternative for what the Stanford Research Institute likes to call "Societally Conscious Achievers," conformist consumers who need to believe they're actually "non-conformists" before they can, "in good conscience," part with their money (Meyer 15-20). Advertisers and politicians know this and purposely cloak their true intent behind a façade of being "Societally Conscious." McDonald's, for example, established Ronald McDonald House to treat children with cancer, a disease no doubt contracted from their own McToad burgers. Vice-President Al Gore—who, by the way, studied neuro-linguistic programming under none other than Col. John Alexander back in 1983 (Bowart Chp. 31, p. 12)—professes to be an environmentalist while not mentioning the fact that he's as much of an oil man as George W. Bush.

In the 9-25-00 edition of the *Los Angeles Times* Michael O'Hanlon reported the following:

> Most tellingly, the budget proposals of [George W. Bush and Al Gore] differ by less than 2%. Remarkably, for perhaps the first time since the 1960s, it is the Democratic candidate who proposes spending more on the country's defense.
>
> Gore proposes allocating $100 billion of the 10-year surplus, or about $10 billion per year, to the armed forces. Bush's budget plan would provide the Pentagon about half as large a real dollar increase. Either way, defense spending would remain about $300 billion a year. That is as much as the world's next 10 military powers spend in aggregate.

Bush and Gore's budgets differed by less than *two percent*. What, then, were those two idiots debating about on television? Answer: nothing. They don't need to debate anything, just so long as they keep their lips moving. The content of the media doesn't matter. Marshall McLuhan was the first to point this out in *Understanding Media,* and you can bet your ass The Powers That Be are well aware of this. There's a reason why the NSA regularly consults McLuhan's book *The Laws of Media* and uses his theory of the Tetrad to manage world affairs (Dobbs). The future of humanity can be predicted by studying the future of its technology. Control technology, and you control humanity.

When Tipper Gore and Senator Joe Lieberman complained about the Hollywood film industry—the very same industry that provided a significant chunk of the financial backing for the Gore/Lieberman presidential campaign—you never heard them mention the fact that the very same ultra-violent virtual reality video games that so offended their delicate sensibilities were specifically created by DARPA (the Defense Advanced Research Projects Agency) to train American soldiers to kill on the battlefield without hesitation (Steinberg 5). The reason you didn't hear Lieberman bring up that particular tasty tidbit is simple: He's as much of a warhawk as Dick Cheney or George W. Bush. As he so proudly stated on more than one occasion during the 2000 Presidential campaign, Lieberman was the first Democrat to express his support for the initial Persian Gulf War on the floor of the Senate. Progressives should be happy that Bush stole the election from Gore. It's better to *know* the killers are coming rather than open the gates for a Trojan Horse. Remember: In a dictatorship you have only one choice, in a democracy you have two choices, and in a cryptocracy you have one choice disguised as two.

The ultimate point is this: The techniques of modern day public education were specifically created, via behaviorist entrainment and Ericksonian negative neuro-linguistic programming, to discourage non-linear thinking among our nation's school children and encourage fragmentation.

We see the fragmentation all around us, from our most brilliant theoretical physicists who have been submerged in unprovable claims for a hundred years, wading through a sea of elementary particles in search of the ultimate irreducible integer of matter... from our major political institutions, bickering amongst themselves, incapable of even stealing an election properly anymore (things have certainly decayed since Kennedy's day)... all the way down to that nice old lady over there, your kid's second-grade school teacher whose body cells are now dividing uncontrollably from years of cigarettes sold to her forty years ago by a bombardment of television, radio, and magazine ads in that long-lost Golden Era when the *Journal of the American Medical Association* claimed smoking was actually good for women... down to that kid standing in front of you right now, the cute one with the hole in his brain and the gun in his hand. He's pointing it directly at your face. His finger is tightening on the trigger. Do you recognize that emotionless look in his eyes? You should. After all, he's your son.

Think fast, daddy.

Works Cited

Bowart, Walter. *Operation Mind Control.* Ft. Bragg: Flatland Editions, 1994.

Cockburn, Alexander. "We're Reaping Tragic Legacy From Drugs." 6 July 1999. On www.latimes.com.

Democracy Now. Pacifica Radio. KPFK, Los Angeles. 18 Sep. 2000.

Dobbs, Robert. Dave Porter Interview. *Genesis of a Music.* Pacifica Radio. KPFK, Los Angeles. 24 Sep. 1994.

Gatto, John Taylor. *Dumbing Us Down.* Philadelphia: New Society Publishers, 1992.

Gatto, John Taylor. Jim Martin Interview. *Flatland* 11 (1994): 6-15.

Grossman, Lt. Col. Dave. *On Killing: The Psychological Cost of Learning to Kill in War and Society.* New York: Little, Brown and Company, 1995.

Hagelin, John. Lecture. State of the World Forum. The Fairmont Hotel. San Francisco, Oct. 1999.

Leary, Timothy. Lecture. Millennium Madness Conference. Scottish Rite Temple. Los Angeles, 29 May 1993.

Mandelbaum, W. Adam. *The Psychic Battlefield: A History of the Military-Occult Complex.* New York: St. Martin's Press, 2000.

McLuhan, Marshall and Wilfred Wilson. *From Cliché to Archetype.* New York: Viking Press, 1970.

Meyers, William. *The Image Makers*. New York: Times Books, 1984.

Rappoport, Jon. *The Secret Behind Secret Societies*. San Diego: Truth Seeker Books, 1998.

Steinberg, Jeffrey. "The Creation of the 'Littleton' Culture." *The New Federalist*, 30 August 1999: American Almanac pp. 5-7.

PART THREE

SECRET SOCIETIES
(THEIR KITH AND KIN)

Confederate General Albert Pike
photo - Matthew Brady

THE HISTORY OF UNKNOWN MEN: THE INFLUENCE OF SECRET SOCIETIES ON EXOTERIC WARFARE

"Esoteric Orders will not become extinct until the purpose which brought them into being has been fulfilled. Organizations may perish, but the Great School is indestructible."
–Manly P. Hall, *The Adepts In the Western Esoteric Tradition Vol. IV: Masonic Orders of Fraternity*, 1950

The true story of the role secret societies have played in history has yet to be written. Indeed, it's a story that can never be fully told due to its very nature. Obfuscation and esoteric word games abound in the realm of the occult. Those who are interested in such subjects, such as the people reading this very book, are left with only dubious sources and half-baked theories. Occasionally, a respectable source will come along and rearrange pre-existing facts into a coherent, scholarly whole. Others will produce voluminous tomes cleverly mixing real information with misinformation and outright disinformation. And still others, bestselling "exposés," are merely dark fantasies wrapped in the garb of journalistic reportage. My personal favorites are those that pretend to be utterly disgusted by the nefarious deeds of various and sundry secret societies while describing, in extreme pornographic detail, all the sordid rites these high acolytes are supposedly committing upon innocent young waifs all across the globe and beyond. I know personally at least one semi-popular lecturer, who's been warning people of these occult forces for years. He delivers very complicated presentations on the dangers of secret societies while never mentioning the fact that he's a member of one of the most infamous. This betrays a rather puckish sense of humor. Either that or he's just up to no good. Who can tell? When one begins investigating the occult, the question of what is real and what isn't eventually goes up for grabs.

The purpose of this particular chapter is not to offer a comprehensive history of secret societies; even if I had an extra thousand pages at my disposal, it *still* couldn't be comprehensive. However, I will offer a brief outline of the most important historical events with which secret societies have been involved.

Ishmael Reed once wrote, in the pages of his classic novel *Mumbo Jumbo*, "The history of the world is the history of the warfare between secret societies." In the realms of the occult, there are two forms of warfare: the exoteric and the esoteric. In this chapter we will be focusing on the exoteric. The exoteric would represent the traditional forms of war with which secret societies have been involved. In can be demonstrated through historical fact that secret societies played an integral role in the American Revolution, the French Revolution, the Greek War of Independence, the Civil War, and World War II, just to name five—rather significant—examples.

The Invisible College

This influence can be seen as both positive and negative. In 1660, a quasi-Masonic secret society called "the Invisible College" was formed by rogue astronomers who wished to practice *real* science without being burned at the stake by the Inquisition. Only thirty years before, in 1633, Galileo was forced to recant by the Inquisitors-General of the Holy Catholic and Apostolic Church for daring to suggest the truth: that the earth revolved around the sun, and not the other way around. This tragedy was no doubt a major impetus for the formation of the "Invisible College" (Lomas 17). These scientific men, who believed in reason over faith, put their lives on the line to promote "free thinking" and to actively oppose religious demagoguery. Such an organization of revolutionaries would require absolute secrecy in order to survive in a totalitarian regime. They would require oaths of loyalty and secret grips and specific rituals to prove one's membership in the College. When an authoritarian government is observing one's every move, secrecy is the only defense for the powerless.

I find the paranoia that surrounds the subject of secret societies to be somewhat bemusing. Rather than be afraid of the idea, I suggest starting your own secret society. Given recent trends in global affairs, you might have to do just that if you wish to go to the bathroom without ending up on a tape somewhere. (I recommend the recent book *Freemasonry and the Birth of Modern Science* by Robert Lomas for more information on "the Invisible College.")

The American Revolution

Manly P. Hall, in his 1944 book *The Secret Destiny of America*, conjures a poetic vision of the vital role Freemasonry played in the formation of the United States. Again, the idea that a ragtag group of revolutionaries would need to meet in secret in order to topple a repressive regime should not be a surprise to either historians or lay people. Respected mythologist Joseph Campbell had much to say about the Masonic symbolism woven into the very fabric of the United States of America; the flags, seals, monuments and icons of the United States all bore great Masonic significance. Discussing the symbols on the dollar bill, Campbell says, "These founding fathers who were Masons actually studied what they could of Egyptian lore. In Egypt, the pyramid represents the primordial hillock. After the annual flood of the Nile begins to sink down, the first hillock is symbolic of the reborn world." Campbell elaborates:

> Now here is the Great Seal of the United States. Look at the pyramid on the left. A pyramid has four sides. These are four points of the compass.... But when you get up to the top, the points all come together, and there the eye of God opens.... These were eighteenth century deists, these gentlemen. Over here we read, "In God We Trust." But that is not the god of the Bible. These men did not believe in a Fall. They did not think the mind of man was cut off from God. The mind of man, cleansed of secondary and merely temporal concerns, beholds with the radiance of a cleansed mirror a reflection of the rational mind of God. Reason puts you in touch with God. Consequently, for these men, there is no special revelation anywhere, and none is needed, because the mind of man cleared of its fallibilities is sufficiently capable of the knowledge of God. All people in the world are thus capable because all people in the world are capable of reason.
>
> All men are capable of reason. That is the fundamental principle of democracy. Because everybody's mind is capable of true knowledge, you don't have to have a special authority, or a special revelation telling you that this is the way things should be....
>
> These were, after all, learned men. The eighteenth century Enlightenment was a world of learned gentlemen. We haven't had that quality in politics very much. It's an enormous good fortune for our nation that that cluster of gentlemen had the power and were in a position to influence events at that time. (Campbell 25-29)

The French Revolution

These learned gentlemen also had an enormous influence on the French Revolution. George Washington, for example, was very close friends with the Marquis de Lafayette, one of the early supporters of the French Revolution. In 1777

General Lafayette had been a volunteer in Washington's army. Both were Masons, and Washington may very well have introduced Lafayette into the ranks of the Brotherhood (Wilgus 29.) Thomas Paine, too, had an enormous impact on the French Revolution. Neal Wilgus, an objective and thorough researcher who nonetheless manages to weave some welcome snatches of humor into his work, relates the travails of Thomas Paine after the formation of the United States. In part, he has this to say about Paine:

> He was in France when the fall of the Bastille touched off the rebellion against monarchy and he was chosen by Lafayette to take the key of the prison to America as a symbol of "the spoils of despotism, and the first ripe fruits of American principles transplanted into Europe," as Paine later wrote to Washington.
>
> More direct involvement came in 1791 when Paine, back in England again, published the first part of *The Rights of Man*, a stirring defense of the early stages of the revolution…. (78-9)

There is no doubt that the same cast of characters who fomented revolution among the American Colonies was hard at work in France bringing about "order out of chaos" as well. Furthermore, that the vast majority of these players were Freemasons is a fact not in dispute.

Neal Wilgus' writing exists on the fringes of popular culture, and perhaps would be dismissed by the more discerning reader. Nonetheless, for more information about the role of secret societies during the French Revolution, I highly recommend chapters two and three of Wilgus' highly informative and amusing 1978 book, *The Illuminoids*. It's an enjoyable compendium of little-known facts about the history of secret societies and political paranoia. When he allows himself to indulge in speculation, Wilgus clearly labels it as such.

If Wilgus is not to your liking, however, perhaps we should refer instead to an extremely well-respected historian who received his doctorate as a Rhodes Scholar at Oxford and taught history for seventeen years at Harvard and Princeton Universities before moving on to become the director of the Woodrow Wilson International Center for Scholars, located in the Smithsonian Institute Building in Washington, D.C. This is a man whose credentials are impeccable. Despite this, strangely enough, hardly any writer interested in conspiracy theories ever mentions James H. Billington or his most important work, *Fire in the Minds of Men: Origins of the Revolutionary Faith*. Published in 1980 by Basic Books in New York, it traces the history of revolutionary movements beginning with "occult Freemasonry" and moving all the way up to the present day. In Chapter Four, "The Occult Origins of Organization," Billington writes:

> Masonry imparted to the revolutionary tradition at birth the essential metaphor that revolutionaries used to understand their own mission down to the mid-nineteenth century: that of an architect building a new and better structure for human society.... The rituals leading to each new level of membership were not, as is sometimes suggested, childish initiations. They were awesome rites of passage into new types of association, promising access to higher truths of Nature once the blindfold was removed in the inner room of the lodge.... Masonry ritualized fraternity and provided upward mobility more easily than outside society. The Masonic title of "brother" fulfilled on the continent some of the function of blending bourgeoisie and aristocracy that was assumed in England by the envied term "gentleman." In the Masonic milieu, normally conservative people could seriously entertain the possibility of Utopia—or at least of a social alternative to the ancient regime. Philip of Orleans was the titular head of French Masonry (the Grand Orient); and most of the pro-revolutionary denizens of the cafes of the Palais-Royal were his Masonic "brothers."
>
> In the early days of the revolution, Masonry provided much of the key symbolism and ritual—beginning with the Masonic welcome under a "vault of swords" of the king at the Hotel de Ville three days after the fall of the Bastille. To be sure, most French Masons prior to the

revolution had been "not revolutionaries, not even re-
formers, nor even discontent"; and, even during the revolution, Masonry as such remained politically polymorphous: "Each social element and each political tendency
could 'go masonic' as it wished." But Masonry provided
a rich and relatively nontraditional foraging ground for
new national symbols (coins, songs, banners, seals), new
forms of address (*tu, frere, vivat!*), and new models for
civic organizations, particularly outside Paris.

Most important for our story, Masonry was deliberately used by revolutionaries in the early nineteenth century
as a model and a recruiting ground for their first conspiratorial experiments in political organization. (92-3)

And to be sure, these "conspiratorial experiments" did not
end with the French Revolution....

The Greek War of Independence

Not many Masons, and certainly not the general public, are
aware of how major a role Freemasonry played in the sev-
en-year-long Greek War of Independence. Today, Freemasons
are not allowed to discuss political or religious matters within
the confines of the Lodge. And yet, in the early nineteenth century, Freemasons actually constituted a "military expedition-
ary lodge to travel to Greece and fight for the independence
of the country" (230). The name of the lodge was *Les Enfants
Adoptifs de Sparte et d'Athenes*, and was formed from the combined members of three Marseilles lodges.

According to retired journalist (and 32nd Degree Freemason)
Andreas C. Rizopoulos:

In 1828 the State of Greece was officially acknowledged,
but it was not until almost 120 years later that the country
obtained its present borders and territories. The occupa-
tion of the country had started in 1453 when Constanti-
nople, the besieged capital city of Byzantium, fell to the
Ottomans. In the following four centuries the Ottomans

controlled most of the areas of the present Greece with the exception of the Ionian Islands and parts of the Peloponnese. The former were successively under the control of the Venetians, the French, the Russians, again the French, and finally were placed under British Protection between 1815 and 1864. The latter was partly occupied by the French. During the four-hundred-year period there have been a number of unsuccessful uprisings. Then in the early part of 1814 the seeds of the War of Independence were indeed sown in a Masonic lodge. (224-25)

General Charles Fabvier, an honorary member of this lodge, played a significant role in the war; this included leading his fellow Masons in a commando-style raid on the Acropolis. There were over five hundred soldiers involved in this raid, the vast majority of whom were regular military; however, almost all the volunteers were members of the newly constituted Marseilles lodge. Five Masons died in the battle, and were buried on the Acropolis. Fabvier and his troops (including the Masonic volunteers) held the Acropolis for six months, until the war finally ended.

F. Vassal, Grand Secretary of the supreme governing body of French Freemasonry, made a speech on December 27, 1825, in which he supported the militaristic, guerilla-like efforts of his brethren. He said, "...we have to admit that Freemasons have a great interest in the liberation of the Greeks. There is the cradle of our initiation...." (228).

Again, covertly inspiring revolutions can either have positive or negative results, depending on which side of the guillotine you're on. The influence of secret societies on American history, in particular, has been both necessary and bloody. And sometimes they've just been bloody....

The Civil War

Consider the Civil War. Investigative journalist Warren Getler has recently published a comprehensive book detailing the role of Albert Pike in the Civil War via a quasi-Masonic secret society known as The Knights of the Golden Circle, which later evolved (or devolved) into the Ku Klux Klan.

Pike is the most influential and enigmatic figure in Freemasonry. He's well-respected by the vast majority of Masons, mostly due to the fact that Pike designed the thirty higher degrees of the Scottish Rite as they are now performed today. Many Masons own copies of his encyclopedic book *Morals and Dogma*, and yet have not bothered to read it. This is not surprising, as its style certainly does not lend itself to a casual read. Most of the esoteric information in *Morals and Dogma* is adapted from previous occult texts; much of it, in fact, is lifted from the works of the famous Cabalist Eliphas Levi. Pike, himself, admits that he "extracted quite half of its contents from the works of the best writers and most philosophic or eloquent thinkers" (iii). The book, and the twenty-nine ritualistic degrees they comment on, was intended to compile the occult knowledge of the ages into one convenient package.

There's no doubt that Pike was a learned man. He was a lawyer, a scholar, a military strategist, and a poet; indeed, his poetry, little known today, was praised by no less an authority than Edgar Allan Poe. What's in dispute is whether he used this impressive intelligence for positive or negative ends. Masonic biographies attempt to paint a picture of Pike as some kind of saint. He did indeed use his knowledge and influence as a successful attorney to help many Indian tribes attain at least some amount of justice from the U.S. government. According to Getler, "... Pike pressed for federal payment of claims due for Indian lands that had been confiscated earlier in the nineteenth century. He obtained a six-figure settlement for the Creeks and went on to win other important suits and financial rewards for the aggrieved tribes" (59).

However, on the other end of the spectrum, Pike was also an "unabashed apologist for slavery" who "saw to it that key supporters of the Southern cause were corralled into the Supreme Council's ranks by the fall of 1859" (56). With these supporters, Pike formed a separate secret society outside the ranks of Freemasonry known as the Knights of the Golden Circle. There are many parallels between the symbols and rituals of the Scottish Rite and the KGC, too many to detail here. These parallels served a strategic purpose for Pike's militaristic goals.

The point that needs to be highlighted here is the central mission of Pike's KGC. Thomas P. Kettell, author of the 1866 *History of the Great Rebellion*, states, "...the Knights of the Golden Circle, having for its primary object the extension and defense of slavery, was organized; and several degrees, as in the Masonic order, were open to the aspirant for high rank in it. To the initiated of the highest rank only was the whole plot revealed, and the others, with but an imperfect idea of its purposes, were employed to further its designs." In other words, the organization had a pyramidal, top-down structure in which the "fully-informed elite" passed "instructions on to cells of obedient, ill-informed foot soldiers," all for the purpose of furthering the Southern cause. According to Getler, "By late 1863, the designs of Pike and the KGC were twofold: to continue to strive for Southern independence by helping to defeat the North on the battlefield, and to prepare, simultaneously, for a future conflagration, post-Abraham Lincoln, if they lost the rebellion then under way" (64-65).

When the South lost the Civil War, that plan was apparently put in operation. Getler demonstrates many intriguing connections between John Wilkes Booth, the assassin of Abraham Lincoln, and the KGC. If you have not yet come across Getler's work, I recommend seeking it out as soon as possible. His book is available in two editions; the 2003 hardcover goes by the evocative title, *Shadow of the Sentinel*; the recent paperback was published by Simon & Schuster under the more literal title, *Rebel Gold*.

World War II

The negative influence of secret societies on history can be seen, as well, in the early days of World War II. A well-organized, shadowy secret society had a major impact on the politics of Adolf Hitler. In this case, the secret society in question was definitely *not* the Freemasons. In fact, Hitler despised Freemasonry with a passion, considering it to be one of the three worst influences at large in 1920s Germany, and did everything in his power to destroy every Masonic Lodge in the country. In his 1927 manifesto *Mein Kampf*, Hitler wrote:

> The general pacifistic paralysis of the national instinct of self-preservation begun by Freemasonry in the circles of the so-called intelligentsia is transmitted to the broad masses and above all to the bourgeoisie by the activity of the big papers which today are always Jewish. Added to these two weapons of disintegration comes a third and by far the most terrible, the organization of brute force. As a shock and storm troop, Marxism is intended to finish off what the preparatory softening up with the first two weapons has made ripe for collapse. (320)

Hitler's objection to the Freemasons must not have been a dislike for the occult. Indeed, Hitler was obsessed with the occult, a fact that is far more well-known among scholars today than it was fifty years ago. It's more than likely that Hitler perceived the Freemasons as being members of a rival gang that simply needed to be eliminated in order to clear the playing field.

To my knowledge, the first writers to discuss Hitler's involvement with the occult were Jacques Bergier and Louis Pauwels in their 1960 book *The Morning of the Magicians*. Though entertaining, the book's claims were not exactly well-documented. And even less well-documented was Trevor Ravenscroft's 1973 book *The Spear of Destiny: The Occult Power Behind the Spear Which Pierced the Side of Christ*. Among its wilder claims was that Hitler experimented with mescaline, which led to his "Luciferic possession" (82), and that his rise to power was made possible by his possession of the Spear of Longinus (the Roman soldier who killed Christ). You'll be happy to know, according to Ravenscroft, that the Spear fell into the hands of the U.S. military at 2:10 P.M. on

April 30, 1945 (342). If true, we can only hope they're using it wisely today.

Since these initial chimerical takes on the legend, professional journalists and historians have picked up the rumor, dusted it off, and found genuine facts lurking just below the surface. In 1992 a scholar at the University of Wales, Nicholas Goodrick-Clarke, wrote a book called *The Occult Roots of Nazism* that delved into these areas in a dry, academic manner. But the best recent book on the subject was written by investigative journalist Peter Levenda. First published by Avon Books in a mass market paperback edition in 1995, it could easily be mistaken for a sensationalistic expose along the lines of *The Spear of Destiny*. Its full title is *Unholy Alliance: A History of Nazi Involvement with the Occult*. (To underscore the book's marginalized status, it might be noteworthy to point out that its only official recognition from the entire publishing world was to be nominated for a "Bram Stoker Award" under the "Best Non-fiction" category by the Horror Writers of America. To add insult to injury, Levenda wasn't even notified of its nomination until long after the award ceremony was over. One wonders what *did* win.) Since then, the book has been reprinted by Continuum with an introduction by bestselling novelist Norman Mailer.

In order to write the book, Levenda flew all the way to South America to investigate rumors that Martin Bormann, Hitler's former *Riechsleiter*, fled to Chile with the help of an "underground railroad" of sympathizers at the end of World War II. Once there, Bormann reportedly settled down in a heavily guarded encampment called "Colonia Dignidad" (i.e., "Colony of Righteousness"). Through circumstances too strange and complicated to detail here, Levenda did manage to locate the stronghold, investigate the place, and come out alive. He discovered that the "Colony" was a Jim-Jones-like compound where the most esoteric rites of Nazism were still being practiced.

This dramatic encounter led to his investigation into the occult roots of Nazism. Over the course of his book, Levenda introduces the reader to an eccentric cast of characters who, under modern conditions, might have ended up living somewhere outside San Francisco, getting stoned every day, telling each other's fortunes, perhaps attending lectures at Esalen once in awhile, and desperately attempting to sell their poetry and artwork to a cold, unsympathetic world. The core members of the Nazi Party were, without a doubt, proto-New-Agers *par excellence.* In the early 1900s, Baron Rudolf von Sebottendorff created a secret society called Thule Gesellschaft whose members mixed paganism, Theosophy and quasi-Masonic rituals to form an overarching, racist, right-wing aristocratic philosophy, the main goal of which was to cleanse the world of "impure" races. These occultists and eugenicists believed that once this goal had been accomplished, the God-like "Hidden Masters" who lived beneath the north pole (i.e., "Thule") would emerge from the inner earth and renew their ancient relationship with Mankind. It was this secret society that created the National Socialist Workers' Party and placed Hitler in power, manipulating him from behind the scenes. Of course, this would not be the last time a major world leader would be manipulated from behind the scenes by racist assholes far smarter than him.

Throughout his regime, Hitler relied heavily on a core group of occultists to advise him on the most crucial aspects of military strategy. This group included Dietrich Eckart, Alfred Rosenberg, Franz Six, Otto Ohlendorf, Erik Jan Hanussen, Wilhelm Gutberlet, Rudolf Hess, Heinrich Himmler, and Karl Haushoffer. All of them believed in ancestor worship, believed they regularly spoke to the dead, believed the earth was hollow, believed the ruins of Atlantis would soon be found (revealing the Aryan roots of pre-historical civilization), believed in the veracity of runes, believed that mating in ancient cemeteries would release the spirits interred within the tombs, believed that the Third Reich would truly last a thousand years.

This *belief*, blind faith in a mystical force that prevented human beings from exercising free will, resembled the faith of the Inquisitors-General of the Holy Catholic and Apostolic

151

Church more than the theosophical and Masonic philosophies the Thule Society appropriated for their own ends. Hitler ended up becoming exactly what he railed against in his book: a "useless eater," a withered appendage dependant on a body far larger than his limited intellect could ever hope to understand; an appendage that, once severed, had no mouth with which to speak, no brain with which to reason, no legs with which to flee from his own worst nightmare. The appendage died, but the body metamorphosed and survived....

The Great School, whether Black or White, is indestructible. Names change, acolytes die, beliefs alter, and reason persists. As long as history itself continues, so will the influence of secret societies.

Works Cited

Billington, James H. *Fire in the Minds of Men.* New York: Basic Books, 1980.

Campbell, Joseph and Bill Moyers. *The Power of Myth.* New York: Doubleday, 1988.

Hall, Manly P. *The Adepts In the Western Esoteric Tradition Vol. IV: Masonic Orders of Fraternity.* Los Angeles: Philosophical Research Society, 1950.

---. *The Secret Destiny of America.* Los Angeles: Philosophical Research Society, 1944.

Hitler, Adolf. *Mein Kampf.* New York: Houghton Mifflin, 1971.

Levenda, Peter. *Unholy Alliance.* New York: Avon, 1995.

Lomas, Robert. *Freemasonry and the Birth of Modern Science.* Gloucester, Massachusetts: Fair Winds, 2003.

Getler, Warren and Bob Brewer. *Shadow of the Sentinel.* New York: Simon & Schuster, 2003.

Rizopoulos, Andreas. "European Freemasons and the Greek War of Independence." *Heredom.* Washington, D.C.: Scottish Rite Research Society, 2005. 223-46.

Ravenscroft, Trevor. *The Spear of Destiny.* York Beach: Samuel Weiser, 1982.

Pike, Albert. *Morals and Dogma.* Richmond: L. H. Jenkins, 1956.

Wilgus, Neal. *The Illuminoids.* Albuquerque: Sun Publishing, 1978.

CHAPTER EIGHT

THE MYSTERY OF ALBERT PIKE

The enigma of Albert Pike is a persistent one. Certain facts are known about him, facts that detractors and supporters alike can both agree upon. He's a little-known figure whose impact upon American history far exceeds his notoriety. He single-handedly created the higher degrees of Scottish Rite Freemasonry (degrees 4 through 33). He was Sovereign Grand Commander of the Southern Jurisdiction of Scottish Rite Freemasonry from 1859 to 1891, the year of his death. He was a Confederate General during the American Civil War. He was a powerful attorney in his day. He was also a prominent poet, whose literary works have been forgotten except by a small handful of devotees. He is the author of one of the most important works on Masonic ritual, philosophy and symbolism, i.e., *Morals and Dogma*.

On these facts, everyone can agree. It's the interpretation of these facts that begins to grow a bit misty.

Pike is a polarizing figure. There seems to be very little objective analysis of his impact on history. Mainstream historians rarely, if ever, refer to him. Therefore, we are left with volumes of questionable interpretations that often draw upon half-truths, rumors, innuendoes, misinterpretations, and outright forgeries. Pick up any book that contains even a minor reference to the man and you will find that the interpretation of the author falls into one of two categories: 1) Pike was a genius and a Saint whose very touch turned men's souls into alchemical gold, or 2) Pike was a Satan worshipper whose noxious acts still stain the very heart of the United States of America—indeed, the entire world.

There is no middle ground among these "researchers." Pike was either good or evil. Of course, the world would be much simpler if everyone were wholly good or wholly evil. Zen Buddhist Alan Watts once wrote a book titled *The Book: On the Taboo Against Knowing Who You Are* in which he advises his readers to drop that dialectic way of thinking, what he calls "the game of Black-versus-White" (30). It only causes confusion because it is a model that does not reflect reality. Human beings are far more complicated than that, and this includes Pike.

With most historical figures, the latter statement could remain unsaid, but strange as it is to say, a very small minority of pundits have indeed implied that Albert Pike was not human at all (he was really a shape-shifting reptilian in disguise). I'm going to immediately crawl out on a limb, right here in the fifth paragraph, and propose we eliminate that theory for lack of evidence.

But first, picture a scene for me, if you will. Picture an underground train depot, a twisted set of metal tracks sunk about ten feet into the concrete. On either side of the tracks people are yelling at each other: men, women, children... all races, all creeds. Strangely, some of the people who are shouting the loudest have no faces at all. A giant bronze bust of Pike is sitting in the middle of the tracks. In the distance, a train is barreling down upon this immense monument. The train is so loud, nobody can hear what anybody else is saying.

Let's slow this scene for a moment, turn the volume down on the train, and turn up the volume only on certain individuals... just one at a time. There's no preferred order amidst this chaos. We'll select our speakers at random....

A. Ralph Epperson, a Fundamentalist Christian and author of the book *The New World Order*, has concluded that Albert Pike was a Satanist whose secret goal was to stamp out all organized religions in the world. (But isn't Satanism itself an organized religion? Oh, wait, sorry about that. Let's leave aside editorial intrusions for a moment and just examine the claims.) Here's Epperson in his own words:

...Pike considers Lucifer to be the God that is good, and the God of the Bible is the devil, the god of evil. That is what [Pike's] statement about "that which is Below is as that which is Above" means. That means that the God in the heavens is the god that is below, and the god who is below is the god in the heavens.

So the Masons do believe in a god: it is in the fallen lightbearer, Lucifer. There can be no other reasonable explanation of what Mr. Pike just wrote. (159)

No other reasonable explanation? This is a common belief among Christians, particularly the Southern Baptists, many of whom are very concerned about the ongoing "threat" of Freemasonry. Most people reading this will no doubt already be aware of the fact that the hermetic dictum "As above, so below" is a common phrase among the ancient practitioners of alchemy and does not refer in any way to either God or Satan. In fact, the belief systems associated with alchemy no doubt existed long before the Christian religion came into being. But when one is viewing the world within a limited framework, the amount of information one has to draw upon will be equally limited... and this may lead to numerous misperceptions, like the one we've just heard.

Now let's pan over to the other side of the tracks, shall we?

Manly P. Hall, a 33rd Degree Scottish Rite Freemason who wrote scores of books attempting to illuminate the esoteric meanings of Masonic symbolism (*The Secret Teachings of All Ages* being the most exhaustive) seems to have an endless supply of adoring adjectives to describe Albert Pike. He variously refers to Pike as "the Plato of Freemasonry," "this Masonic Prometheus," "the Homer of America," "the Master Builder," "the Real Master of the Veils," "the Oracle of Freemasonry," and (perhaps most confusing) "the Zoroaster of modern Asia" (37-8). And that's just scraping the surface.

Hall chooses to introduce Pike in his illustrated review of occultism and Philosophy, *The Phoenix*, with the following anonymous tribute:

Albert Pike was a king among men by the divine right of merit. A giant in body, in brain, in heart and in soul. So majestic in appearance that whenever he moved on highway or byway, the wide world over, every passer-by turned to gaze upon him and admire him. Six feet, two inches, with the proportions of a Hercules and the grace of an Apollo. A face and head massive and leonine, recalling in every feature some sculptor's dream of a Grecian god.... (37)

Hall does not mention who wrote the preceding tribute or where it was originally published. It's hard to imagine what sort of prostrate position the writer was in when these words flowed from his (or her) pen. Perhaps Pike himself wrote it. Or maybe even Manly P. Hall. When it comes to attribution in Hall's writing, everything's in doubt. He had a bad habit of being rather too lackadaisical about citing his sources—a habit he shared with Pike himself. For this reason alone much of his writing is considered useless by mainstream historians, and I understand their dismissal of him on those grounds. But it could be that Hall didn't *want* his work to be useful to historians. Like Pike himself, Hall was interested in history only on his own terms, and those terms involved the practice and explication of metaphysics. Every aspect of the mundane world somehow related back to the big Masonic "G"—whether that G stood for the initial letter of the Hebrew alphabet, "Geparaith," "God," "Geometry," or "the generative principle" is entirely open to interpretation. Pike cites them all as possible candidates. (On pp. 780, 640, 40, and 632 of *Morals and Dogma*, respectively.)

Hall saw himself reflected in Pike and came to admire him accordingly. They were both preeminent scholars of the arcanum, perhaps the *most* knowledgeable of their respective centuries, having each compiled his occult knowledge in encyclopedic works. Therefore it might be no surprise that Hall would place Pike on a such a lofty pedestal. And here we come to an important point about the enigma of Albert Pike: Because so much of Pike's real life and career is shrouded in mystery, it's easy for him to become a polymorphous Rorschach blot upon which people with an intense interest in the esoteric can project their own highest hopes or darkest fears.

To Anton Chaitkin, author of *Treason in America*, Albert Pike is nothing more than...

> ...one of the most physically and morally repulsive individuals in American history. Horribly obese—easily 300 lbs. or more—Pike was known in his adopted state of Arkansas as a practitioner of Satanism. His reported sexual proclivities included sitting astride a phallic throne in the woods, accompanied by a gang of prostitutes. He would bring to his revels one or more wagon-loads of food and liquor, most of which he would consume over a period of perhaps 48 hours, until he passed into a stupor.
>
> Pike was thrilled at the chance he got to kill Spanish-Americans in the Mexican War; he pushed himself forward in Arkansas politics with noisy anti-Negro and pro-slavery rhetoric; and in the 1850s he became the leading Southern organizer and boss of the American Party or "Know-Nothing"—the third-party grouping based on hatred and fear of immigrants. (234-35)

Where Chaitkin is getting some of his information, particularly the bit about the prostitutes in the woods and the phallic throne (what *is* a phallic throne?), I have no idea. He doesn't cite a source for these allegations.

In a Labor Day lecture delivered to the Schiller Institute in Washington, D.C., Chaitkin later attempted to delineate what he called "the Scottish Rite's KKK Project" by attempting to connect Pike to the founding of the Ku Klux Klan. He said, "The Knights of the Ku Klux Klan was a terrorist counterattack, beginning in Tennessee, designed to block Reconstruction and reverse the outcome of the Civil War. *The Klan and the Scottish Rite were one and the same enterprise*, continuing the imperial effort behind the slave owners' rebellion."[1]

---

1   Chaitkin's truncated lecture can be found online at www.theforbidden-knowledge.com/hardtruth/scottishriteproject.htm.

But to James T. Tresner II, author of the anecdotal biography *Albert Pike: The Man Beyond the Monument*, Pike is nothing less than...

> ...one of the most amazing men who has ever lived. During his long life, he was a teacher, an explorer of the American frontier, a poet, a newspaper editor, a lawyer—in fact he is still regarded as one of the outstanding legal scholars of the 1800s—a short-story writer, a linguist, a worker for reform in both education and the criminal justice system, an active advocate for the rights of women and the rights of Native Americans, an orator whose speeches are still reprinted in collections of Southern literature, a general in the Civil War, and a philosopher.
>
> He made and gave away fortunes. He built the finest home in Little Rock, Arkansas. The society columns of the Washington, D.C. newspapers spoke of him as one of the most graceful dancers, cordial hosts, and knowledgeable connoisseurs of food in the capital city. He always had a joke to tell his legion of friends, and his hearty laugh was famous.
>
> When, in the last years of his life, he moved to an apartment in the House of the Temple, his personal library contained thousands of books. He was a profound student of religion and philosophy. (39)

When researching this article, I decided to give Pike the benefit of the doubt. I wondered if writers like Epperson and Chaitkin might have given Pike short shrift; after all, facts can always be misinterpreted to bring about a negative conclusion. My first goal, therefore, would be to visit the library established by Manly P. Hall at the Philosophical Research Society in Los Angeles, one of the largest repositories of occult texts in the United States. Since Manly P. Hall was one of Pike's most ardent admirers, I concluded that this might be the best place to go in order to get a more positive view of Pike and his work.

The librarian at the Philosophical Research Society is Maja D'Aoust, who has lectured frequently over the years on the subject of alchemy and has recently co-authored a book on hermeticism titled *The Secret Source*. I asked Ms. D'Aoust to comment on Pike and his contributions to Freemasonry, as well on the study of the occult in general:

Guffey: Do you know anything about Pike's life?

D'Aoust: Not a lot. Albert Pike was a member of the Ku Klux Klan. He was a Grand Wizard. And, of course, I read *Morals and Dogma*.

Guffey: I'd like to talk about the KKK angle in a minute, but first let's talk about *Morals and Dogma*. You've read the entire book?

D'Aoust: Oh, yeah.

Guffey: Would you say it's a mélange of different sources?

D'Aoust: Oh, he takes stuff from *everywhere*.

Guffey: What do you mean? Just straight out rips off another text?

D'Aoust: *Completely*.

Guffey [Laughs]: He uses the cut-up technique?

D'Aoust: Cut-and-paste, is more like it.

Guffey: Is he upfront about that?

D'Aoust: Oh, no, no, no. No![2] [Laughs] And not that that's

---

2   In all fairness to Pike, D'Aoust's interpretation here is not exactly accurate. In the preface to *Morals and Dogma*, Pike couldn't be more upfront about his intentions: "In preparing this work, the Grand Commander has been about equally Author and Compiler; since he has extracted quite half its contents from the works of the best writers and most philosophic or eloquent thinkers. Perhaps it would have been better and more acceptable if he had extracted more and written less.

"Still, perhaps half of it is his own; and, in incorporating here the thoughts and words of others, he has continually changed and added to the language, often intermingling, in the same sentences, his own words with theirs. It not being intended for the world at large, he has felt at liberty to make, from all accessible sources, a Compendium of the Morals and Dogma of the Rite, to re-mould sentences, change and add to words and phrases, combine them with his own, and use them as if they *were* his own, to be dealt with at his pleasure and so availed of as to make the whole most valuable for the purposes intended. He claims, therefore, little of the merit of authorship, and has not cared to distinguish his own from that which he has taken from other sources, being quite willing that every portion of the book, in turn, may be regarded as borrowed from some old and better writer" (iii-iv).

159

a bad thing. I mean, we all do the same thing in our lives, right? We're taking bits and pieces from everywhere we go. Pike's main source was this gentleman by the name of Eliphas Levi, and Arthur Edward Waite. Those are the two main people Albert Pike is reading when he makes his *Morals and Dogma*. And almost all Masons base their information on that book by Pike. So the first thing that I would think to do is ask, where did Albert Pike get his information? He's getting it from Eliphas Levi, whose information is all coming from hermeticism and Kabbalah... and Arthur Waite, who gets all *his* information from hermeticism and Kabbalah. Albert Pike did it so that he could amass a text which then people could use to get the information from, right? Instead of having to read twenty bazillion books to get it from, he made this nice encyclopedic volume that, from then on, any Mason who needed the information could just look in that book and there it would be. Same with [Madame] Blavatsky. [Her book] *The Secret Doctrine* is also meant to be an encyclopedic volume.

Guffey: Would you say that Blavatsky was like Pike? In that she had a lot of contradictions in her personality?

D'Aoust [Laughs]: She was a mess of a person. First of all, she was so fat before she died she had to be wheeled around in a cart by, like, three men. And meanwhile she's writing about all these disciplines that take a lot of will power. If you see what happens to her physical body....

Guffey: Are you saying she wasn't practicing what she was preaching?

D'Aoust: There's a lot of different levels of practice. Some people can be astral projection masters but they can't get out of bed to go to the bathroom, so... there are so many different levels of "practice," who knows?

Guffey: Well, in terms of not practicing what you preach... when you mention the thing about Albert Pike and the KKK, that's something I've actually been trying to research and pin down. Anton Chaitkin was the first person I ever read who mentioned Pike's supposed KKK connection. Pike's a very elusive fellow. If you read a book by a Freemason, Pike's a wonderful guy who was against slavery and—

D'Aoust: Of course. Sure! And if you read a book about Hitler by a Nazi, they'll say the same thing.

Guffey: Oddly enough, you can easily find another book about Pike in which you'll have the exact opposite information, but both stories will seem equally plausible somehow.

D'Aoust: They probably are both true, because he had different faces for different parts of the community. There are bridges and elementary schools built to him in his home town because he was such a helpful member of the community, and to that part of the community he *was* very helpful. He was *very* helpful to many people, but not to—you know, unfortunately—the black Americans who he probably strung from a tree.

After the interview Ms. D'Aoust referred me to Paul Austad, the Director of Technology at the Philosophical Research Society. Mr. Austad provided several valuable sources that dealt with Pike's involvement in the Ku Klux Klan.

The 1905 book *Ku Klux Klan: Its Origin, Growth and Disbandment* by J.C. Lester and D.L. Wilson contains an introduction by Dr. Walter L. Fleming, who was a professor of History at West Virginia University and held a Ph.D. in History from Columbia University. In his introduction he lists "[s]ome well-known members of the Klan" and states, "General Albert Pike, who stood high in the Masonic order, was the chief judicial officer of the Klan" (24).

The 1924 book *Authentic History, Ku Klux Klan, 1865-1877* by Susan Lawrence Davis contains an oil portrait of General Pike given to the author by Pike's own son (Yvon Pike of Leesburg, Virginia) for the specific purpose of including it in her book. In Chapter XVIII, titled "Arkansas," Davis reports:

General Pike organized the Ku Klux Klan in Arkansas after General [Nathan] Forrest appointed him Grand Dragon of

161

that Realm at the convention at Nashville, Tenn. He was also appointed at that time Chief Judicial Officer of The Invisible Empire. He advised in this capacity that the Ku Klux Klan memorize their Ritual and to never make it public....

General Pike appointed Mr. Henry Fielding and Mr. Eppie Fielding of Fayetteville, Arkansas, to assist him in organizing Dens in that state. They were members of the Athens, Ala., Klan from its beginning and went to Arkansas, to live in 1867. They were Confederate soldiers, and gave me much information about the powerful influence General Pike had over the people of Arkansas during the dark days of reconstruction.

In 1872 Arkansas had two governments operating at one time and civil war was threatened and great excitement prevailed against the Washington Government. General Pike called a mass meeting at Little Rock, Ark., in the Capitol building and appealed to the people to be patient until better times would come and assured them that he would go to Washington and intercede for them, which he did many times.

At this meeting General Pike unfurled the Stars and Stripes and in a most beautiful manner, asked the people to follow it, which thousands of them did, promising him to be patient until the Ku Klux Klan could redeem the state. (276-77)

In his 1929 book *The Tragic Era: The Revolution After Lincoln,* a former Ambassador to Spain and Chile named Claude G. Bowers writes, "In the earliest phase [of the Klan] only men of the highest order were in control." He lists the leaders in each of the Southern states in which the Klan had planted their roots including Alabama, Mississippi, North Carolina, Texas, and Georgia—leaders such as "[i]n Arkansas, General Albert Pike, poet and journalist, scholar and jurist, solider and explorer, and a commanding figure in Masonry for half a century..." (310).

Far more recently, Wyn Craig Wade's 1987 overview of the White Supremacy movement, *The Fiery Cross: The Ku Klux Klan in America,* identifies Pike as having served as the Grand

Dragon of Arkansas during the early days of the Klan's inception. But Wade also adds this clarification:

> [T]he leadership of these men, originally appointed by Memphis officials, was usually in name only and nowhere lasted longer than 1869; such experienced veterans quickly realized the impossibility of governing *in secret* such widespread bands of young hellions and wanted no responsibility for it. (58)

In a very rare book, *History and Evolution of Freemasonry*, written in 1954 by a Freemason named Delmar D. Darrah, Pike's own words seem to clarify his sympathies further. Regarding the establishment of the Prince Hall Masonic Lodges for African-Americans, Pike wrote a letter in 1875 in which he stated, "I took my obligations from white men, not from negroes. When I have to accept negroes as brothers or leave masonry, I shall leave it" (329). He goes on to declare that he is dedicated to keeping "the Ancient and Accepted Rite uncontaminated, in *our* country at least, by the leprosy of negro association" (Upton 215). Some Masons claim these quotes are being taken out of context. Interested readers, however, can see the entire text in Appendix 12 of William H. Upton's 1902 study titled *Negro Masonry: Being a Critical Examination of Objections to the Legitimacy of the Masonry Existing Among the Negroes of America*, a book written by a Freemason. The entire letter can also be see at this pro-Masonic website: www.masonicinfo.com/pikesracism.htm. Feel free to judge for yourselves.

Even earlier, in 1868, Pike published an editorial in his own newspaper named the *Daily Appeal* in which he wrote:

> With negroes for witnesses and jurors, the administration of justice becomes a blasphemous mockery. A Loyal League of negroes can cause any white man to be arrested, and can prove any charges it chooses to have made against him.... The disenfranchised people of the South... can find no protection for property, liberty or life, except

in secret association…. We would unite every white man in the South, who is opposed to negro suffrage, into one great Order of Southern Brotherhood, with an organization complete, active, vigorous, in which a few should execute the concentrated will of all, and whose very existence should be concealed from all but its members.

The preceding quote can be found on a website dedicated to documenting the history of nineteenth century racism: www.geocities.com/ru00ru00/racismhistory/19thcent.html.

There are still more voices to be heard amidst the turmoil: The Grand Lodge of British Columbia and Yukon have published a lengthy essay on their website countering the claims that Albert Pike had any connection to the Ku Klux Klan. The title of their essay is "Albert Pike Did Not Found the Ku Klux Klan" (the full text of this essay can be found at: http://freemasonry.bcy.ca/anti-masonry/kkk.html). This title is, in fact, a true statement: Albert Pike did *not* found the Ku Klux Klan. During the American Civil War, he founded a secret society called the Knights of the Golden Circle which later *transformed* into the Ku Klux Klan.

The Knights of the Golden Circle is the X factor in this debate. What *was* the Knights of the Golden Circle? What was Albert Pike's intention in forming it? Was it an esoteric secret society with a benign interest in hermetic rites that was then later *twisted* into what we now know as the Ku Klux Klan? In 2003 journalist Warren Getler published a fascinating history of the Knights of the Golden Circle, *Shadow of the Sentinel*, a book that's been sadly overlooked despite the fact that it's a highly readable, true-to-life detective story. Getler claims that the main purpose of the Knights of the Golden Circle was to overcome the North on the battlefield and prepare for a contingency plan to continue the war underground, secretly, in the event that the South was defeated. This book is the best and most comprehensive analysis of Pike's involvement with both the Knights of the Golden Circle and the Ku Klux Klan. (I've written more extensively about the Knights of the Golden Circle's involvement in the Civil War in Chapter Seven.)

There's no doubt that Pike was involved in these secret societies. The question is, why? Let's now turn up the volume on another member of the crowd, shall we?

James Tresner II, a 33rd Degree Scottish Rite Freemason, attempts to defend Pike's connection to the Knights of the Golden Circle by putting words in his mouth. In a strange videotape produced by the Scottish Rite Research Society, Tresner dresses up like Pike and answers questions from a contemporary Mason who's sent back in time into Pike's library for a late night chat. Here is what Tresner, in the role of Pike, has to say about the American Civil War:

> Have the people of your time reduced the terrible and complex issues of the war to a simple-minded belief that the North wanted to free the slaves and the South wanted to impose slavery? [...] Oh, sir. No, no. I knew no one personally who argued that slavery was a good thing, though there may have been such people. But how do you end it? Decree, in a day, that the slaves are free? No, I believed that the only way to end slavery was to make it unnecessary economically. And I hoped for better conditions in the South than in the North; for there were slaves there, too—women and children who worked in the manufactories for so low a wage that they starved to death even as they worked. To that end, I worked and argued to increase shipping and manufacturing in the South.
>
> When the Southern Convention met in 1856 and introduced a resolution in favor of resuming the slave trade, I took the floor and spoke against it. I ended that speech by saying that I looked forward to the day when ALL men would be free. And for that I was booed off the floor, my character was attacked, and I was threatened with physical assault.
>
> No, sir, I was no lover of slavery. But to me, and to many of us, that was not the issue of the war. The issue was whether the states or the federal government was to control. I

feared the despotism of a large government, and I believed in my heart that the states were better suited to governing the citizens and protecting their interests. (Tresner 60)

Some of these statements strike me as plausible. Indeed, the central issue of the American Civil War was *not* the abolition of slavery, though high school history books have encapsulated the war as such in order to make it more easily digestible by students whose knowledge of American history has been bastardized by years of just such oversimplification. Other statements strike me as outright dissimulation, particularly the notion that Pike never once came into personal contact with a single person in the antebellum South who argued "that slavery was a good thing." In complex technical language, this statement could be categorized as "a shuck and a jive." Quite frankly, for me, that comment alone strains the credibility of the rest of Tresner's statement.

Let's return to what can be documented: not Tresner's words, but Pike's. How do we reconcile Pike's incendiary, overtly racist comments with his own magnum opus, the apex of Masonic philosophy, *Morals and Dogma*? Let's turn the volume up on Pike's own words at the moment. Is *Morals and Dogma* the work of a man who advocates slavery or violence in any form? Let's allow the monument to speak for himself at last....

> Might, in an army wielded by tyranny, is the enormous sum total of utter weakness; and so Humanity wages war against Humanity, in despite of Humanity. So a people willingly submits to despotism, and its workmen submit to be despised, and its soldiers to be whipped; therefore it is that battles lost by a nation are often progress attained. Less glory is more liberty. When the drum is silent, reason sometimes speaks.
>
> Tyrants use the force of the people to chain and subjugate—that is, *enyoke* the people. Then they plough with them as men do with oxen yoked. Thus the spirit of liberty and innovation is reduced by bayonets, and principles struck dumb by cannonshot. (*Morals and Dogma* 3)

...[I]t is one of the fatalities of Humanity to be condemned to eternal struggle with phantoms, with superstitions, bigotries, hypocrisies, prejudices and the pleas of tyranny. Despotisms, seen in the past, become respectable, as the mountain, bristling with volcanic rock, rugged and horrid, seen through the haze of distance is blue and beautiful. The sight of a single dungeon of tyranny is worth more, to dispel illusions and create holy hatred of despotism, to direct FORCE aright than the most eloquent volumes. The French should have preserved the Bastile [sic] as a perpetual lesson; Italy should not destroy the dungeons of the Inquisition. (*Morals and Dogma* 4)

[The Mason] labors equally to defend and to improve the people [...]. He knows that the safety of every free government, and its continuance and perpetuity depend upon the virtue and intelligence of the common people; and that, unless their liberty is of such a kind as arms can neither procure nor take away; unless it is the fruit of manly courage, of justice, temperance, and generous virtue—unless, being such, it has taken deep root in the minds and hearts of the people at large, there will not long be wanting those who will snatch from them by treachery what they have acquired by arms or institutions.

He knows that if, after being released from the toils of war, the people neglect the arts of peace; if their peace and liberty be a state of warfare; if war be their only virtue, and the summit of their praise, they will soon find peace the most adverse to their interests. It will be only a more distressing war; and that which they imagined liberty will be the worst slavery. For, unless by the means of knowledge and morality, not frothy and loquacious, but genuine, unadulterated, and sincere, they clear the horizon of the mind from those mists of error and passion which arise from ignorance and vice, they will always have those who will bend their necks to the yoke as if they were brutes; who, notwithstanding all their triumphs, will put them up to the highest bidder, as if they were mere booty made in war; and find an exuberant source of wealth and power, in the people's ignorance, prejudice, and passions. (*Morals and Dogma* 177)

To honor the Deity, to regard all men as our Brethren, as children, equally dear to Him, of the Supreme Creator of the Universe, and to make himself useful to society and himself by his labor, are [Freemasonry's] teachings to its Initiates in all the Degrees. (*Morals and Dogma* 329)

Quotes such as these are often used by Freemasons to "prove" that Pike could not have been a racist or a supporter of slavery. The Freemasons are right: These are *not* the words of a man who supports either racism or slavery. These words have as much relevance today, perhaps even more so, as they did when Pike first wrote them. Does that mean that the man who wrote them was not a racist?

No, it doesn't. No one can know, at this late date, exactly what Pike was like in his private life. This would not be the first time in the fields of philosophy, religion, or literature when the words a man penned were far nobler than his actions. Do a man's actions invalidate a man's work? Does the fact that Ezra Pound was a fascist anti-Semite lessen the artistic quality of his *Cantos*? Does the fact that Lewis Carroll had a penchant for taking nude photographs of prepubescent children invalidate *Alice in Wonderland* as a classic in British literature? Does the fact that William S. Burroughs shot and killed his wife cancel out his status as one of the great innovators in American literature in the 20th century?

Perhaps they do.

And perhaps the fact that neither Ezra Pound, Lewis Carroll, nor William S. Burroughs ever deigned to pen a 1,086-page didactic tome titled *Morals and Dogma* should be taken into consideration here as well.

If so, it should also be kept in mind that the words inscribed in the Declaration of Independence are clearly not those of men who support the slavery of fellow human beings... and yet, nonetheless, most of the learned gentleman who signed that auspicious document did indeed own slaves and continued to own them once their revolution was complete.

Listen to the clamor growing: These are the arguments of the crowd still milling around in that underground depot, cut off from the rest of society. Few people today, above ground, care whether or not Albert Pike was a member of the Ku Klux Klan. Few people today even know what Freemasonry is, and far fewer have ever heard the words "Knights of the Golden Circle." Quite frankly, it's not something they really need to know in order to pursue their daily lives.

But still, here in the dusty underground, the war continues to be waged as if there were never a better war worth fighting. The masses can barely hear each other over the noise of the oncoming train, the apocalyptic clamor of a bronze statue being shattered into tiny shards. The masses stand agape, staring dumbly as the train whizzes past.

Would these paralyzed fellows be shocked to see who's driving this train, the very same coal-black engine that just reduced Pike's larger-than-life-sized monument into copper-colored dust? Look closely through the front window and you can almost make out the engineer's bedraggled, wizened features: It's him all right, the one person who went the farthest to encourage all this mystery and obfuscation in the first place: Grand Commander Albert Pike, Confederate General and Master of the Royal Secret... yes, the "Zoroaster of modern Asia" himself.

There's no doubt in my mind Pike would be pleased to learn that his *mystery*, at the very least, still persists even as the amount of people in the world who actually read his cryptic words dwindle ever further into non-existence.

After all, there's something to be said for *mystery*... one notion with which everyone huddled in this underground depot can agree.

"What does it matter what you say about people?"
—Marlene Dietrich, Orson Welles' *Touch of Evil*, 1958

Works Cited

Bowers, Claude G. *The Tragic Era: The Revolution After Lincoln*. New York: Blue Ribbon, 1929.

Chaitkin, Anton. "The Scottish Rite's KKK Project." http://freemasonry.bcy. ca/anti-masonry/kkk.html.

---. *Treason in America: From Aarron Burr to Averell Harriman*. 1985. Washington, D.C.: Executive Intelligence Review, 1999.

Darrah, Delmar D. *History and Evolution of Freemasonry*. Chicago: C. T. Powner, 1954.

Davis, Susan Lawrence. *Authentic History, Ku Klux Klan, 1865-1877*. New York: American Library Service, 1924.

Epperson, A. Ralph. *The New World Order*. Tucson: Publius Press, 1990.

Getler, Warren and Bob Brewer. *Shadow of the Sentinel*. New York: Simon & Schuster, 2003.

Hall, Manly P. *The Phoenix: An Illustrated Review of Occultism and Philosophy*. 1956. Los Angeles: The Philosophical Research Society, 1995.

Lester, J.C. and D.L. Wilson. *Ku Klux Klan: Its Origin, Growth and Disbandment*. New York: Neale P, 1905.

Pike, Albert. *Morals and Dogma*. 1871. Richmond: L.H. Jenkins, 1956.

Touch of Evil. Perf. Charlton Heston, Janet Leigh, and Orson Welles. Universal, 1958.

Tresner II, James T. "A Visit with General Albert Pike." *Heredom* 10 (2002): 39-62.

Upton, William H. *Negro Masonry: Being a Critical Examination of Objections to the Legitimacy of the Masonry Existing Among the Negroes of America*. 1902. New York: AMS Press, 1975.

Wade, Wyn Craig. *The Fiery Cross*. 1987. New York: Oxford University Press, 1998.

Watts, Alan. *The Book: On the Taboo Against Knowing Who You Are*. New York: Collier, 1967.

CHAPTER NINE

WAS SHAKESPEARE A FREEMASON?: MASONIC SYMBOLISM IN MACBETH

I n 1933 Past Master Alfred Dodd published a book that purported to contain evidence linking William Shakespeare
with the creation of Freemasonry, an international secret
society built around an interest in esoteric knowledge, including the ancient art of alchemy. In the book, *Shakespeare: Creator of Freemasonry*, Dodd focuses on the Masonic symbolism
in two plays, *Love's Labours Lost* and *The Tempest*. Except for
two brief references he ignores *Macbeth*, an indispensable play
in establishing Shakespeare's ties to Freemasonry. The play appears to have been written as an allegory for the bloody murder of Hiram Abiff, the core figure of Masonic ritual.

Upon reaching the third degree the Masonic initiate is led
through the mock ritual killing of Hiram Abiff, one of three
original Grand Masters of Freemasonry. According to legend,
Abiff had promised his architects that he would reveal to them
all the secrets known by a Master Mason once the construc-
tion of Solomon's Temple was completed. Three of the build-
ers—Jubela, Jubelo, and Jubelum—were too impatient to wait
and attacked Abiff, demanding to hear "the Master's Word"
immediately. Abiff refused, after which the three "unworthy

craftsmen" committed the ultimate betrayal by killing their master (Robinson 218, 219).

From the previous paragraph alone one might notice the uncanny recurrence of the number three in Masonic ritual. In addition, not only are there three original Grand Masters, three assassins, and a total of thirty-three degrees of the Masonic hierarchy, but there are also three Principal officers, three symbolic steps "from this life to the source of all knowledge" (Downard, "Sorcery" 81), three obligations, three lights upon the Altar, three "pillars" that support the Lodge, and three knocks that gain the candidate admission into the Lodge, followed by three more knocks to summon the Brethren (Pike 548). This last example is paralleled in Act Two, Scene Three, where the porter utters the line "knock, knock, knock" twice until he allows entrance to Macduff, the future murderer of the "unworthy" Macbeth.

Both the number three and the concept of alchemy play an integral role in the story of Macbeth's downfall. In Act One, Scene One, we are introduced to three witches who utter the words, "Fair is foul, foul is fair" (1110). James Shelby Downard has pointed out that this is a well known principal of alchemy. Just as lead can be transformed into gold, the ostensibly noble Macbeth and his wife can be transformed into serial murderers by greed and ambition. Macbeth and Lady Macbeth might be seen as deliberate representations of the mystical *nagari*, an androgynous dragon that symbolizes the alchemists' ultimate goal of separating "the cosmic she and he" (Downard, "Call to Chaos" 309). Certainly, the Macbeths might be viewed as a warning to those who would take this separation to an extreme.

The number three appears again in relation to Hecate's appearance in Act *Three*, Scene Five. Though some scholars attribute the authorship of this scene to a writer other than Shakespeare, nevertheless it's interesting to note that in classical mythology Hecate has three roles—some of them infernal, some of them divine. Downard writes, "...she is Diana on

Earth, Luna in Heaven, and Hecate in Hell" ("Sorcery" 63). This parallels the triune godhead Jah-Bul-On, an entity mentioned prominently in the thirteenth degree of the Scottish Rite, whose name is said to be comprised of Jahweh, Baal, and Osiris (Knight 236). The melding of the positive and the negative are common elements of both alchemy and the Brotherhood. As Grand Commander Albert Pike has written, "The true name of Satan, the Kabbalists say, is that of Yahveh reversed; for Satan is not a black god.... For the initiates this is not a Person, but a Force, created for good, but which may serve for evil" (102). "The conviction of all men that God is good led to a belief in a Devil, the fallen Lucifer or Lightbearer, Shaitan the Adversary, Ahriman and Tuphon, as an attempt to explain the existence of Evil, and make it consistent with the Infinite Power, Wisdom, and Benevolence of God" (Pike 324). "Man is a free agent, though Omnipotence is above and all around him. To be free to do good, he must be free to do evil. The Light necessitates the Shadow" (Pike 307). In other words, "Fair is foul, foul is fair."

Macbeth can easily be viewed as a mingling of these forces. He is a bundle of paradoxes: nobleman and murderer, murderer and coward, coward and warrior. He is the perfect vessel for Shakespeare's retelling of the ritualistic killing inherent in the third degree, for the three "unworthy craftsmen" possess many of the same contradictory traits.

In Act Two, Scene Three, Shakespeare presents a subtle analogy to a fragment of the Hiram story. According to the ritual, confusion erupted among Hiram's architects after his murder, for only the Grand Master knew the location of the building's plans. Without these, the architects could not finish constructing the Temple of Solomon, which was to have been the masterpiece of Hiram Abiff. Instead it remained half-completed for a long time, and eventually deteriorated into ruins. It was not to be finished until years later, by architects who had no knowledge of Abiff's original intentions. Essentially, the life had been stolen from the building by the "unworthy craftsmen."

Similarly, confusion abounds when the noblemen learn about the death of King Duncan. In feigned surprise Macduff yells "horror" *three* times in a row, followed by these lines:

> Confusion now hath made his masterpiece:
> Most sacrilegious murder hath broke ope
> The Lord's annointed temple and stole thence
> The life o' th' building! (1118)

The parallels between the Abiff legend and these lines are obvious. Shakespeare further extends the Abiff metaphor only a few lines later when Macbeth describes what the King looked like in death:

> His silver skin laced with his golden blood;
> And his gashed stabs looked like a breach in nature
> For ruin's wasteful entrance... (1118)

Of course, silver and gold are colors respectively attributed to the moon and the sun, both of which are prominent alchemical symbols. According to Albert Pike they also "correspond to the two columns of the [Masonic] Temple, Jachin and Boaz" (776). Reinforcing this connection, Shakespeare uses an evocative simile to describe Duncan's wounds. The word "ruin's" brings to mind the dilapidated state of an old building—no doubt the unfinished "anointed temple" of Solomon.

Perhaps the most blatant parallel between the death of Abiff and Shakespeare's tragedy occurs during the next murder scene. Haunted by the witches' prophecy that Banquo would be "father to a line of Kings," Macbeth hires a pair of assassins to exterminate Banquo and his son Fleance. In the following scene, this pair mysteriously transforms into a trio. To the uninitiated this might seem like a discrepancy. However, after all the evidence presented so far it becomes obvious that Shakespeare is purposely waving a red flag in order to attract the audience's attention to this "irrelevant" detail. For the Bard's "fellows" it would have been immediately obvious that the three assassins were to be associated with Jubela, Jubelo, and Jubelum. Certainly it's no coincidence that the assassins kill Banquo in Act *Three*, Scene *Three*. As stated before, there are thirty-three degrees in Freemasonry. To underscore the symbolism, Shakespeare begins the very next scene with these words, "You know your own degrees" (1122).

In scenes like these Shakespeare is constantly toying with figure and ground. The figure is the plot itself, while the ground is the mystical symbolism fueling the direction of the plot. For example, on the surface "You know your own degrees" simply refers to the revelers at Macbeth's banquet measuring how much they can eat and drink, but beneath the surface may lurk the true, symbolical meaning. Another example of this occurs in this very same banquet scene when one of "night's black agents" returns to inform Macbeth of Banquo's murder. To Macbeth's question, "Is he dispatched?" the assassin replies, "My lord, his throat is cut:/That I did for him." Relieved, Macbeth says, "Thou art the best o' th' cutthroats" (1122). The figure here is a mere plot device, a continuation of Macbeth's killing spree. The ground is something quite different, a subtle reference to the oath of the first degree in which the slitting of the throat plays a significant role (Morgan 22).

Like light melding with shadow, figure and ground perform a delicate dance throughout the entire play. Sometimes, however, the symbolism subsumes both figure and ground. When Macbeth confronts the witches a second time, for example, he is assailed by *three* apparitions. These apparitions cannot be interpreted on a rational, surface level. The first one, described as "an Armed Head," is clearly symbolic of the first Sephiroth of the Kabbalah. As Albert Pike has written, "First of these [ten Sephiroth], in each, is Kether, the Crown, ring, or circlet, the HEAD" (768). Freemasons believe that Hiram Abiff's "Word," lost upon his death, can only be found "in certain great texts known to scholars under the generic name of Kabalah" (Waite 417). The search for the Lost Word is a central goal of Freemasonry.

The second and third apparitions are inextricably tied together. The second takes the form of a bloody child, while the third appears as "a Child Crowned, with a tree in his hand" (1126). This may recall the Mysteries of Samothrace, one of many ancient cults upon which the Freemasons based their hierarchical system of degrees. On the island of Samothrace very young children were initiated into the Mysteries. They were presented with the sacred robe, the crown of olive, and directed to sit upon a throne. Pike describes the details:

> In the ceremonies was represented the death of the youngest of the Cabiri, slain by his brothers, who fled into Etruria, carrying with them the chest or ark that contained his genitals: and there the Phallus and the sacred ark were adored. Herodotus says that the Samothracian Initiates understood the object and origin of this reverence paid the Phallus, and why it was exhibited in the Mysteries. (427)

The second apparition represents the object of the mimed ritualistic sacrifice, the Hiram Abiff of the Samothracian Mysteries, while the third is to be identified with the Initiate himself, holding aloft a tree that is both phallic and reminiscent of the Kabbalistic Tree of Life, thus connecting the final apparition with the first. Of all the symbols in *Macbeth* these are the most overt, and at the same time the most obscure. Appropriate for a play filled with paradoxes.

The preceding has explored merely a fraction of the Masonic symbolism that can be found in *Macbeth*. Any of these examples viewed in isolation would not mean much. However, as in alchemy, when the various elements are combined, something strange and unexpected rises to the surface. Though new, one feels as if it has always been there, just out of sight.

The idea of Shakespeare having been a Freemason will probably be a controversial theory to literary scholars, but then again anything not generally known since before the Cretaceous Period is controversial to literary scholars. Meanwhile, most mainstream historians believe that Freemasonry was founded in 1717, long after Shakespeare's death. Other, more esoteric authors trace the origins of the Brotherhood all the way back to Ancient Egypt. True or not, neither theory erases the fact that obvious Masonic symbolism is woven into the tragedy of Macbeth, written over a hundred years before traditional history says that such symbolism ever existed.

Gloria Dei Est Celare Verdum.

Works Cited

Dodd, Alfred. *Shakespeare: Creator of Freemasonry*. London: Rider & Co., 1933.

Downard, James Shelby. "The Call to Chaos." *Apocalypse Culture*. Ed. Adam Parfrey. Portland: Feral House, 1990. 307-27.

---. "Sorcery, Sex, Assassination and the Science of Symbolism." *Secret and Suppressed: Banned Ideas & Hidden History*. Ed. Jim Keith. Portland: Feral House, 1993. 59-92.

Knight, Stephen. *The Brotherhood*. New York: Dorset Press, 1986.

Morgan, William. *Illustrations of Masonry*. Batavia: Miller, 1827.

Pike, Albert. *Morals and Dogma*. Richmond: L.H. Jenkins Inc., 1948.

Robinson, John J. *Born in Blood*. New York: M. Evans & Co., 1989.

Shakespeare, William. *Macbeth. The Pelican Shakespeare*. Ed. Alfred Harbage. New York: Viking, 1977.

Waite, Arthur Edward. *A New Encyclopedia of Freemasonry*. New York: Weathervane Books, 1970.

Pierre Athanase Marie Plantard (March 18, 1920 – February 3, 2000)

CHAPTER TEN

THE ILLUSION OF CONTROL: THE PRIORY OF SION AND THE ILLUMINATI

This whole secret society business is a slippery one. What are secret societies? How far back do they go? Human beings have been forming exclusive clubs ever since the first moment they developed enough intelligence to distinguish differences among their fellow human beings. Women had their own club, the warriors had another, and the priests still another.

In ancient Egypt the simple act of reading was considered sacred knowledge, meant only for the priest caste. Not even the Pharaoh knew how to read. Imagine the leader of an entire country being dependent on a small sect lurking behind the scenes in order to enact even the simplest of proclamations. How would such a country ever survive?

Perhaps this is what poet T.S. Eliot meant when he wrote in 1936, "You have to consider that any esoteric occult ritual is today socially acted out by the daily publishing and consuming of newspapers." The simple act of reading would have been considered a magical ritual to the "uninitiated" of ancient Egypt. Therefore, merely by reading these words, you can consider yourself part of the original Inner Circle. How does it feel to be illuminated?

It always serves the purpose of the Inner Circle to keep as much knowledge away from the profane as humanly possible.

If you're dependent on *me* to interpret the holiest of sacred texts, then my job security is considerably higher than it would be otherwise, isn't it? The job of any priest caste is to convince the underlings that God (i.e., the Mysteries) is accessible only through them.

For example, Jesus was not officially made divine until the Council of Nicea voted on the issue in 325 A.D. (Baigent, Leigh and Lincoln 368). Amusingly, Jesus almost lost out on this, the Heavyweight Championship Title of the Cosmos, having won by only a few votes. It was necessary to transform Jesus into the Son of God because the Church wished to maintain control over the image of Godhood in the minds of the masses. If Jesus isn't divine, why do people need to flock to our Church Leaders who act as a direct conduit to Him? No one goes to Church every Sunday to talk to Gandhi, no matter how many great deeds he performed in his lifetime. Nobody ever sees Gandhi in a tortilla or on a billboard on the side of the freeway. There is no religion organized around kind-hearted philanthropists like Martin Luther King or Mother Theresa, regardless of the devotion they inspire. No, the only game in town is divinity, and if you don't have that you don't have a Church, and if you don't have a Church you don't have parishioners, and if you don't have parishioners you don't have money flowing into the coffers of the Vatican or the Evangelicals on a daily basis. Simply put, the Council of Nicea had to trademark the image of God, and the only way to do it was to make Jesus "theirs," to make him divine. Those who dared to remove the thin veil of divinity from Jesus, particularly in the fourteenth century, were burned at the stake.

Unfortunately for the Church, the Gnostics and the Knights Templar were doing just that. Both organizations could be considered remnants of the Essenes, a hermetic secret society of Jews who flourished in Palestine from the 2nd century BC to the 1st century AD. They were questioning the divinity of Jesus, which is one of the main reasons these "secret societies" were considered so dangerous. This is what forced them to go underground and develop secret signs and handshakes in order to pursue the rigors of genuine knowledge as opposed to the dogma of religious belief. Some of the most significant elements of the Essenes' philosophy are embedded in the Rose Croix degrees of Scottish Rite Freemasonry, particularly the 17th degree. In his encyclopedic book *Morals and Dogma,* which concerns itself with the esoteric roots of Freemasonry, Albert Pike writes extensively about the Essenes and their connection to Jesus. Pike believed that Jesus himself was an initiate of the Essenes.

Thus, we see that the need for secret societies emerged from two groups with different impulses: One group feels the need to control, while the other feels the need to defend itself *against* control. The Hegelian dialectic as warfare between opposing human impulses... between opposing secret societies. Fortunately, as William Burroughs once said, "Control is controlled by its need to control" (Burroughs, *Dead City Radio*). Some people need to feel as if they are in control every second of the day; this requires knowing what other people are doing at all times instead of tending to their own business. But if one is clever enough, it's not difficult to control the controllers while allowing them to maintain the illusion they're still calling the shots.

Knowing the enemy is on your trail, it's sometimes necessary to create false fronts—red herrings, as it were—to keep the controllers off-balance and confused. When a lizard knows it's being pursued by a predator, it will often shed its tail in order to distract its would-be killer. The predator will waste time pouncing on the tail; meanwhile, the lizard is scurrying off into the underbrush, where it can recoup and wait to reemerge, stronger than before.

The same is true of secret societies. It's sometimes necessary to create *faux* secret societies in order to divert the public's attention, while the really important deeds are being performed in the shadows. What's the use of a secret society even your mother is fully aware of?

Most mainstream Americans—indeed, mainstream citizens of any country—would be amazed at how many obscure secret societies are operating under their noses at all times. Some of these societies are insignificant, others quite powerful indeed. From their names alone, most people wouldn't be able to separate the wheat from the chaff. For example, have you ever heard of The Royal Order of the Jesters? How about The Mystic Order of the Veiled Prophets of the Enchanted Realm? Or the Order of the Trapezoid? Or the Royal Order of Quetzalcoatl?

By now, almost everybody has heard at least a whisper of such secret societies as the Priory of Sion and the Illuminati. They were real organizations—that much is certain—but in both cases their actual influence was very short-lived.

The Priory of Sion

As anybody who has read the bestselling novel *The Da Vinci Code* already knows, the Priory of Sion is said to be an ancient secret society that has controlled world affairs for centuries. In truth, the man who started the Priory of Sion in 1956 was a rightwing confidence man named Pierre Plantard who was eventually imprisoned over allegations concerning fraud, embezzlement, and child corruption. His reputation as a charlatan was established early on. A French police report in 1941 states:

> Plantard, who boasts of being in contact with numerous men of politics, appears to be one of those *illumines* and pretentious young people, heads of more or less fictitious groups, wanting to give themselves importance and who take advantage of the current movement in favor of youth to attempt to get themselves taken into consideration by the government. (Picknett and Prince 65)

Plantard loved to weave tall tales about the Priory, boasting an impressive list of Grand Masters that stretched all the way back to the fourteenth century, perhaps even earlier. Alchemists like Nicolas Flamel and Robert Fludd, scientists like Leonardo da Vinci and Isaac Newton, and accomplished novelists like Victor Hugo and Jean Cocteau were all High Muckety-Mucks of the Priory at one point or another, according to the good Monsieur Plantard. This reminds me of Ambrose Bierce's definition of Freemasonry from his classic satirical work *The Devil's Dictionary*:

> An order with secret rites, grotesque ceremonies and fantastic costumes, which, originating in the reign of Charles II, among working artisans of London, has been joined successively by the dead of past centuries in unbroken retrogression until now it embraces all the generations of man on the hither side of Adam and is drumming up distinguished recruits among the pre-Creational inhabitants of Chaos and the Formless Void. The order was founded at different times by Charlemagne, Julius Caesar, Cyrus, Solomon, Zoroaster, Confucius, Thothmes, and Buddha. Its emblems and symbols have been found in the Catacombs of Paris and Rome, on the stones of the Parthenon and the Chinese Great Wall, among the temples of Karnak and Palmyra and in the Egyptian Pyramids—always by a Freemason. (Bierce 109)

Plantard even claimed the Priory of Sion linked back to The Knights Templar and the Crusades. The Priory, however, is actually far younger. Researchers Lynn Picknett and Clive Prince determined that although the Priory "was established in 1956, it draws almost exclusively on late-nineteenth-century material for its history and folklore, suggesting that whoever the shadowy figures were behind Plantard and the Priory, they belonged to that era" (317-18). After a great deal of detective work, Picknett and Prince determined that a group of French synarchists were the true architects of the Priory of Sion myth.

The concept of synarchy was developed in the late nineteenth century by Joseph Alexandre Saint-Yves as a response to the anarchist movement so prevalent in Europe at that time:

Saint-Yves' concept of synarchy was essentially a reaction to the rise of anarchy and therefore its opposite—a highly ordered method of government based on what he believed were universal laws and principles. Everything and everybody has its place and purpose; harmony is achieved by keeping to that place and fulfilling that purpose, whereas any circumvention of those natural laws leads to disaster. Everyone has to remain in his or her allotted station in life. ([Gerard Encausse] Papus likened the individual's relationship to a nation or race to the cells' relationship to the body. As each was preordained to fulfill a specific function, attempting to do anything else would only cause problems for both the individual and the organism as a whole.)

His works outlined an ambitious, visionary program for establishing synarchy in France and beyond. Each state must be highly organized at every level, with everyone in his or her own specific place; otherwise anarchy would triumph. Challenging one's status would not be tolerated. (338-39)

William L. Shirer, the journalist who authored *The Rise and Fall of the Third Reich*, described synarchy as "a sort of first step towards the half-baked idea of the Fascist corporate state" (389). Picknett and Prince choose to believe that the synarchist influence, and therefore the Priory influence, has been influential to this very day in forging a European Union.

Though Picknett and Prince both admit the Priory story is a hoax, they suspect it is a hoax "in the same way that intelligence deceptions are hoaxes" (429). They believe the Priory is a mask the synarchists have worn over the years for various reasons. In 1956 the purpose was to act "as a front for groups plotting Charles de Gaulle's return to power [...]. Later, in the 1960s, it was revived with a new purpose, a misinformation exercise" that popularized the myth of an existing bloodline of Jesus Christ for the purpose of diverting "other esoteric groups from seeking out certain archives" (430).

The truth of Picknett and Prince's theories is impossible to know. Some simply do not wish to know. For many people, the truth about the origins of the Priory does not matter. After all, the theories of Picknett and Prince were colorful enough to pique the imagination of Dan Brown, who based his novel *The DaVinci Code*, in part, on their 1997 book *The Templar Revelation: Secret Guardians of the True Identity of Christ*. Dan Brown and Plantard are very similar in some ways. Brown, like Plantard, has a vivid imagination and a gift for telling an exciting tale. Plantard, like Brown, employed almost every significant historical figure and esoteric organization, such as the Knights Templar, in order to make his myth seem palatable. But if Plantard was right—that the Priory links all the way back to the Knights Templar—the connection is a tenuous one. The two organizations are as much connected as a severed tail is to a panicked lizard.

The Illuminati

The same can be said of the Illuminati, a secret society formed in Germany on May 1, 1776 by Adam Weishaupt, the dean of the faculty of law at Ingolstadt University. According to Masonic historian Manly P. Hall, Weishaupt's secret society sprang out of the academic setting in which he worked every day: "There can be no doubt that Dean Weishaupt found himself in the midst of scholastic plotting and counterplotting. To him, the campus of the university was a microcosm of the world, and the conspiracies which flourished in the school symbolized the larger strife between reactionary and progressive factions" (76-77). Anyone who has had the slightest contact with modern academia can sympathize with Weishaupt's position. The struggle between conservative and progressive factions has never been more Machiavellian than now. In this context I am by no means using the traditional political terms of "conservative" and "progressive." In fact, the conservative factions in academia are, for the most part, represented by people who would be considered "liberal" by the outside world; alas, their liberal views do not extend toward their students. They are authoritarians who wish to control the minds of their students with extreme regimentation and useless rules. It is this same type of authoritarianism that Weishaupt found himself up against in the 1700s.

Two Freemasons named Baron Adolf von Knigge and Johann Joachim Christoph Bode helped Weishaupt form the Illuminati for the purpose of combating this authoritarian strain, not only in academia, but in German society in general. The Illuminist Order never boasted more than two thousand members at a time, but these members were some of the brightest and most influential intellectuals of the day. However, their political goals did not constitute the entire purpose of the organization; these goals were merely a natural outgrowth of their esoteric philosophies. As Hall states:

> Certainly there was an undercurrent of things esoteric, in the most mystical sense of that word, beneath the surface of Illuminism. In this respect, the Order followed exactly in the footsteps of the Knights Templar. The Templars returned to Europe after the Crusades, bringing with them a number of choice fragments of Oriental occult lore, some of which they had gathered from the Druses of Lebanon, and some from the disciples of Hasan Ibn-al-Sabbah, the old wizard of Mount Alamut.
>
> If there was a deep mystical current flowing beneath the surface of Illuminism, it is certain that Weishaupt was not the Castalian Spring.... Weishaupt emerged as a faithful servant of a higher cause. Behind him moved the intricate machinery of the Secret Schools. As usual, they did not trust their full weight to any perishable institution. The physical history of the Bavarian Illuminati extended over a period of only twelve years. It is difficult to understand, therefore, the profound stir which this movement caused in the political life of Europe. We are forced to the realization that this Bavarian group was only one fragment of a large and composite design....
>
> The ideals of Illuminism, as they are found in the pa-

gan Mysteries of antiquity, were old when Weishaupt was born, and it is unlikely that these long-cherished convictions perished with his Bavarian experiment. The work that was unfinished in 1785 remains unfinished in 1950. (78-80)

Indeed, just as it remains unfinished today. Like a magician waving a handkerchief in order to distract his audience from the shenanigans occurring in the shadows, the Secret Schools sometimes find it necessary to feed bread and circuses to the profane in order to satiate their own uncontrollable need to feel in control at all times. Bread and circuses can take many forms. Recently, they've taken the form of pulp bestsellers and multi-million dollar movies. In the past, they took the form of sermons and impressive stained glass windows and bells ringing atop church steeples all across the countryside. The opiate of the masses is constantly morphing and adapting to the times.

Control is controlled by its need to control.

Works Cited

Baigent, Michael, Richard Leigh and Henry Lincoln. *Holy Blood, Holy Grail*. New York: Dell, 1983.

Bierce, Ambrose. *The Devil's Dictionary*. Cleveland: World Publishing, 1943.

Burroughs, William S. *Dead City Radio*. Island Records, 1990.

Hall, Manly P. *The Adepts In the Western Esoteric Tradition Vol. IV: Masonic Orders of Fraternity*. Los Angeles: Philosophical Research Society, 1950.

Pickett, Lynn and Clive Prince. *The Sion Revelation*. New York: Simon & Schuster, 2006.

Frontispiece for *The Constitution of the Free-Masons*, (London, 1723)

Engrav'd by John Pine in Aldersgate Street London

CHAPTER ELEVEN

TRACING THE
HERMETIC ROOTS
OF FREEMASONRY

"Symbols embody power—the power to understand
and therefore influence the world around us—the power to bring much needed rain to a dry land—the power
to grant good fortune to a tribe's hunters—the power
to unite people together in a single belief. In the wrong
hands, this power can be a dangerous thing. And so rituals developed to pass these symbols safely from one person to the next.

"The sharing of symbols is the ultimate expression of
trust. Through this sharing, you give some of your own
power to another person while at the same time gaining
some of theirs."

–Anonymous, *A Sharing of Symbols*, 2007

In the Fall of 1995, while pursing an undergraduate degree
in English at CSU Long Beach, I was assigned the task of
writing yet another in a long line of critical interpretations
of William Shakespeare's *Macbeth*. Somehow I needed to find
a new take on a subject that had been autopsied, dissected,
analyzed, and re-re-analyzed under the cold, sterile glare of
four centuries of smudged, professorial lenses eager to mag-
nify, scorch and extract the beauty out of something that had
once been alive. Not *just* alive, but subversive as well. Politically dangerous. A violent spectacle designed to illuminate the

masses through esoteric symbolism woven into a melodrama about murder.

I decided to view *Macbeth* through the lens of Freemasonry and hopefully shine new light into the well-trodden niche of Shakespeare criticism. It seemed clear to me, after encountering the text for a second time, that the play was filled with very obvious Masonic symbolism and that the author of the play must have been initiated into the first three degrees of Freemasonry in order to have written it.

The essay I wrote was eventually published, first in a conspiracy magazine called *Paranoia*, then on the official website of Torrance Masonic Lodge #394. I recently allowed it to be reprinted a third time on a website called www.rosslyntemplars.org.uk/. It appears in this book as Chapter Nine.

After completing the essay, I received the grade of "D" because (said the learned professor) Freemasonry didn't come into existence until 1717 and, therefore, William Shakespeare could not have been a Freemason.

Oh?

I once believed that Freemasonry existed only as an oral tradition prior to 1717, thus explaining why mainstream historians insisted the first Masonic Lodge was established in 1717. Just because this was the first year in which there was *written* evidence of Freemasonry's existence didn't mean Freemasonry bloomed out of the virgin soil of the eighteenth century fully formed; however, it turns out that even *this* assumption is merely that—an ill-informed assumption.

Consider these words by Pierre G. Normand, a 33rd Degree Freemason and editor of *The Plumbline—The Quarterly Bulletin of The Scottish Rite Research Society*:

> [L]odges in Scotland began accepting non-operatives during the early 1600s, a century before the formation of the grand lodge of 1717. We know this to be an historic fact as the records and minutes of those Scottish lodges still exist. The earliest appearance of a non-operative Freemason is recorded in the minutes of the Lodge of Ed-

inburgh on 8 June 1600. The practice increased throughout Scotland and the British Isles during the century
prior to 1717....

The old theory (now proven false) that "Freemasonry
was a new thing in 1717" denies the existence of the many
Scottish lodge records.... Thankfully, due to the formation of the Irish, Scottish and Ancients' grand lodges,
most other grand lodges today can trace their Masonic
ancestries back to the early operative lodges of the British
Isles, and not just to the four speculative London lodges
of 1717. ("Coil's Definition of Freemasonry" 3)

Since the earliest documented Masonic Lodge was established in 1600, this makes it more than possible for Shakespeare to have been initiated in the first three degrees before
1605, the year *Macbeth* was probably written.

But even 1600 might be considered a late date, if one were
attempting to trace the true roots of Freemasonry. It's impossible to study the origins of Freemasonry, as well as most of the
other secret societies that emerged in the wake of the Enlightenment, without also exploring the history of alchemy, hermeticism, and the Kabbalah. The essential principles of Freemasonry predate any organization bearing that specific name.
We do know that modern Freemasonry grew out of the medieval fraternity of operative stoneworkers. As Normand says,
"The Freemasons of the middle ages were so-called because
they were free men, and worked in freestone" ("A Definition of
Freemasonry" 6).

But these Masons weren't simply master architects. In private, they spent much of their time studying and practicing "the
doctrines of Gnosticism, Neoplatonism, and Manichaeism.
Later, they were influenced by... the much-persecuted Templars. But... they had learned discretion in the school of sad
experience" (Hall, *Adepts* Vol. I 13). One of the best encapsu-
lations of the origins of Freemasonry is Manly P. Hall's book
*The Adepts in the Western Esoteric Tradition Vol. IV: Masonic
Orders of Fraternity*. First published in 1950, this small book

draws upon a wide range of important and voluminous sources (such as J. S. M. Ward's 1921 book *Freemasonry and the Ancient Gods*) to paint a concise picture of a very complex historical development:

> Assemblies of men specially skilled in architecture descended from antiquity and flourished in both Europe and Asia. These guilds of artisans were called upon whenever it was resolved to build new cities, to erect monumental structures, or to restore or enlarge shrines, temples, and palaces....
>
> It was considered indelicate to inquire into the secrets of these associations of builders. Apparently they combined religious and philosophical speculations with the more prosaic rules of construction. The normal boundaries of prevailing racial and religious prejudices were relaxed in favor of these skilled bands of craftsmen, who were permitted to live according to their natural instincts and preferences while laboring in various districts and countries. Great edifices, such as the cathedral churches, often required centuries to complete. Thus several generations of artisans were employed on a single project, and the camps or towns which they established contiguous to their work became comparatively permanent communities. Like the gypsies, these bands of wandering craftsmen never mingled with other people. (11-12)

The "religious and philosophical speculations" Hall is referring to here could be described, in broad terms, as hermeticism. According to Lewis Spence's *Encyclopedia of Occultism*, the word "hermeticism" is derived from Hermes Trismegistus, the "name given by the Greeks to the Egyptian god Thoth or Tehuti, the god of wisdom, learning and literature." Of Hermes, Spence writes:

> To him was attributed as "scribe of the gods" the authorship of all sacred books which were thus called "Hermetic" by the Greeks. These, according to Clemens Alexan-

drinus were forty-two in number and were sub-divided into six portions, of which the first dealt with priestly education, the second with temple ritual and the third with geographical matter. The fourth division treated of astrology, the fifth of hymns in honour of the gods and a text-book for the guidance of Kings, while the sixth was medical. It is unlikely that these books were all the work of one individual, and it is more probable that they represent the accumulated wisdom of Egypt, attributed in the course of ages to the great god of wisdom.

As "scribe of the god" Thoth was also the author of all strictly sacred writing. Hence by a convenient fiction the name of *Hermes* was placed at the head of an extensive cycle of mystic literature, produced in post-Christian times. Most of this Hermetic or Trismegistic literature has perished, but all that remains of it has been gathered and translated into English.... Hitherto these writings have been neglected by theologians, who have dismissed them as the offspring of third century Neo-Platonism. According to the generally accepted view, they were eclectic compilations, combining Neo-Platonic philosophy, Philonic Judaism and Kabalistic theosophy in an attempt to supply a philosophic substitute for Christianity. The many Christian elements to be found in these mystic scriptures were ascribed to plagiarism. By an examination of early mystery writings and traditions it has been proved with some degree of certainty that the main source of the Trismegistic Tractates is the wisdom of Egypt.... (208-09)

The history of hermeticism is so intimately intertwined with the history of Freemasonry that members of Masonic Foshay Lodge #467 in Culver City, CA have recently established a club for the purpose of becoming California's next traditionally-oriented Masonic lodge, and the name they chose for this club is none other than the "Hermes Trismegistus Masonic Club."

We see now that Hermes was another name for the Egyptian god Thoth. Egypt is the key to tracing the roots of Masonic symbolism, if not the Brotherhood itself. Researcher

Ralph Ellis, for example, has done a commendable job of tracing the origins of Freemasonry to Ancient Egypt. This notion is by no means new. Freemasons have been trying to prove this connection (to themselves, if no one else) since the rise of what C.W. Leadbeater calls "the Anthropological School," a movement of Masonic students that was still under development even in the early nineteenth century. These researchers attempt to extend the pedigree of the Brotherhood into antiquity by locating Masonic "signs and symbols, both of the Craft and higher degrees, in the wall-paintings, carvings, sculpture and buildings" of various ancient civilizations throughout the world (Leadbeater 4). These attempts can sometimes descend into absurdity. Ralph Ellis, however, makes several intriguing connections between *uniquely* Masonic terms and the Egyptian language:

> Apart from the one or two terms that are taken from the Bible, these terms are unique to Masonry and are not to be found within the English language....
>
> While masonic history, myths and teachings are valuable in divining the true history of the Craft, so too are the signs, grips, knocks and recognition words that form masonic initiations and entrance to Lodge. Since these words and phrases have been largely handed down by rote, and often without any knowledge of their true meanings, their original pronunciation may have survived the centuries. The distortions of the Chinese-whisper syndrome only apply to words that are thought to have a real meaning, and so the receiver tries to derive this meaning out of the odd-sounding syllables that they have heard. But if the word is known to be a nonsense word, like *hocus pocus* or *abracadabra*, it is likely that the syllables will be simply learned and transmitted phonetically without interpretation or distortion.
>
> But while Masonry uses and preserves these ancient words and phrases, the list of presumed meanings given for them are so bland and contrived, it is almost certain that the true meanings have been lost.... (207-08)

One fascinating example of Ellis' research is his analysis of the word "Jahbulon." This single three-syllable word has caused a great deal of trouble for Freemasons in recent years. Many anti-Masons cite it as the prime reason one cannot be a Christian and a Freemason at the same time. These Christians claim the word is simply another name for "Satan." The word appears in some versions of the York Rite's Royal Arch Degree (the Seventh Degree), or the Scottish Rite's Royal Arch of Solomon Degree (the Thirteenth Degree). In his 1984 book *The Brotherhood*, anti-Masonic journalist Stephen Knight claimed that Jahbulon represented nothing less than the secret God of Freemasonry. Knight believed that "[t]his grotesque manifestation of evil" was "a specific supernatural being—a compound deity composed of three separate personalities fused in one" (236), and that those three personalities were Jahweh (JAH), Baal (BUL), and Osiris (ON). Though imaginative, there are obvious problems with this interpretation. (How Knight derived the word "Osiris" from "ON" has always troubled me.) Alas, there are equal problems with the definition provided by pro-Masonic researchers Arturo de Hoyos and S. Brent Morris who claim that "Jahbulon" means "Jehovah, powerful Lord" or "Jehovah, the Lord, the I AM" or "Lord in Heaven, the Father of All" (de Hoyos and Morris). The pro-Masons say "God" and the anti-Masons say "Satan." Is there no deeper interpretation available?

In *Eden in Egypt* Ralph Ellis writes:

> [T]he syllable "On" most likely referred to the biblical On, or Heliopolis, a name that was derived from the Egyptian An or On. In its turn, the syllable Baal could refer as much to "lord" or "king" as the god Baal....
>
> The term Yah was originally derived from Yah, the Moon-god; but of course Yah is only another name for Djehuti or Thoth. The... other amendment is to the translation of "bul" or "bal." The obvious connection to make is with Baal, as we have seen, but an alternative is the link to Babel.... [T]he Tower of Babel actually referred to the Great Pyramid, since the Egyptian term *belbel* referred to pyramids.

195

Thus, the final translation of the masonic god-name
Jahbulon or Yahbulon could well be "Thoth, Lord of He-
liopolis," or perhaps even the "Thoth Pyramid of Heliopo-
lis." Both of these phrases again display the true Egyptian
origins of Masonry.... (224)

The idea that the "true omnific word" (Mackey 112) in Freemasonry would be a reference to "Thoth, Lord of Heliopo-
lis" makes a great deal of sense given the fact that Thoth, or
Hermes, was the god of "sacred writing." Or as Albert Pike
writes at the very end of his book *Morals and Dogma*, "Gloria
Dei Est Celare Verbum" (861). Translation: "It is to the glory of
God to conceal a word."

Let's now skip ahead to the year 1832, which marked the publication of a compelling work of scholarship titled *Sullo Spirito
antipapale che produsse la Riforma, etc.* by Professor Gabriele
Rossetti (1783-1854). According to the late Manly P. Hall, Rossetti's central thesis can be summarized as follows: "A Secret Society... whose original is lost in the mysterious twilight of Oriental religion, has continued from the earliest historical point at
which its workings can be traced to exercise an almost universal influence on the condition of the civilized world" (Hall, *The
Adepts Vol. I* 73). The teachings of these secret societies passed
from Egypt and Persia to the early Christian heretics, the Gnostics. Because of the political power arrayed against the Gnostics
in Rome, they had to be very careful in practicing these ancient
rites. Complicated signs, grips, and passwords, all of which required great discipline to memorize, were used to protect the
ancient Mysteries. These Mysteries were passed on to various
other religious orders opposed to the Catholic Church, specifically the Manicheans, the Paulicians, the Albigenses, and the
Knights Templar. From the smoldering ashes of the Templars,
wiped out by the Catholic Church in 1314, rose the phoenix of
the Freemasons and related societies such as the Rosicrucians.

In the 11th and 12th centuries, these "illuminated" individuals
armed themselves with "a new weapon far more terrible than
any they had hitherto employed, and capable of being directed

to a thousand purposes of attack and defense" (Hall, *The Adepts Vol. I* 73-74). This new weapon was called literature. Rossetti claimed that the Brotherhood had planted their illuminist seeds, surreptitiously, within songs, poems, histories, and the sciences.

Including the plays of Shakespeare? Perhaps so.

Eventually, I received an "A" on that *Macbeth* paper. I wrote a six-page letter to the Grade Appeal Committee outlining the significance of Masonic symbolism as it related to the culture in which Shakespeare wrote and lived. The letter must have persuaded somebody. Either that or they just didn't want to deal with me anymore.

At the time I wasn't aware of Gabriele Rossetti. If I had been, I definitely would have cited his work in my letter to the Grade Appeal Committee. Rossetti's book is quite significant, as he appears to be the first scholar to promote what would now be called "a conspiracy theory" with regard to the development of Western literature. As with most controversial theories of this sort, there soon arose a counter-argument in the form of Arthur Henry Hallam's *Remarks on the Disquisizion* (in which the author stated quite baldly that Rossetti's theory was ingenious, but utterly impossible), thus establishing a pattern that continues to this day: First there appears the illuminist text, followed immediately by the Papal response.

A further example: Following the earliest known Rosicrucian publications—such as *The Fame and Confession of the Fraternity of R: C:* (1614) and *The Chemical Marriage* by the pseudonymous Christian Rosencreutz (1616)—there appeared the inevitable anti-thesis in the form of a book titled *Grease For the Fall* written by an anonymous Catholic authority warning the masses that Rosicrucianism can only lead to disgrace and eternal damnation.

A cursory glance at today's pop culture—not just in literature, but in films and art and comic books as well—will bear out the persistence of this seemingly never-ending dialectic.

These "illuminist seeds" can be found in many great works within the Western Canon, and yet this hermetic symbolism is rarely discussed in literature classes, even at the post- graduate level. This hermetic symbolism continues to be the hidden ground of literary analysis. The fact is that the writers who have utilized this symbolism in their work often strike a chord in the mass mind of public consciousness, almost subliminally.

This symbolism begins to crop up among writers in the early 1600s, around the same time that the first speculative Masonic Lodges are being established in the British Isles. This hermetic knowledge appears, encoded, in Shakespeare's plays *Midsummer Night's Dream* (c.1594-96), *Measure For Measure* (1603), *The Winter's Tale* (1610), *The Tempest* (1610), and of course *Macbeth* (c.1605). It appears in Miguel de Cervantes' *Don Quixote* (1615), John Milton's *Paradise Lost* (1674), Alexander Pope's *The Rape of the Lock* (1714), Jonathan Swift's *Gulliver Travels* (1726), Jean Terrasson's *The Life of Sethos* (1734), Sir Edward Bulwer Lytton's *Zanoni* (1842), Sir Walter Scott's *Redgauntlet* (1824), Goethe's *Faust* (1832), Herman Melville's *Moby Dick* (1851), and on and on. This field is ripe for further investigation. The delicate trick would be to find a method of analyzing this symbolism in such a way that one does not extract the beauty out of something that should simply *be*.

Perhaps it might be best to leave this hermetic symbolism where it belongs, in the shadows, where it is most powerful; those who need to find it no doubt will.

Such is the chameleonic nature of hermeticism itself.

Gloria Dei Est Celare Verbum.

Works Cited

Anonymous. *A Sharing of Symbols*. Tallinn, Estonia: Ukrainian Cultural Center, 2007.

de Hoyos, Arturo and S. Brent Morris. "Is It True What They Say About Freemasonry?: The Methods of Anti-Masons." www.srmason-sj.org/web/SRpublications/deHoyos-chapter3.htm#i4.

Ellis, Ralph. *Eden in Egypt*. Kempton: Adventures Unlimited, 2004.

Hall, Manly P. *The Adepts in the Western Esoteric Tradition Vol. I: Orders of the Quest*. Los Angeles: Philosophical Research Society, 1949.

---. *The Adepts In the Western Esoteric Tradition Vol. IV: Masonic Orders of Fraternity*. Los Angeles: Philosophical Research Society, 1950.

Knight, Stephen. *The Brotherhood*. New York: Dorset Press, 1986.

Leadbeater, C.W. *Ancient Mystic Rites*. 1926. Wheaton: Theosophical Publishing House, 1986.

Mackey, Albert G. *An Encyclopedia of Freemasonry*. Philadelphia: Louis H. Everts, 1905.

Normand, Pierre G. "Coil's Definition of Freemasonry." *The Plumbline: The Quarterly Bulletin of The Scottish Rite Research Society*. Vol. 14, No. 3 (2006): 3.

---. "A Definition of Freemasonry." *The Plumbline: The Quarterly Bulletin of The Scottish Rite Research Society*. Vol. 14, No. 2 (2006): 6, 7.

Spence, Lewis. *An Encyclopedia of Occultism*. 1920. Secaucus: Citadel Press, 1993.

Wᴹ. MORGAN,

From an original picture of A. Guley.

Printed according to Act of Congress the 1st day of June 1826 by Jn. Seller at the State of N. York

CHAPTER TWELVE

THE SOLOMON KEYHOLE: THE MASON/MORMON CONNECTION

From Morgan to Mormon

Since the publication of Dan Brown's bestseller, *The Da-Vinci Code*, public interest has been piqued by former-ly "fringe" subjects such as secret societies, ceremonial magic, and the hidden origins of the most powerful religions of the world. Rumors have been flying around regarding the subject of Dan Brown's sequel ever since its tentative title, *The Solomon Key*, was announced by Brown's publisher.[1] Three books have already been published that speculate about the contents of a novel that hasn't even been finished yet, an in-dication of the unprecedented interest generated by Brown's previous thriller. One of these books, *Secrets of the Widow's Son* by David A. Shugarts, briefly speculates that Brown will be exploring the curious and little-known connections between Freemasonry and the Church of Latter-day Saints.

The Church of Latter-day Saints, also known as the Mor-mon Church, was founded in 1830 by a man named Joseph Smith, Jr. Harold Bloom, the influential literary scholar, has called Smith "a far more crucial figure than Jesus could be" (Owens 2). Bloom regards Smith as a visionary American poet,

---

1 Since this chapter was written, Brown's novel has been published by Dou-bleday and is called *The Lost Symbol*. The plot primarily concerns itself with Masonic symbolism in Washington, D.C.

more important than Ralph Waldo Emerson and Walt Whitman, a prophet with uniquely American qualities. According to Bloom's voluminous book *The American Religion*, Smith's main intent in starting his church was to revive interest in the God of the ancient Kabbalists and Gnostics. This might not surprise some Mormons; however, what *would* surprise them is the extent to which their religion is inextricably entwined with one of the most ubiquitous secret societies in the world. To understand these connections, we must travel back to the summer of 1826....

On September 11, 1826, a tragedy occurred that had devastating repercussions for the brotherhood known as the Freemasons. This tragedy also directly inspired the book called the *Book of Mormon* authored by Joseph Smith Jr.

The tragedy in question was the wrongful arrest of a man named Captain William Morgan who lived in the town of Batavia, New York. Morgan had been initiated into the Royal Arch Degree of Freemasonry on May 31, 1825 in LeRoy, New York (Voorhis 253). Only about a year after receiving the Royal Arch degree, Morgan found himself barred from joining a new Chapter of the Royal Arch constituted in Batavia. According to some Masonic historians, Morgan had lied about his previous initiation in a Lodge in Canada in order to convince the Masons in LeRoy to initiate him into the Royal Arch. When this became known, Morgan found himself out in the cold (Palmer 173).

Whatever the circumstances, all that is known for certain is that in the Spring of 1826, not long after being barred from the Lodge, Morgan filed with the Clerk of the northern district of New York a copyright application for a book to be titled "Illustrations of Masonry by one of the Fraternity. *God said let there be Light and there was light.*" News of this spread throughout the network of Lodges in Central New York. To make matters worse, Morgan would often brag about the book's imminent publication in barrooms and on the street.

Matters escalated. On the night of September 10th, 1826, the printing offices that had agreed to publish Morgan's book were deliberately set on fire. The flames were extinguished quickly, and the damage was minimal. The culprits were never caught.

The next day Morgan was arrested by six men headed by "Holloway Hayward, constable of Canandaigua, N.Y., who carried a warrant sworn to by Ebeneezer Kingsley, a tavern keeper of Canandaigua, charging Morgan with the theft of a shirt and cravat, taken five months before" (Voorhis 256). Within mere hours Morgan was acquitted of the charge due to the fact that he could prove the articles in question had been loaned to him. However, he was immediately arrested again for a debt of less than three dollars and jailed when unable to furnish bail.

The next evening Morgan was released from the jail only to find himself being forced into a closed carriage by several unknown people, who took him on what must have been a rather unpleasant ride to Fort Niagara a hundred miles away. He was confined in an unused powder magazine for a week until September 19. Nobody knows for certain what happened to Morgan after that. At the time, many believed he was bound and gagged and taken out into the middle of the Niagara River, where he was thrown overboard. Over a year later, a corpse did indeed wash ashore about forty miles below Ft. Niagara in Oak Orchard Harbor, New York, but a Coroner's jury determined the body to be that of a man named Timothy Munroe, who had drowned only a couple of weeks earlier. Nonetheless, Morgan's widow and some of his friends still insisted the body was that of Morgan.

If the purpose of Morgan's abduction was to prevent the public revelation of Masonic secrets, it had the exact opposite effect. Morgan's book, or at least some version of it, was published on December 15, 1826. It remains in print to this day, and the entire text can be found online at: www.utlm.org/onlinebooks/captmorgansfreemasonrycontents.htm. The furor caused by Morgan's arrest and subsequent disappearance led to the formation of the very first third party in American politics: the Anti-Masonic Party. Its entire purpose was to stamp out Masonic influence in government. What was once a prestigious organization, the mere acceptance into which was certain to lead to heightened stature and financial benefits in one's community, was now tainted by public ire and suspicion. Dark rumors floated around concerning the dangerous effect secret oaths and penalties had been having on the objectivity of police officers, judges, and elected politicians. Masons fled the Brotherhood in droves, and Lodges closed down all over the country.

But what does any of this have to do with the *Book of Mormon*?

Joseph Smith and the Gadianton Bands

In the midst of this social turmoil, a different drama was unfolding only twelve miles away in the town of Palmyra, New York. Joseph Smith, Jr. had lived in Palmyra with his poverty-stricken family since he was ten years old (ca. 1815-1816). Joseph, only twenty at the time, had spent the majority of his life searching for buried treasure in the company of his father. Smith's parents supposedly recognized when he was still a child that the boy had "paranormal abilities." Between 1822 and 1827, the future prophet of the Mormon Church was enlisted to act as a "seer" for several different treasure-hunting groups. He used magical implements, such as two "seer-stones" he would place in a hat, in order to divine the location of treasure. Whether or not he actually found treasure is unknown; however, the fact that the family remained poverty-stricken might allow us to come to a reasonable conclusion.

Smith was trained in ceremonial magic, the hermetic arts, and the principles of alchemy at a very early age. His father raised all his children not only to believe in the power of magic, but to actively practice it. In fact, many of Smith's ancestors were involved in the occult as well. Ironically, in 1692 two women were hanged in Salem, Massachusetts based on the accusations of Smith's great-great-grandfather (Quinn 31). (Then again, perhaps irony was involved in this incident less so than strategy. After all, it's often a good idea to accuse somebody else of a crime before the inquisitors get around to accusing *you*.) Smith, Jr. was also schooled in the occult through the tutelage of a physician named Dr. Luman Walter, a member of the aforementioned treasure-hunting circle. Besides being a traditional medical doctor, Walter was also an expert in mesmerism and Paracelcian medicine; his bag of tricks no doubt included alchemy, astrology, and hermetic practices as well. In addition to these influences, Joseph's older brother Hyrum was initiated into Freemasonry in Mount Moriah Lodge No. 112 of Palmyra, New York the same year as William Morgan's disappearance (Durham 1).

Smith's treasure-seeking ventures also ended around this time, and gave way instead to an important new phase in his short life. Few people, including members of the Mormon Church, are aware that the *Book of Mormon* was directly inspired by the Captain Morgan affair. It would have been impossible to live in New York during this period and not have some opinion on Morgan's abduction. Given Smith's connection to occult circles in Central New York, and the fact that Smith only lived twelve miles away from Morgan, it's natural that Smith's curiosity would be strongly piqued by the ongoing drama of the Captain's disappearance. In fact, it's not out of the realm of possibility to suggest that Smith knew Morgan personally, and perhaps even had some influence on his plan to release the *Illustrations of Masonry* in the first place. This notion is supported by the fact that Morgan's widow, Lucinda, would later become one of Smith's many wives (Brooke 232).

As stated earlier, Morgan was arrested on September 11, 1826 and disappeared the next evening. Joseph Smith began writing the *Book of Mormon* almost exactly a year later, on September 22, 1827, after claiming that an angel named Moroni appeared to him in his room and revealed to him that a set of sacred golden tablets was buried in a nearby hill. Inscribed upon the tablets was a condensed history of the ancient inhabitants of the American continent written in a language Smith called "reformed Egyptian," an unknown language only he could understand by gazing into a pair of "seers" (two stones he called the "Urim and Thummin") delivered to him along with the tablets. After the grueling work of translation was finished, Moroni the angel conveniently showed up and took his precious tablets back.

Three thousand copies of the completed text, the *Book of Mormon*—named after the record's final scribe from the ancient days in which it was originally written—was published on March 26, 1830. Only a few weeks after its publication, Joseph Smith founded the Church of Christ (the name would later be changed to its present moniker, the Church of Latter-day Saints). In the coming years, the membership of Smith's fledgling church would keep on growing as a multitude of other supernatural beings appeared to Smith with even more revelations; these apparitions included John the Baptist, Christ's apostles Peter, James and John, Moses and Jesus Christ himself. These later visitations would result in further holy texts, but the *Book of Mormon* remains the cornerstone of the church to this day.

To those familiar with the tragedy of William Morgan, the *Book of Mormon* can be seen as a thinly veiled allegory of his kidnapping and murder. No less a scholar than John L. Brooke—an Associate Professor of History at Tufts University whose book on the roots of Mormonism, *The Refiner's Fire: The Making of Mormon Cosmology, 1644-1844,* received several book awards—has been intrigued by the similarity between the name "Morgan" and the word "Mormon." Martin Harris, an early Mormon leader, was "elected to an Antimasonic committee for Palmyra by the Wayne County Antimasonic convention in October 1827; he was quoted in 1831 as announcing that the *Book of Mormon* was the 'Antimasonic Bible'" (Brooke 169).

A major plotline in the *Book of Mormon* involves an ominous secret society known as the Gadianton Bands, "an organization founded anciently by Cain entering into a pact with Satan, sometimes renewed by satanic revelation, internally protected by covenants of the blackest sorcery, and established for the purpose of murder and robbery" (Quinn 207). After mentioning the chaos caused by the Morgan affair, John Brooke states in *The Refiner's Fire*, "When viewed against these contemporary hermetic dramas and in light of Masonic mythology, the conflict between good and evil that occupies so much of the *Book of Mormon* can be read in terms of a contest between... pure, 'primitive' Freemasons and corrupt, 'spurious' Freemasons" (164-65).

Some writers, like David Shugarts in his recent book *Secrets of the Widow's Son*, have speculated that Dan Brown will be using the Masonic roots of Mormonism as a major plotline in *The Solomon Key*. If so, this will be no great revelation. The connection between Freemasonry and Mormonism has been an open secret since the original publication of the *Book of Mormon*.

In early 1835, only a few years after the publication of the *Book of Mormon*, a British scholar named E.S. Abdy published a three-volume study of the United States titled *Journal of a Residence and Tour in the United States of North America, from April, 1833, to October, 1834*. Despite the fact that the Mormon Church was only in its infancy, Abdy had the foresight to devote a considerable number of pages to its formation. One paragraph in particular is worth quoting at length, as it reveals how obvious the Masonic/Mormon connection was from the very beginning:

> The chief peculiarities of the sect are the gift of preaching in unknown tongues, plainness of apparel, and gratuitous services in all who are chosen to minister to the secular and spiritual wants of the community. One passage in this curious Koran clearly points to the place of its concoction, and the prepossessions of its author; who would doubtless ground a claim for the prophetic spirit on this very objection from the unbeliever. It alludes, most unequivocally, to the freemasons; Ontario county, in the State of New York, being the place where Morgan's murder excited such a spirit of hostility to "the craft." "Satan", says the plate, "did stir up the hearts of the more parts of the Nephites, insomuch that they did unite with their oaths, that they would protect and preserve one anoth-

er, in whatever [sic] difficult circumstances they should be placed; that they should not suffer for their murders, and their plunderings, and their stealings. And it came to pass, that they did have their signs, yea, their secret signs, and their secret words: and this that they might distinguish a brother, who had entered into the covenant, that, whatever [sic] wickedness his brother should do, he should not be injured by his brother, nor by those who did belong to his band, who had taken this covenant: and whosoever of their band should reveal unto the world their wickedness and their abominations, should be tried, not according to the laws of their country, but according to the laws of their wickedness which had been given by Gadianton and Kishkumen." (Hogan 293-94)

The preceding interpretation, published only five years after the founding of the church, was written by a scholar who wasn't even living in the United States, so imagine how much clearer the Morgan/Mormon connection would have been to those living in Central New York at the time.

According to Past Master Mervin B. Hogan, Secretary of the Masonic Research Lodge of Utah, by the early 1840s almost the entire Mormon hierarchy, with only a few exceptions, had been initiated into the sublime degree of Master Mason (Hogan 290). Joseph Smith himself became a Master Mason in March of 1842 (Brooke 242). At this point, the reader might be wondering, "If Smith had such a negative opinion of the Freemasons, why did he join them?" All available evidence, including Smith's own letters, indicates that he strongly believed Freemasonry was descended from the Ancient Mysteries he was so obsessed with, but that the Brotherhood had been corrupted slowly over the generations. Smith's intent was to alter Masonry to fit his own cosmology, to bring it back to its pure, uncorrupted state. He took what he learned from the Masonic rituals and adapted them to his own purpose.

The similarities between Masonic and Mormon rituals are numerous. According to John Brooke:

Masonic symbolism... runs through the story of the discovery of the Golden Plates. Most obviously, the story of
their discovery in a stone vault on a hilltop echoed the
Enoch myth of Royal Arch Freemasonry, in which the
prophet Enoch, instructed by a vision, preserved the Masonic mysteries by carving them on a golden plate that he
placed in an arched stone vault marked with pillars, to be
rediscovered by Solomon. (Brooke 157)

In a 1974 lecture, Dr. Reed C. Durham, Jr., president of the
Mormon History Society, commented on other similarities:

[T]he inner courts of the temple were fashioned in such a
way that officers could preside on platforms at either end,
east or west, was... similar to Masonic Lodges and Tem-
ples.... The use of secret penal oaths, accompanied with
signs, hand clasps, and tokens involved therein, also reflected Masonic life practices.... There is absolutely no question
in my mind that the Mormon ceremony which came to be
known as the Endowment introduced by Joseph Smith to
Mormon Masons initially, just a little over one month after
he became a Mason, had an immediate inspiration from
Masonry. This is not to suggest that no other source of inspiration could have been involved, but the similarities between the two ceremonies are so apparent and overwhelming that some dependent relationship cannot be denied.
They are so similar, in fact, that one writer was led to refer
to the Endowment as Celestial Masonry.... (2-3)

These similarities include the wearing of aprons and sacred
undergarments embroidered with the square and compass,
the vows of non-disclosure, the division between lesser and
greater ceremonies, the presentation of the Mysteries through
participatory drama, the symbols of the sun and moon, and
the wording of the oaths themselves (Quinn 230-34). Durham
mentions further connections:

[T]he Nauvoo Temple architecture was, in part at least,
Masonically influenced. Indeed, it appears that there was

an intentional attempt to utilize Masonic symbols and motifs. The sun stones, and the moon and star stones, were examples. An additional example was the angel used on the weather vane on the top of the Temple.... [A] beautiful compass and square, in typical Masonic fashion [can be see hanging above the angel]. (3)

One of the major alterations Smith made in these rituals adopted from Masonry was in allowing the initiation of women. This practice is more closely aligned with a French version of Freemasonry, known as Co-Masonry, which was emerging in Europe at that time. (In the present day, there are two branches of Co-Masonry, one based in France and the other in the United States; the U.S. headquarters is in Larkspur, Colorado. As is typical with such organizations, the two branches despise each other, and the initiates of each believe they alone possess the "one true path" to enlightenment. *C'est la vie.*)

Apparently, Smith's numerous alterations and refinements were perceived as outright desecration and thievery by some Masons at the time. On June 27, 1844, Joseph Smith and his older brother Hyrum were shot to death when the Carthage jail in which they were imprisoned was attacked by a mob of about two hundred armed men. According to many reports, there were Masons among the crowd who led the assault. Smith was halfway through shouting out a Masonic distress signal when the first bullets hit him in the chest. (Smith and his brother had been arrested for violating freedom of the press, as they had forcibly shut down a newspaper critical of the Mormon Church. Oddly enough, the strong arm tactics Smith used to quiet dissent against his church seem not at all dissimilar to the action the Batavia Freemasons took against the printing press that had agreed to publish Morgan's book criticizing the Brotherhood.)

The aforementioned Secretary of the Utah Masonic Research Lodge, Past Master Mervin B. Hogan, prepared a history of the Mormon Church for the express purpose of recording the Masons' intersection with Joseph Smith. The study was published in 1977 and was titled *Mormonism and Freemasonry: The Illinois Episode.* In that report Hogan had this to say about Smith's murder:

> The Mormons knew who the principals were in the killing of Hyrum and Joseph Smith. They were also well informed as to who the individual Masons were who participated in that lynching. Significantly, the Mormons also knew and realized the vital distinction between individual Masons acting solely on their own initiative and the fact that the Masonic Order had in no sense participated as an organization. Brigham Young [who became the head of the Church after Smith's death] was especially cognizant of the fact that every organization of people is constituted of human beings. Every organization has regrettable examples of members who are constitutionally unable to measure up to the demanding but admirable tenets and admonitions of the association.
>
> The above factors are but some of the numerous reasons which prompted Brigham Young to declare a ban of silence on the Mormon experience with Illinois and Iowa Freemasonry. (Hogan 308)

With the kind of symmetrical tidiness more appropriate to a piece of fiction than a tragic moment in history, Joseph Smith ended up dying under circumstances as dramatic as those that surrounded the arrest and abduction of Captain William Morgan, whose untimely death inspired the Prophet to form his church in the first place.

Smith's life was certainly a strange one, filled with all the twists and turns of a Shakespearean tragedy—or perhaps a dark comedy. He built his church on the claim that he had been the recipient of divine revelation—not once, but numerous times. Never having been the recipient of such illumination, I can't say whether Mormon cosmology is sound or unsound. Perhaps an angel named Moroni really did present the keys of the secrets of Solomon to Joseph Smith, Jr. in a modest farmhouse in Central New York in September of 1827. All I do know is that when one peers past the official story as presented by the Mormon Church, takes a peek through the keyhole as it were, and sees the events that led up to Smith's "revelation," one finds a curious story that casts Smith's cosmology in a very different light, one that reframes the revelation more as autobiography than divine inspiration.

Consequences of the Morgan Affair and the Murder of Joseph Smith

The deaths of William Morgan and Joseph Smith impacted Freemasonry to a significant degree. Membership in the Brotherhood has been on a steady decline ever since. It's important to point out that no one knows for certain how Morgan died, or even if he was murdered. Many more facts are known about the murder of Joseph Smith, and yet even the details of his death are still shrouded in uncertainty. Given the circumstances, the notion of Freemasons being responsible for Morgan's disappearance seems likely. However, individual Masons being involved does not mean that Morgan's kidnapping or Smith's murder came about due to official directives from the Supreme Council. After all, kidnapping Morgan did not represent strategic thinking at its finest. The group most harmed in the long run by Morgan's disappearance were the Masons themselves. Any intelligent person, particularly people as cunning as the Masons are accused of being, surely would have the ability to peer into the future far enough to predict these obvious consequences.

A letter published in a local newspaper ten days before Morgan's abduction proves that while some Masons were growing more and more enraged by Morgan's publishing plans, others were calling for a peaceful solution to the problem:

> Sober minds counseled silence, advising against any action against Morgan. They predicted that if let severely alone, the book would fall stillborn. September 1, 1826, ten days before Morgan's disappearance, the Batavia *Spir-*

it of the Times published a letter from Henry Brown (a Mason) in which he strongly deprecated the indiscreet excitement of some Masons, as well as the violent asperity of the enemies of the Order. "No man in his sober senses," said he, "can credit the perjured wretch who commences his career by publishing his infamy. The attempt has often been made before and always has proven abortive, terminating in disgrace to those concerned." (Palmer 174)

The clumsiness of the kidnapping, performed in such a way that it could only draw attention to itself, would seem to indicate an operation initiated by desperate, foolish men. The Masons' desire to shut down Morgan's book publishing venture was futile from the very beginning. Most of the Masonic "secrets" revealed in Morgan's book had already been available in an English book called *Jachin and Boaz* published as early as 1798 (Palmer 182). The Central New York Masons' hatred of Morgan perhaps had more to do with personal affronts than with any grand strategy on the part of the entire Brotherhood.

It seems as if some Masons in Batavia were arrogant enough to think that their rituals, the exact details of which had already been publicly available for twenty-eight years, were precious enough to kill for. But no secret is ever sacred enough to justify murder. Ironically, this is one of the symbolic teachings of the third degree of Freemasonry, the very same degree these men were trying to protect from "profane" eyes. This blind fanaticism, tantamount to religious fervor, was the same kind of irrational authoritarianism that the earliest Freemasons in Europe had supposedly banded together to combat. Alas, when any organization grows too powerful and forgets its true roots, it sometimes flips into its opposite extreme: Rationality becomes Irrationality, Illumination becomes Obfuscation, and Light becomes Dark.

Works Cited

Brooke, John L. *The Refiner's Fire: The Making of Mormon Cosmology, 1644-1844*. Cambridge: Cambridge University Press, 1994.

Durham, Dr. Reed C. "Is There No Help For the Widow's Son?" www.xmission.com/~country/reason/widowson.htm.

Hogan, Mervin B. *Mormonism and Freemasonry: The Illinois Episode. Little Masonic Library Book II.* Richmond: Macoy Publishing, 1977.

Owens, Lance S. "Joseph Smith: America's Hermetic Prophet." http://gnosis.org/ahp.htm.

Palmer, John C. *The Morgan Affair and Anti-Masonry. Little Masonic Library Book II.* Richmond: Macoy Publishing, 1977.

Quinn, D. Michael. *Early Mormonism and the Magic World View.* Salt Lake City: Signature Books, 1998.

Voorhis, Harold Van Buren. "What Really Happened to William Morgan?" *Little Masonic Library Book II.* Richmond: Macoy Publishing, 1977.

CHAPTER THIRTEEN

WILLIAM S. BURROUGHS: 20ᵀᴴ CENTURY GNOSTIC VISIONARY

I n 1984, in Boulder, Colorado, the poet Gregory Corso asked William S. Burroughs, "What religious persuasion would you consider yourself?" Without hesitating, Burroughs replied, "Gnostic, or a Manichean" (Corso Interview).

Upon reading those words, suddenly everything made sense.

Perhaps it's appropriate that the above conversation occurred in 1984. In many ways, Burroughs was a far more lucid and accurate analyst of twentieth century politics than even George Orwell, whose concept of "newspeak" in his 1948 novel *1984* was quickly overshadowed by the real-world machinations of post-WWII Madison Avenue advertising techniques and Washington D.C. Public Relations firms. Superior to Aldous Huxley's brilliant 1958 collection of essays, *Brave New World Revisited*, Burroughs' 1974 book *The Job* is an essential guide to charting the opaque labyrinth of obfuscation and lies regularly constructed by the Reality Studio to protect itself from the light of scrutiny. Unlike his more naïve contemporaries among the Beat literary movement, Burroughs never took his eye off the twitchy sharpshooter in the corner, the wild card in the deck known as *Control*.

With the precision of a surgeon (he studied medicine at Harvard, acquiring specialized knowledge that would eventually serve him well in his novels), Burroughs performed an autopsy on the body politic in a multitude of bleak and humorous novels, foremost among them *Junky* (1953), *Naked Lunch* (1959), *The Soft Machine* (1961), *Nova Express* (1964), and *The Place of Dead Roads* (1983).

But Burroughs never limited his vision to merely charting the intricate connections that make up the system of control. Like Huxley before him, who eventually followed his dystopian novel *Brave New World* with a Utopian counterpoint titled *Island*, Burroughs himself attempted to construct his own vision of a Utopia in such novels as *The Wild Boys* (1971) and *Cities of the Red Night* (1981). In both cases, Burroughs seemed to suggest that a Utopia was not possible except within an isolated oasis, what Hakim Bey would call "a temporary autonomous zone" (*T.A.Z.* 99). In the first case, the autonomous zone takes the form of an all-male enclave in the jungles of North Africa; these commandos, trained in combat for defensive purposes, can reproduce without the aid of women and travel through the trees on prehensile hemorrhoids. In *Cities of the Red Night*, Burroughs' Utopia is based on historical fact and manifests as an island settlement established by Captain Mission, an actual pirate who lived in the eighteenth century.

> Mission explored the Madagascar coast and found a bay ten leagues north of Diego-Suarez. It was resolved to establish here the shore quarters of the Republic—erect a town, build docks, and have a place they might call their own. The colony was called Libertatia and was placed under Articles drawn up by Captain Mission. The Articles state, among other things: all decisions with regard to the colony to be submitted to vote by the colonists; the abolition of slavery for any reason including debt; the abolition of the death penalty; and freedom to follow any religious beliefs or practices without sanction or molestation. (*Cities of the Red Night* xii)

In both *Wild Boys* and *Cities of the Red Night*, Burroughs celebrates the notion of an autonomous zone kept separate from the madding hordes through potentially violent defensive measures, where a human being is allowed to pursue life free from the constant surveillance of overly authoritarian social structures. In Burroughs' hands, William Golding's *Lord of the Flies* would no doubt have a very different outcome.

Burroughs' libertarian brand of morality was based on Jack Black's notions of the "Johnson family" as chronicled in Black's 1926 autobiography *You Can't Win*. The impact this book had on Burroughs when he was still a young man can't be overestimated. In Burroughs' own words, the Johnson creed can be described as follows:

> "The Johnson family" was a turn-of-the-century expression to designate good bums and thieves. It was elaborated into a code of conduct. A Johnson honors his obligations. His word is good and he is a good man to do business with. A Johnson minds his own business. He is not a snoopy, self-righteous, troublemaking person. A Johnson will give help when help is needed. He will not stand by while someone is drowning or trapped under a burning car. (*Place of Dead Roads* ix)

Surely in Burroughs' world this would be the only mandatory social stricture established for his personal temporary autonomous zone.

Burroughs' vision of a Utopian autonomous zone could be seen as a metaphor for the Gnostic concept of "the pneuma," an infinitesimally small fragment of the divine that exists in all human beings. Gnosticism, an early form of Christianity, flourished in the Middle East until approximately the 4th century A.D. when the movement was violently suppressed by Roman Catholic authorities. Dr. Stephan Hoeller, the current bishop of the Gnostic Church in Los Angeles, distinguishes Gnosticism from traditional forms of Christianity in this way: "[Gnosticism is] much more orientated toward the personal, spiritual advancement and transformation of the individual, regarding figures such as Jesus as being helpers rather than sacrificial saviors. It is a form of religion that has... a much more ecumenical and universal scope in terms of its relationship to spiritual, religious traditions other than the Christian" (Guffey Interview).

According to literary scholar Gregory Stephenson:

> ...[T]he attitude that characterizes all the Gnostic systems is that the world, the body, and matter are unreal and evil. They are illusions that are the products of malevolent powers called Archons, chief among whom is Sammael (the god of the blind or the blind god), also called Ialdabaoth or the Demiurge. These creator-gods are not the Deity of the Supreme Being, though they make claim to being so. The Deity is completely transcendent—absolutely distinct, apart, and remote from the created universe. However, a portion of the divine substance, called the pneuma, is enclosed in the human body—within the human passions and the human appetites.... The aim of Gnosticism is to liberate the pneuma from its material, delusional prison and to reunite it with the Deity. The Archons seek to obstruct this liberation and to maintain their dominion. (60)

This basic theological structure applies to almost all of Burroughs' work. Burroughs' strong sense of morality, of the distinct difference between right and wrong, is often lost in the lurid morass of details concerning his personal life. His heroin addiction, his homosexuality, his arrest in Mexico for the accidental death of his wife, his early experimentation with yage in South America and his later fascination with Wilhelm Reich's unorthodox theories regarding orgone energy—all of these unusual aspects of his life, though admittedly intriguing, are often reduced to gossipy anecdotes that threaten to diminish the importance of the work itself. Burroughs was never the star of his own novels, not even in his highly autobiographical debut, *Junky*. The central figure in all his novels is *war*—a continuous war between Freedom and Control, what Burroughs himself might very well refer to as "good and evil."

The conflict between good and evil is considered to be a hollow theme by most literary scholars. After all, is this not the purview of Tolkienesque sword and sorcery epics and four-color superhero comics? Surely no major literary figure of the twentieth century ever bothered to waste his time on such silliness.

But that's not quite true. In the work of no other American writer do we find this theme explored in as complex and harrowing a manner as in the novels and essays of William Burroughs. As quoted at the beginning of this chapter, Burroughs described himself as a "Manichean." Burroughs defined this term as follows:

> The Manicheans believe in an actual struggle between good and evil, which is not an eternal struggle since one of them will win in this particular area, sooner or later. Of course, with the Christians there was this tremendous inversion of values where the most awful people are thrown up as this paragon of virtue for everyone to emulate... (Corso Interview 4-5).

The Manichean sect of Gnosticism spread across three continents over the course of eleven hundred years beginning, approximately, in A.D. 240. It was founded by the Persian prophet Mani, who was eventually imprisoned at the age of 61, tortured for 26 days, and assassinated. According to Dr. Hoeller, Mani is among "two of the great luminaries of the Gnostic tradition" (*Gnosticism* 135).

Dr. Hoeller sums up Mani's basic doctrine as follows:

> In the beginning, said Mani, the kingdoms of Light and Darkness coexisted in uneasy peace. While Light had no quarrel with the existence of Darkness and would have remained content existing side-by-side with it, Darkness would have it otherwise. Darkness was in a state of agitation and wrath and decided to attack and invade the realm of light.

219

As the legions of Darkness approached the realm of Light, the primal light needed to defend itself. It called upon the Mother of Life to bring forth the Primal Man (a cosmic figure, not related to Adam or other human beings except in an indirect way). The Primal Man in turn had five sons, and together the six expelled the Dark forces from the kingdom of Light and pursued them onto the battlefield of the lower aeons. Unfortunately, on the battlefield the chief demons of Darkness overpowered the Primal Man and his five sons and devoured them, incorporating their luminous essence into their dark forms. This is how the first terrible intermingling of Light and Darkness occurred....

In the course of the rescue efforts the Primal Man is freed, and he gloriously ascends to the Godhead. The souls of the human beings, however, have been left behind, along with Light particles that derive from the captivity of the Primal Man and of his sons. It is only at this point that the material world as we know it comes into being. The earth is created as an alchemical vessel of purification and transformation where the Light can be extracted from dark matter. The sun and the moon are both vessels of Light that serve as vehicles to transport Light upwards out of earthly darkness. (*Gnosticism* 140-41)

In Burroughs' world, evil disguises itself as good and good disguises itself as evil. The Archons are Christians and politicians and "jus' good folk." The Gnostics are roving bands of criminals and thieves known only to themselves as "the Johnsons." The visionaries, the ones who have attained genuine *gnosis* (i.e., "knowledge") can see through the illusions forged by control, identify the face of the enemy, and from that point begin the quest for true freedom. These visionaries regularly employ unorthodox and seemingly "insane" methods to overthrow the hypnotic bonds of control: opiates, orgone energy, tape recorders that are used to cut up, analyze, and reconfigure the endless barrage of shallow media used to keep the masses docile, astral travel through time and space, hermetic magic, telepathy, etc.

These are the tools of the 20th century Gnostic in Burroughs' re-vitalized Libertatia. The goal of these latter day Gnostics is to establish an autonomous zone, a physical approximation of the pneuma, while having as much fun as possible trying to "wise up the marks," a paraphrase of a key sentence in the third chapter of his 1964 novel *Nova Express*: "And you can see the marks are wising up, standing around in sullen groups and that mutter gets louder and louder" (*Three Novels* 196).

The Archons are represented on Earth by parasite-infected control-freaks Burroughs aptly calls "the shits": "...my contention is that evil is quite literally a virus parasite occupying a certain brain area which we may term the RIGHT center. The mark of a basic shit is that he has to be *right*" (*The Adding Machine* 16). The shits will use all the power they have on this planet in order to prevent the Johnsons from waking up the marks.

This conflict between good and evil is played out in Burroughs' fiction over and over again, perhaps most prominently in *Nova Express*. In this novel the Johnsons are "The Nova Police" and the shits are "The Nova Mob," or simply "The Board": "All right you board bastards, we'll by God show you 'Operation Total Exposure.' For all to see. In Times Square. In Piccadilly" (*Three Novels* 197). Operation Total Exposure represents an attempt by the Nova Police to pull back the illusory curtain that protects the parasite-infected Reality Studio from being seen in its true form, to induce *gnosis* in the madding hordes, to transform the "marks" into "Johnsons."

In chapter one of *Nova Express*, Inspector J. Lee of the Nova Police addresses the human race: "What scared you all into time? Into body? Into shit? I will tell you: '*the word.*' Alien Word '*the.*' '*The*' word of Alien Enemy imprisons 'thee' in Time. In Body. In Shit. Prisoner, come out. The great skies are open" (*Three Novels* 186).

Chapter two, titled "Prisoners, Come Out," is an open letter addressed to the "peoples of the earth" and is signed by Inspector Lee. In this letter the Inspector explains that the purpose of his novels is "... to expose and arrest Nova Criminals. In *Naked Lunch*, *Soft Machine* and *Nova Express* I show who they are and what they are doing and what they will do if they are not arrested. Minutes to go. Souls rotten from their orgasm drugs, flesh shuddering from their nova ovens, prisoners of the earth to come out. With your help we can occupy The Reality Studio and retake their universe of Fear Death and Monopoly—" (*Three Novels* 189).

In his 1978 collaboration with Brion Gysin, *The Third Mind*, Burroughs wrote in reference to *Nova Express*: "A new mythology is possible in the space age where we will again have heroes and villains with respect to intentions toward this planet—" (97).

The arch-nemesis of Inspector Lee and his Nova Police is a Demiurge-like figure named Mr. Bradly Mr. Martin who leads the extraterrestrial Nova Mob, and through this Mob he has kept the earth enslaved for thousands of years. In *The Third Mind*, Burroughs describes Mr. Bradly Mr. Martin in terms that are overtly Gnostic:

> Mr Bradly-Mr Martin, in my mythology, is a God that failed, a God of Conflict in two parts so created to keep a tired old show on the road, The God of Arbitrary Power and Restraint, Of Prison and Pressure, who needs subordinates, who needs what he calls "his human dogs" while treating them with the contempt a con man feels for his victims—But remember the con man needs the Mark— The Mark does not need the con man—Mr Bradly-Mr Martin needs his "dogs" his "errand boys" his "human animals"—He needs them because he is literally blind. They do not need him. In my mythological system he is overthrown in a revolution of his "dogs"— (97)

Throughout the novel, Inspector Lee explicitly warns the people of earth about some of the most insidious tools the Mob is using against them:

> Their drugs are poison designed to beam in Orgasm Death and Nova Ovens—Stay out of the Garden of Delights—It

is a man-eating trap that ends in green goo—Throw back
their ersatz Immortality—It will fall apart before you can
get out of The Big Store—Flush their drug kicks down
the drain—*They are poisoning and monopolizing the hal-
lucinogen drugs—learn to make it without any chemical
corn*—All that they offer is a screen to cover retreat from
the colony they have so disgracefully mismanaged. To
cover travel arrangements so they will never have to pay
the constituents they have betrayed and sold out. Once
these arrangements are complete they will blow the place
up behind them (*Three Novels* 188).

The succeeding chapters introduce us to members of Mr.
Bradly Mr. Martin's Archon-like Nova Mob: "'Sammy the
Butcher,' 'Green Tony,' 'Iron Claws,' 'The Brown Artist,' 'Jacky
Blue Note,' 'Limestone John,' 'Izzy the Push,' 'Hamburger Mary,'
'Paddy the Sting,' 'The Subliminal Kid,' 'The Blue Dinosaur'"
(*Three Novels* 236).

In a section eerily redolent of current events, a chapter titled
"Coordinate Points," The Inspector does us the favor of outlining the Mob's plan to bring about global destruction:

The basic nova mechanism is very simple: Always create as many insoluble conflicts as possible and always aggravate existing conflicts—This is done by dumping life
forms with incompatible conditions of existence on the
same planet—There is of course nothing "wrong" about
any given life form since "wrong" only has reference to
conflicts with other life forms—The point is these forms
should not be on the same planet—Their conditions of
life are basically incompatible in present time form and
it is precisely the work of the Nova Mob to see that they
remain in present time form, to create and aggravate the
conflicts that lead to the explosion of a planet that is to
nova—At any given time recording devices fix the nature
of absolute need and dictate the use to total weapons—
Like this: Take two opposed pressure groups—Record
the most violent and threatening statements of group one
with regard to group two and play back to group two—

> Record the answer and take it back to group one—Back
> and forth between opposed pressure groups—This pro-
> cess is known as "feed back"—You can see it operating in
> any bar room quarrel—In any quarrel for that matter—
> Manipulated on a global scale feeds back nuclear war and
> nova—These conflicts are deliberately created and aggra-
> vated by nova criminals— [...] In all my experience as a
> police officer I have never seen such total fear and degra-
> dation on any planet—We intend to arrest these crimi-
> nals and turn them over to the Biological Department for
> the indicated alterations— (*Three Novels* 235-36)

Jack Kerouac once wrote, "Burroughs is the greatest satirical writer since Jonathan Swift," but the truth is that Burroughs never wrote a word of satire in his life. He was writing about life as he *saw* it, exactly as he *experienced* it. The Nova Mob and the virus parasites from outer space were not metaphors for him. They were real. Burroughs, perhaps more so than F. Scott Fitzgerald or even Ernest Hemingway, was the prime mimetic writer of the twentieth century. He never wrote anything other than realistic novels. Marshall McLuhan, author of *Understanding Media* and *The Gutenberg Galaxy*, might have been the first to catch onto this subtle but significant point when he wrote in 1964, "It is amusing to read reviews of Burroughs that try to classify his books as nonbooks or as failed science fiction. It is a little like trying to criticize the sartorial and verbal manifestations of a man who is knocking on the door to explain that flames are leaping from the roof of our home" (Murphy 145). Indeed, Burroughs wasn't trying to satirize modern culture, nor was he trying to create a hypothetical, science fictional representation of it. He was simply explaining his society within the only context that seemed appropriate to him, and that context was undoubtedly a Gnostic one.

Even the so-called science fictional elements of his books were not intended as satire or metaphor. Burroughs could very well have been introduced to the *Nova Express* model of invading extraterrestrials (and/or intrusions from alternate dimensions) at a very young age. In various interviews, for example, Burroughs has recounted one of his earliest childhood memories. When he was four, he woke up early in the morning and saw little gray men playing in a block house he had made. "I felt no fear," he said, "only stillness and wonder" (Bockris xx). When asked about this incident in 1987, interviewer Larry McCaffery offhandedly referred to such experiences as "hallucinatory." Burroughs replied, "I wouldn't call them hallucinatory at all. If you see something, it's a shift of vision, not a hallucination. You shift your vision. What you see is there, but you have to be in a certain place to see it" (Hibbard 182).

This image of "little gray men" evokes more recent, popular conceptions of extraterrestrials as seen on the mass market covers of any number of books by Whitley Strieber, the author of *Communion* (1987), *Transformation* (1988) and several others in which his ostensible contacts with alien beings are delineated. Burroughs was so convinced of the reality of invading extraterrestrials that in 1989 he wrote a letter to Strieber asking to visit him and his family in their cabin in upstate New York. The 1996 revised edition of Victor Bockris' *With William Burroughs: A Report from the Bunker* contains an in-depth interview about this meeting:

> I was very interested in his first books and I was convinced that he was authentic. I felt he was not a fraud or fake.... I wrote a letter to Whitley Strieber saying that I would love to contact these visitors.... His wife, Anne Strieber, wrote back saying, "We, after talking it over, would be glad to invite you to come up to the cabin." So we spent the weekend there. I had a number of talks with Strieber about his experiences, and I was quite convinced that he was telling the truth.... (Bockris 242)

Burroughs follows this comment by exploring the idea of "invasion" on all levels. He genuinely believed the human race was, and *is*, being infected by hostile intelligences on a regular basis:

> When I go into my psyche, at a certain point I meet a very hostile, very strong force. It's as definite as somebody at-

tacking me in a bar. We usually come to a standoff, but I don't think that I'm necessarily winning or losing.... Listen, baby, I've been coping with this for so many years. I know this invasion gets in. As soon as you get close to something important, that's when you feel this invasion, and that's the way you know there's something there. I've felt myself just marched up like a puppy to go and do something that would get me insulted or humiliated. I was not in control.... There are all degrees of possession. It happens all the time. What you have to do is confront the possession. You can do that only when you've wiped out the words. You don't argue.... You have to let it wash through. This is difficult, difficult; but I'll tell you one thing: You detach yourself and allow this to wash through, to go through instead of trying to oppose, which you can't do.... The more you pull yourself together the further apart you get. You have to learn to let the thing pass through. I am a man of the world; I understand these things. They happen to all of us. All you have to do is understand them or see them for what they are, that's all. (Bockris 242-46)

John Lash, co-founder of Metahistory.org, a website that concerns itself with Gnosticism and related topics, has many Burroughs-like perceptions regarding the Gnostic model of spiritual "intrusion." Lash states:

It might be said that Gnostics believed that only by confronting what is insane and inhumane in ourselves, can we truly define what is human. In essence, to define humanity is to defend it against distortion. Gnostics asserted that the capacity for distortion of *humanitas*, or dehumanization, is inherent in our minds, *but this capacity alone is not potentially deviant.* Since we are endowed with *nous*, a dose of divine intelligence, we are able to detect and correct distorted thinking.... In a practical sense, Gnostic teachers in the Mystery Schools instructed the neophytes in how to face the Archons both as alien intruders, comparable to the Greys and Reptilians of contemporary lore, and as tendencies in their minds. The detection of...

intrusion in *both* these modes of experience seems to be unique to the finely nuanced noetic science of the [Gnostic] Mysteries. (www.metahistory.org/gnostique/archon-files/GnosticCatechism.php)

And it is this "finely nuanced science" that Burroughs attempted to keep alive in the form of fiction. Burroughs' many readers were all potential recruits, "marks" who had "wised up" just enough to see a hint of light behind the illusion. His sincerest hope was that at least *some* of them were paying attention, would pick up the tools he left behind within his books, and use them to storm through the mass of Nova Mobsters whose unenviable job is to surround and protect the ramparts of the fragile Reality Studio until its dying day.

Works Cited

Bey, Hakim. *T.A.Z.* Brooklyn: Autonomedia, 1991.

Bockris, Victor. *With William Burroughs: A Report From the Bunker*. New York: St. Martin's Griffin, 1996.

Burroughs, William S. *The Adding Machine*. New York: Seaver, 1986.

---. *Cities of the Red Night*. New York: Holt, Rinehart and Winston, 1981.

---. Corso Interview. "Attack *Anything* Moving." *Burroughs Live: The Collected Interviews of William S. Burroughs 1960-1997*. Ed. Sylvere Lotringer. New York: Semiotext(e), 2000.

---. *The Place of Dead Roads*. New York: Henry Holt, 1983.

Burroughs, William S. and Brion Gysin. *The Third Mind*. New York: Viking, 1978.

Burroughs, William S. *Three Novels: The Soft Machine, Nova Express, The Wild Boys*. NewYork: Grove Press, 1988.

Hibbard, Allen. *Conversations with William S. Burroughs*. Jackson: University Press of Mississippi, 1999.

Hoeller, Stephan A. *Gnosticism: New Light on the Ancient Tradition of Inner Knowing*. Wheaton: Quest, 2002.

---. Guffey Interview. "The Suppressed Teachings of Gnosticism." *Paranoia*. www.paranoiamagazine.com/hoeller.html.

Lash, John. "A Gnostic Catechism: Encounters with Aliens in a Mystery School Text."

227

www.metahistory.org/gnostique/archonfiles/GnosticCatechism.php.

Murphy, Timothy S. *Wising Up the Marks: The Amodern William Burroughs*. Los Angeles: University of California Press, 1997.

Stephenson, Gregory. *The Daybreak Boys: Essays on the Literature of the Beat Generation*. Carbondale: Southern Illinois University Press, 1990.

PART FOUR

CONSPIRACIES AND THE THREE DOMINANT RELIGIONS OF THE WEST: CHRISTIANITY, JUDAISM AND ISLAM

CHAPTER FOURTEEN

PROGRAMMING ARMAGEDDON IN THE MIDDLE EAST

You're probably not aware of this, but for some time now the fate of the world has hinged on the color of a cow.

In the early 1990s Reverend Clyde Lott, a cattleman in Mississippi, came up with a brilliant notion—so brilliant it was no doubt divinely inspired. According to scripture, Numbers 19:2 to be exact, the birth of a red heifer is one of the most important preconditions for the advent of Armageddon and the return of the Messiah. The other precondition is the removal of the Muslim-controlled Dome of the Rock from the Temple Mount in East Jerusalem.

A brief history lesson: On June 7, 1967, during the bloody Six-Day War, Israeli troops took control of the Temple Mount for the first time in almost two thousand years. Despite this victory, the decision was made by the Israeli government to allow the Temple Mount to remain in Muslim hands. One reason was political: to prevent a catastrophic holy war. However, that was not the main reason. The main reason was that the most influential rabbis in Israel forbade any further action from being taken. According to Jewish religious law, no Jew is allowed to enter the sacred gates of the Mount until he is purified. Alas, the only method by which one can be made "clean" is to bathe oneself in the ashes of a pure red heifer. And in 1967 a pure red heifer did not exist.

Enter: a former Southern Baptist turned Pentecostal minister whose family has been raising cattle for generations. Employing the most sophisticated biotech methods, Rev. Clyde Lott has been attempting to breed a pure red heifer in the Holy Land itself. He is being helped financially by some of the most extreme members of Israel's religious right, such as the Temple Institute in Jerusalem's Old City, to create an unblemished red heifer per the specifications of the Old Testament. The word "unblemished," by the way, is meant very precisely. Even a single strand of white hair will disqualify the cow. Who knows how many isolated white hairs have saved a lucky little heifer from the sacrificial altar?

According to some Christian fundamentalists, like televangelist Jack Van Impe, these Temple purification ceremonies cannot begin until the heifer is three years old. Lott and his associates in Jerusalem have been at this game for over a decade. Who knows how close they are to their goal?

Most people, unconcerned with the minute details of ancient scripture, would dismiss this talk of ritual sacrifice and Biblical prophecy as the obsession of a few fringe lunatics. Who cares how they choose to waste their time? Let them go about their business. After all, who could they harm?

Try the whole world.

Armageddon, for these people, is not an abstract concept destined to occur in humanity's far distant future. For them, we are living in the End Times. The End could be written by Our Lord at any moment. It's only days, even seconds away. Jesus is coming, says Chicken Little, Jesus is coming. All the signs are lining up.

It began, for them, with the establishment of the state of Israel in 1948. That was the first precondition, the first sign that The End was not far off. In the 1970s and 1980s the Christian fundamentalist Hal Lindsey published bestseller after bestseller exalting over the coming nuclear war between the United

States and the Soviet Union. Surely these two Cold War enemies could be none other than Gog and Magog identified in Revelation? Now that the Soviet Union has been dissolved, a new enemy has been targeted and groomed for the role: Islam.

Obviously, interpreting Biblical prophecy is very important to these people. Rarely does a minute go by when scripture is not being applied to current events. An outside observer might be tempted to stop for a moment and ask the obvious question: Is any of their time spent feeding the poor, finding homes for children abandoned by parents who couldn't afford to raise them, helping urban areas blighted by neglect and random violence—"minor" deeds that Jesus himself (or rather, the person we think Jesus might have been, if he existed) would no doubt have taken part in if he were alive today? Of course not. How silly to think otherwise. No. It's easier to spend one's time interpreting mistranslated, two-thousand-year-old words for armchair Armageddonists, people who long for death but are too passive to slip a gun barrel in their mouths and pull the trigger.

The amount of money being spent in Jerusalem at this very moment, for the sole purpose of breeding a cow whose every last strand of hair is the color of rust, is astronomical. According to Gershom Gorenberg, an investigative journalist who lives and works in Jerusalem:

> [Clyde] Lott appeared at churches, raising funds, and on Christian TV. Donation cards, adorned with sepia photos of grazing cows, allowed supporters to sponsor the purchase of "1 red heifer—$1,000.00," a half-heifer or quarter, or "1 air fare (1 cow)" at $341. A fundraising letter exhorted, "Remember, Gen. 12:2-3: 'I will bless those who bless you, and whoever curses you, I will curse'"—a verse often cited by evangelicals as a reason to support Israel—and expressed thanks for "this opportunity to share a portion of this monumental work that the God of Abraham, Isaac and Jacob is doing at the hands of these simple men of faith in these last days." (25)

This prophecy business gets easier and easier with every passing moment. Indeed, it's not that difficult at all when you spend twenty-four hours a day doing everything in your power to make your predictions come true.

But how, you might ask, can a small group of "fringe loonies" bring about something as improbable as Armageddon? It's not as hard as you might imagine, particularly when said lunatics are living and working in the White House.

The cozy relationship between Ariel Sharon, the prime minister of Israel, and U.S. President George W. Bush was representative of the co-dependent relationship between the religious right in Israel and fundamentalist Christians in the U.S. It's often been said that politics makes strange bedfellows, but religion can make even stranger ones. Both groups are clearly religious fanatics, and yet neither see the final outcome of their enthusiastic collaboration—a systematic attempt to literally program Armageddon in the Middle East—as the same. How could they? According to the views of fundamentalist Christians, the moment Armageddon begins, the "faithful" will be transported from the material plane and delivered to Paradise while all the heathens remain down here to fry. This moment is referred to by the "faithful" as The Rapture, but this experience won't be so rapturous for all those left behind (that includes the Jews, even the ones helping to shell out the cash to breed the red heifer that will theoretically bring about all this jabberwocky in the first place).

The above view, known as "dispensationalism," is not a new one. It was first proposed by a nineteenth century minister of the Church of England named John Darby. This branch of Christian fundamentalism sprang up out of an environment already brimming with the kind of madness that occurs at the turn of every century. Dispensationalism seems to have emerged mostly as a reaction to several factors prominent at that time: the chaos and uncertainty of the Civil War, the growing acceptance of Darwinism, and the technological advances of the Industrial Revolution. This movement, beginning in the

1870s and continuing to flourish until about 1920, is sometimes referred to as "Darbyism." Darby's small-minded, literalist interpretation of scripture, particularly the Tribulation of Revelation, remains the most important influence on fundamentalists today. That, of course, includes George W. Bush.

In the Spring of 2005, the President of the Unites States and the Prime Minister of Israel seemed to be doing everything in their power to prevent peace in the Middle East. Their true goal seemed, instead, to be the creation of the ripest environment for Armageddon. Did Ariel Sharon care that his colleague George W. Bush believes, in the very heartmeat core of his Born Again soul, that Sharon and everyone who shares his heritage will meet the fate of a kosher hotdog trapped in a microwave oven the second the Big Blowout Superbowl Doomsday Extravaganza is kickstarted? No, he didn't. Nor do the members of the right-wing Temple Institute forking over big bucks to Rev. Lott to help him breed the red heifer. These Israeli extremists know they're being used by the Christian fundamentalists in the U.S. But so what? They're being used to bring about a scenario they "know" will never happen. They "know" the fundamentalist Christians aren't being transported to Heaven when the Israelis gain sole control of the Temple Mount. Their attitude is: Let the fundamentalist *meshuginahs* think what they want. The members of the Temple Institute only care about one thing: the Christian knack for fundraising.

On the other hand, the Christian fundamentalists don't care that the Divine Plan calls for all their Jewish cohorts to burn in eternal hellfire. Guy Garner, one of Rev. Lott's business associates, has been quoted as saying, "It's not pleasant to think about... but God's going to do what He's going to do" (Gorenberg 27). In other words, each side is hoodwinking the other. Meanwhile, each continues to help the other initiate the Divine Plan—whether that be the Jewish Divine Plan or the Christian Divine Plan remains to be seen. Unfortunately for the rest of us, both scenarios end in an apocalypse of some kind... but most assuredly not a supernatural one.

Many experts in geopolitics concur that the birth of a pure red heifer, leading to a concerted raid on the Temple Mount by extremist Jewish settlers, could very well set off the holy war to end all holy wars. Rod Dreher, writing for the *National Review*, interprets it this way:

> The world media covered [the attempt to breed a pure red heifer] as a joke, but it wasn't funny to David Landau, columnist for the Israeli daily *Ha'aretz*. He called the red heifer "a four-legged bomb" that could "set the entire region on fire." Muslim leaders worried about the red heifer too, as they would see an attempt by Jews to take over the Temple Mount as a sign of the Islamic apocalypse. [. . .]
>
> [The heifer] arrives at a time when Israel is fighting a war for survival with the Palestinians, who are almost entirely Muslim, and a time in which Islam and the West appear to be girding for battle with each other, as Islamic tradition predicts will be the state of the world before the Final Judgment.
>
> "These kinds of circumstances are exactly what people are waiting for," says Richard Lands, a Boston University history professor and director of its Center for Millennial Studies. "We could be starting a war. If this is a real red heifer, and strict Orthodox rabbis have declared her worthy of sacrifice, then a lot of Jews in Israel will take that as a sign that a new phase of history is about to begin. The Muslims are ready for jihad anyway, so if you have Jews up there doing sacrifices, talk about a red flag in front of a charging bull."
>
> Lands says there is immense anger among Israelis, both religious and secular, at the ingratitude of Muslims, whom the conquering Israeli army allowed to occupy and control the Temple Mount in 1967. Add to this the fury of a nation under attack by Islamic suicide bombers, and, says Lands, "it's entirely conceivable that this [red heifer] could trigger a new round of attempts to blow up the Dome of the Rock."

Presiding over all this chaos was Ariel Sharon, a man who went out of his way to derail peace in the Middle East. One of his highly publicized insults to Muslims, perhaps brought about by his own religious fanaticism, occurred on September 28, 2000, when he staged an unmistakable act of provocation against the Muslim world by visiting the Temple Mount and touching the third holiest shrine of Islam, known as Hiram al-Shari, while surrounded by armed guards. The message was clear: This shrine will soon be ours once more.

Meanwhile, in New York City, Palestinian and Israeli negotiators had only been hours away from concluding an agreement that would have paved the way for a renewed peace process. But Sharon's strategic provocation destroyed any chances for peace in the near future. As if that weren't enough, his actions soon ignited violent protests all over Jerusalem, the West Bank and Gaza. Hundreds died as a result. Make no mistake: Sharon could not have been ignorant of what would happen in the wake of his actions. Did he care? I suspect not. Paraphrasing a bit of homespun wisdom: You can't make a good Armageddon without breaking a few eggs.

All evidence indicates this is a philosophy President Bush and his flag-sucking cronies also subscribed to. If you don't believe me, perhaps we should listen to what former President Jimmy Carter has to say on the subject. Not only did Carter go on record opposing Bush's war in Iraq, calling it "completely unnecessary," but he also addressed Bush's dispensationalist view of the Bible, calling it

> ...a completely foolish and erroneous interpretation of the Scriptures. And it has resulted in these last few years with a terrible, very costly, and bloody deterioration in the relationship between Israel and its neighbor.... [T]his administration, maybe strongly influenced by ill-advised theologians of the extreme religious right, has pretty well abandoned any real effort that could lead to a resolution of the problem between Israel and the Palestinians. (McGarvey, "Carter's Crusade")

In the Spring of 2005, reports began coming out of the Middle East concerning an imminent raid on the Temple Mount being planned by two extremist Jewish organizations: "Chai v'Kaiyam" and "The Temple Mount and Land of Israel Faithful Movement." Samer Khuwayera, a correspondent for IslamOnline.net, reported: "Leaders of Jewish settlers are planning to storm the holy mosque in a bid to perform Jewish 'religious rituals' in the holy place .... Leaflets are being distributed by Jewish settlers to urge Jews to join the storming of the Islamic holy site on April 10." Though there is no way to know if this information was accurate in its exact details, there was no doubt that a similar assault of some kind was being planned by right-wing extremists in Jerusalem at that time. Such a terroristic move can lead only to needless human fatalities in the Middle East... and rapture among the Born Again community in the United States.

All thanks to the color of a cow.

Works Cited

Dreher, Rod. "Red Heifer Days: Religion Takes the Lead." *National Review Online*. 11 Apr. 2002. www.nationalreview.com/dreher/dreher041102.asp.

Gorenberg, Gershom. *The End of Days: Fundamentalism and the Struggle For the Temple Mount*. New York: Oxford University Press, 2000.

Halsell, Grace. *Prophecy and Politics: The Secret Alliance Between Israel and the U.S. Christian Right*. Chicago: Lawrence Hill, 1986.

Khuwayera, Samer. "Jewish Settlers Plan to Storm Al-Aqsa." 8 Mar. 2005. www.islam-online.net/English/News/2005-03/08/article05.shtml.

McGarvey, Ayelish. "Carter's Crusade." *American Prospect*. 5 Apr. 2004. http://prospect.org/cs/articles?article=carters_crusade.

CHAPTER FIFTEEN

1001 Nights with Ali
(Or)
My Prescription for Peace in the Middle East
(A Fable)

"To proceed, I should like to inform the honorable gentlemen and noble readers that the purpose of writing this agreeable and entertaining story is the instruction of those who peruse it, for it abounds with highly edifying histories and excellent lessons for the people of distinction, and it provides them with the opportunity to learn the art of discourse. This story, which I have called '1001 Nights With Ali,' abounds also with splendid anecdotes that teach the reader to detect deception and to protect himself from it, as well as delight and divert him whenever he is burdened with the cares of life and the ills of this world. Always remember, it is the Supreme God who is the True Guide. Praise be to Allah, the Beneficent King, the Creator of the world and man."

–a paraphrase of the foreword to *The Thousand and One Nights*

Is Islam a Peaceful Religion?: An Afternoon of Fire & Brimstone With Abdel Malik Ali

I spent Cinco de Mayo trapped in a room full of Muslims and Jews. I barely got out of the place alive.

    I wish the above paragraph were true, but I just said that to catch your attention. The truth is, I spent Cinco de Mayo trapped in a room full of robots. Now pull up a chair, dear Shahrazad, and please let me tell you about it. You've tired yourself out enacting so many of your delightful stories for me. It's about time I did the same for you, eh?

Listen:

* * *

Have you ever heard of an Ontological Engineer? No? Neither had I until a couple of years ago when I was dating a Philosophy major. She once asked me, "What am I going to do when I graduate?" As anyone knows, the only careers for which Philosophy majors are suited are 1) Teaching philosophy, 2) whacking off, 3) being a bum, and 4) being Ontological Engineers.

An Ontological Engineer is a Philosophy major who also has a degree in computer science. The Pentagon hires them to devise philosophical quandaries to test artificial intelligence programs. As you no doubt know, despite the sophistication of modern-day computers, even the most cutting-edge AI program is incapable of distinguishing between certain subtleties that humans should be capable of navigating rather easily. For example, these programs find it very difficult to distinguish between metaphor and reality, fiction and non-fiction, truth and lies.

If a programmer asks the AI a question like, "Who is Dracula?" the program might respond with something along these lines: "Dracula was a vampire who lived in Transylvania until 1893 when he moved to London. He was subsequently murdered in the Borgo Pass by a Texan named Quincey Morris. He has no known descendants." Conversely, the programmer might ask, "Who is George Washington?" to which the computer might respond, "George Washington was the first President of the United States."

The computer would have no way of distinguishing between Dracula and George Washington, metaphor and reality, truth and fiction. To the AI, both biographies would be of equal significance.

Back to Cinco de Mayo: I hopped on a bus and went to California State University at Long Beach because my friend had a sculpture featured in an exhibit at the University Art Gallery. The exhibit was scheduled to open at 6:00 P.M. I arrived on campus at around 12:30 P.M. and somehow got roped into attending a talk by an African-American Islamic lecturer named Abdel Malik Ali, Amir of Oakland, California's Masjid Al Islam mosque. My friend's family is from Israel, and she was attending the lecture for the express purpose of protesting it.

The protestors stood quietly in the back and held up signs bearing slogans like, "PREACH LOVE NOT HATE" throughout the two-hour lecture. To their credit they did not try to shout Ali down and allowed him to complete the entire speech. No attempt was made to strong-arm the protestors out of the room. The proccedings remained fairly civil throughout. I give both sides credit for that.

Too bad they're a bunch of robots, though. They're not necessarily destined to remain that way their entire lives, of course, but as long as they insist on misinterpreting metaphors as reality both sides are going to continue to get their kids ripped to pieces, whether from homemade bombs strapped to the chests of gung-ho Palestinians or from lead flying out of an Israeli M16. Meatball Fulton once said, "What's coming at you is coming from you." Both the Palestinians and the Israelis would do well to take heed of that rather simple dictum rather than its twisted corollary: MY METAPHOR IS BETTER THAN YOURS.

When I was a teenager I watched an interview with Joseph Campbell, the twentieth century's foremost scholar on mythology. He and the interviewer (it might have been Bill Moyers) were talking about interpreting religion purely as metaphor. The interviewer seemed to have some trouble grasping this concept. He said, "But would somebody actually die for a metaphor?" Campbell spread his hands in the air and said, "They do all the time."

Throughout Ali's lecture I was sitting among the protestors in the very back of the room. Occasionally one of the protestors would turn to her companion and mumble something like, "Everything he's saying is a lie, everything, every bit of it, 100%, God, I can't beli—!"

I was tempted to pause the tape of reality for a moment and give her a brief lecture on the dangers of Aristotelian thinking. As Count Alfred Korzybski, the great Polish mathematician and philosopher, demonstrated in his classic 1933 book *Science and Sanity*, to use terms like "all" or "none" is ineffectual and counterproductive in rational debate. Mathematically, of course, one can never know *all* or *none* of any given set. It implies that you've actually studied every member of that set in order to come to your conclusion. For example, one would have to carefully interview every Jew who ever lived in order to successfully make the statement, "All Jews are usurious," or interview every Palestinian who ever lived in order to claim, "All Palestinians are suicide bombers." To prevent oneself from making such a mistake, Korzybski recommends that people avoid using terms like "all" or "none" since they serve no useful function and lead to prejudicial, backward thinking. In terms of mathematics, the statement, "Everything Abdel Malik Ali says is a lie" is the same as the statement "All Jews are usurious." Mathematically, they're equally invalid and just as impossible to prove. This is the thinking of pre-programmed robots, not human beings.

Let's examine the claim. "Everything Abdel Malik Ali says is a lie." I took extensive notes during the lecture, and can prove this is untrue. During the course of the two-hour lecture Ali uttered a number of statements that were valid and worthy of consideration. He also uttered a number of statements that indicated he'd mixed a few too many Fruit Loops with his halvah that morning.

Let's Start With the Positive, Shall We?

1) He criticized the Patriot Act as being a flimsy excuse to erode the civil rights of Americans, a charge all too few Americans are making these days. To hear this subject addressed in a public lecture on a University campus was more than welcome.

2) He rightly pointed out a linguistic bit of silliness that has always bugged me, namely the strange assumption that the term "Semite" applies only to Jews. As a professor of English, I think it's only fair that words be used properly. The truth is that both Arabs and Jews who are indigenous to the Middle East are Semites. Therefore, if someone maligns an Arab unfairly on the basis of his race then that person is being "Anti-Semitic" just as much as he would have been if he had persecuted a member of the Jewish race. If I had time, I'd tell you all about the misuse of the word "momentarily" which also grinds my gears, but that would take too much time. Onward....

3) He made the point that the U.S. government has used the tactic of fear since at least the 1940s to appropriate more money for the military. First, they falsely magnified the threat of the Russians following World War II and manufactured Cold War paranoia for the express purpose of maintaining a grip on war-time-level appropriations. He pointed out that when he was growing up, the people of the United States lived in absolute terror of Russians attacking U.S. soil, so much so that they were building shelters in their own homes to survive an imminent nuclear attack. Yesterday it was the Russians, Ali said, now it's Islamic terrorists. And the purpose of this fear-mongering, as in the 1950s, is to appropriate more money for the military-industrial complex. Corporations like Raytheon run this country, he said, and make profits through manufactured wars. As an example of this fear-mongering, Ali made the point that the U.S. government is constantly making official statements such as, "We're surprised terrorists haven't hit the food supply because it's so vulnerable." If you were really concerned about such a possibility, would you actually go out of your way to an-

nounce your Achilles' Heel on national television? Ali underscored the fact that such statements are not to be taken at face value. The statement is not intended to be a genuine warning at all, but a trigger: a trigger of fear.

4) To top it all off, even while his personal friends are getting rich off the war in Iraq, President Bush is rapidly driving the U.S. into bankruptcy.

Valid statements all.

Now Let's Move Onto the Negative, Shall We?

1) He claims that the Bush family is entirely controlled by Zionist Jews. That's odd, considering the fact that Prescott Bush, Dubya's grandfather, was convicted under the Trading With the Enemy Act back in 1942 of conducting business deals with the Nazis during World War II (Loftus and Aarons 360). If the Bush family has ever been controlled by any shadowy group of imperialist demagogues, Zionist Jews would be the last people to be included on the invitation list. Except, maybe, to provide entertainment after the borscht-eating contest.

2) Speaking of entertainment, Ali believes that the entire entertainment industry is controlled by Zionist Jews. In fact, *all* media are controlled by Zionist Jews. Here's an exact quote: "Zionist Jews own the media. That's common knowledge. C'mon, everyone knows this" (shrugs).

3) His main evidence for this assertion was that a close friend of his knows Whoopi Goldberg. Whoopi, you see, confided in this friend during a rare moment of candor (*extreme close-up on* the sweat beads trickling down Whoopi's neck as she swivels her head from side to side looking to see if any spies have managed to infiltrate the alleyway) that she changed her name to "Goldberg" because that's what you have to do in order to get steady work in Hollywood. Okay. I'm sure that name change must have *really* flummoxed all those Jews in Hollywood. ("Funny, Sol, she don't look Jewish.") That'd be as improbable as an African-American man willingly changing his Christian name to something silly like "Abdel Malik Ali" simply to become famous on the Islam-

ic lecture circuit. I hear it's good work if you can get it. Those dudes make a bundle in donations. Maybe Whoopi should think about changing her name again and starting a whole new career. Whoopi 14X has a nice ring to it. Come to think of it, I haven't seen Whoopi in a movie in a long time.

4) Ali claims that Palestinian "freedom fighters" don't target children—not on purpose, at least. The children who are killed, however, should be considered nothing more than "collateral damage." Minor *faux pas* like this happen during every struggle for liberation, didn't you know? During the course of the lecture Ali made it clear that he didn't have a very high opinion of George Bush. I wonder why. After all, they seem to speak the same language.

5) After a homosexual Jewish man asked Ali a pointed question, I learned that Muslims can indeed be homosexuals, but they have to keep their mouths shut about it. Ali said to the man, "I get it. All y'all got your little thing goin' on, but we can't go into your bedrooms to see what's happenin' in there. That's up to you. If you keep it to yourself, we can't stop you. But the fact is, homosexuality's wrong. If you want me to stand here and condone it, I can't. To any Muslim, it's an illegal sexual activity." As this report progresses, Bush and Ali start to look more and more similar, don't they? If these two gentlemen are ever trapped in an elevator together, at least they'll have a lot to discuss. Perhaps they might find themselves becoming a little more intimate than mere friends....

6) If the U.S. invades Iran, this will not only lead to Muslim control of the Middle East, but eventually Muslim control of the entire planet. Allah be praised. I can't wait. Let's get this party started. After having spent an entire afternoon with a whole room full of these dudes, I can imagine the bright and happy world that would rise from the ashes of this Zionist-controlled hell-planet. Only one problem: Who will be left behind to feed us our daily news and entertainment?

7) Another headline from Ali: "There's no such thing as a Muslim who believes in the separation of Church and State."

Which can only mean that this imminent Muslim-controlled paradise will be a theocratic one. It certainly can't be a democracy. I find this interesting. During the entire lecture, Ali would invoke various amendments of the U.S. Constitution. Ali is definitely for Freedom of Speech—when it suits him, of course. He's definitely for the Freedom to Bear Arms—when it suits him, of course. But he's strongly against one of the main pillars of American democracy, namely the separation of Church and State. Therefore, to sum it all up: Ali is pro-theocracy, anti-democracy, and anti-American. Why don't we make him President? He's got all the qualifications.

8) I learned that people often come up to Mr. Ali and ask him questions like, "Is Islam a peaceful religion?" I learned the answer to that question. Here it is: "If you're friendly to us, you will find us to be a friendly religion. If you're not friendly, well, you might not find us to be so peaceful. If you steal our resources, if you rape our children, if you murder our people, you will find Islam to be a religion of terror. We are not going to sit back and allow ourselves to be oppressed by you." In situations like these, it's always important to keep in mind Mark Twain's famous dictum: "The only people qualified to use the word 'we' are kings, lawyers, and tapeworms." I also learned that "The two-state solution is off the table. We will have one-state. In order for there to be peace in the Middle East, the Muslims have to control it. Just like we controlled it before, we have to control it again." However, Ali did offer one ray of sunshine in all this madness: "We'll give you the right of return. You can go back to Germany or Poland or Brooklyn, wherever all y'all came from. You can go back there." So, you see, he's not entirely hateful.

9) When asked if he hated Jews, Ali replied, "I hate Zionist Jews." He was then asked, "Do you believe most Jews are Zionists?" Ali replied, "Of course I believe most Jews are Zionists; that's the problem." He was then asked, "So does that mean you hate most Jews?" Ali replied, "If most Jews are Zionists, and I hate Zionists, then that means I hate most Jews. So, yeah?" (Shrugs.)

10) Possibly the weirdest thing about the event was what I call "the Muslim death-chant." The first time it happened it almost made me leap out of my skin. It happened like this: For emphasis, Ali pointed at a woman in the front row and said, "We two are not meant to get along. You are I.D.F. [Israeli Defense Force]! And I... I *am Hezzbollah!*" At which point, in perfect synchronization, every single Muslim in the room did their best Pavlov's dog impersonation and launched into a guttural death-chant that sounded something like "HOHDIMAHOHDIMAH-HUHR!" At the end of the last syllable they kind of beat their chest, crossed their arms, then resumed their robotic demeanor. The only other times I've ever seen such well-rehearsed synchronization was in German newsreels from the 1930s, or maybe back in high school when I used to watch all the cheerleaders practicing their moves during lunch time. Sometimes I got the feeling Ali was making up excuses to say the word "Hezzbollah" just to see that crazy routine all over again. Why not? I would if I were him. Hell, man, that's real *power*.

11) Ali claims that all children are innocent, perfect beings. In fact, he said (and I quote), "All children are Muslims." Let's explore the logic of that statement for a moment. A true Muslim, you see, is a perfect being; therefore, all children are Muslims, no matter their ethnic background. Even Jews are born Muslims. Even gazelles are born Muslims. Even Jennifer Lopez was born Muslim. When some people are born, they fall out of the stupid-tree and hit every branch on the way down; there must be a hell of a lot of broken branches at the bottom of Ali's tree.

12) Let's discuss the assassination of Malcolm X for a moment. Ali's all bent out of shape about it. He has a right to be. The ironic part of it is that he thinks Zionist Jews did Malcolm in—of course, their Kabbalistic super powers of hypnosis and Svengali-like mind control would have been perfect for the job. The truth is, however, that the real research indicates the exact opposite: that members of the Nation of Islam itself helped engineer the assassination. The fact that the FBI's COINTELPRO program had infiltrated the organization probably accelerated its dissolu-

tion considerably. That such a politically powerful organization would be so thoroughly infiltrated by government spies shouldn't be too much of a surprise. More to the point, political researcher Dave Emory has underscored the fact that Louis Farrakhan, who managed to take up Malcolm's mantle in the wake of his assassination, publicly called for the death of Malcolm X immediately after Malcolm broke with the Nation of Islam and condemned Elijah Muhammad's leadership. Malcolm broke away from both the Nation of Islam and Elijah Muhammad for four reasons:

A) The Nation of Islam barred any cooperation between black people and white people. Malcolm supported this segregation himself until he visited South Africa and saw for himself how successful the cooperation between whites and blacks had been in fighting the apartheid regime. He concluded that a political alliance between the white and black communities in America was the only hope for the liberation of both races.

B) Malcolm uncovered the hypocritical, unethical behavior of Elijah Muhammad. Muhammad demanded strict moral behavior from his followers including outright celibacy, and yet had impregnated a bevy of his own secretaries behind the scenes. The true irony of the situation is this: All these women gave birth out of wedlock, and were then fined and censored by the Nation of Islam for their "immoral behavior." This was a great blow to Malcolm who quickly became disillusioned with the organization.

C) Another problem that Malcolm had with the Nation of Islam was its sources of funding. Despite the fact that Elijah Muhammad condemned any cooperation between blacks and whites, he had no problem accepting massive donations from none other than George Lincoln Rockwell, the leader of the American Nazi Party, and H.L. Hunt, an avowed racist who promoted the return of all black Americans to Africa – beyond a doubt one of the most far-right oil barons in Texas. As anyone who has studied the murder of John F. Kennedy will know, H.L. Hunt and his associates had so many connections to the assassination plot that his involvement is almost beyond question. (Dallas journalist Jim Marrs touches on some of these connections in his comprehensive 1989 book *Crossfire: The Plot That Killed Kennedy*.) Why a white racist like Hunt would be funding a radical black organization should be obvious, and ties into why Louis Farrakhan later developed such close connections to white supremacists like Tom Metzger and Robert Miles, a Ku Klux Klansman who was eventually imprisoned for firebombing school buses as a way of protesting compulsory busing in Michigan. The reason is that both organizations have the same goal: the segregation of the races. Malcolm realized what a mistake this was politically and did not wish to hop into bed with the very same people whose influence he was attempting to defeat. Given Hunt's known connections to various U.S. intelligence agencies, his financing of the Nation of Islam might also have been connected to the government's infiltration of the organization as a vehicle for agitation and provocation.

D) The last reason is the strangest. As Fortean journalist Frank Edwards used to say, "Strange but true!" One of the central tenets of the Nation of Islam was that the entire white race had been genetically engineered in a laboratory by a mad scientist named "Yakob" many centuries ago. I would give anything to go back in time and be a fly on the wall when Malcolm was presented with this stunning information. I imagine it was probably similar to the looks of consternation on the faces of the "true believers" who have worked hard to ascend through the various degrees of Scientology only to be told in the end that the sins of the human race were manufactured 75 million years ago by an extraterrestrial warlord named Xenu who is now imprisoned in a wire cage on a remote island in the Atlantic Ocean just off the coast of Morocco (Corydon 365). I imagine the reaction would be two-fold: 1) I very much wish to believe this, because to reject it would require admitting that I've been a fool for the past _____ number of years, and 2) Where's my chainsaw? Obviously, Malcolm managed to find some sort of middle ground and left the organization without dismembering anybody. It should also be noted, as Dave Emory has pointed out in his lectures, that promoting pseudo-scientific ideas (like that of the white race having been "evil mutations" genetically engineered in a laboratory) serves the purposes of segregationists like Robert Miles, Tom Metzger, George Lincoln Rockwell, and H.L. Hunt because such jabberwocky can only discredit the Nation of Islam and any related black organization in the eyes of mainstream America. Farrakhan, by the way, promulgates this bizarre science fictional genesis story to this very day. Is it possible that this nonsense was a direct result of COINTELPRO influences in the organization?

A full investigation of COINTELPRO's involvement in The Nation of Islam and the assassination of Malcolm X can be found in Karl Evanzz's 1992 book *The Judas Factor*. I recommend it for anyone who wants to know how easy it is for certain intelligence agencies to yank the cranks of the same political organizations who profess hatred for them.

Much of the preceding information about Malcolm X and the Nation of Islam was derived from an excellent lecture by Dave Emory titled "The Assassinations of Dr. Martin Luther King, Jr. & Malcolm X" delivered on Feb 27, 1993 at Foothills College in Palo Alto, CA. A transcript of the lecture is available at www.theconspiracy.us/9408/0027.html. Recordings of other lectures by Emory concerning related topics are available at www.spitfirelist.com.

So ends our interlude concerning the life and death of Malcolm X, dear Shahrazad. Care to take a hashish break or would you prefer to continue? Very well, my child. I can see you're eager to hear the rest of the tale....

My Lunch With the Elders of Zion

The first session of this Woodstock-like love-fest ended at around 2:30 P.M. The Muslim Association drifted off to the Food Court for lunch. So did the Jewish protestors. (The Food Court is right next to the Student Union, where the meeting was held.) Since I was with my friend, of course, I sat with the protestors. Some of them seemed to wonder what I was doing there. I was going to tell them in a thick Irish brogue that I was a drunken mick looking for a limey to blow up and had staggered into the wrong meeting by accident. Thankfully, nobody asked.

The Muslims sat at one table. About fifteen feet away, the Jewish protestors sat at another. A more motley crew I've never seen. Sitting at one table was a Jewish African-American gentleman in his late 50s dressed like Bob Marley, holding in his hand an immense bamboo staff that had a silver Star of David attached to the top. Sitting next to him was the homosexual Jewish man who'd asked Ali the question about homosexuality's place in the Muslim religion. Next to him were two bleach-blonde girls in their late teens who would have looked right at home in drill team outfits. Another guy was a rabbi who taught classes on the Kabbalah at UC Irvine; he identified himself as a professional comedian and could do pretty good impersonations of Detroit rap singers. I sat between my friend and a big dude in his early twenties who looked like he'd been weight-lifting hundred-pound Torahs a few too many years.

It was a strange mélange of personalities. At a certain point one of the blonde girls gestured at the black man's sandwich and said, "I want what he has!" Instantly Bob Marley said, "Honey, you can have *all* of what I got!" The girls sort of backed away slowly and retreated to the far end of the table. I was the only one who laughed, whereas everyone else either didn't hear it or chose to ignore it. The black dude caught my eye and winked. I held up my thumb. He went back to seductively stroking his bamboo staff.

My friend began talking to the big dude in the red shirt sitting next to me. The conversation revealed some interesting details. It turned out these same protestors have followed Ali around from University to University. I guess they distribute the same flyers before each lecture, to which Ali responds by delivering exactly the same speech all over again. I imagine the entire assembly simply teleporting from room to room, reenacting the same scene from campus to campus like Sisyphus in that old Greek myth, condemned to roll the same rock up a hill for all eternity. In a way, it could be seen as a metaphor for the entire Israeli-Palestinian conflict: the same circular arguments replayed over and over again just in case a single carbon-based life form was born in the past two minutes who hadn't yet experienced the profound pleasure of being forced to hear them. Apparently, neither side has anything better to do; helping the sick and the poor would be too trivial a task. Let me tell you, the day I find myself in a room full of religious fanatics who've taken even *two* seconds out of their lives to give a quarter to a homeless man on the street is the same day I'll grow wings and hit a high-C note on a bagpipe. Onward with the story, fairest Shahrazad....

Red Shirt raised his big beefy arm and gestured toward the table full of Muslims fifteen feet away. In a tick-tock monotone he said, "LOOK AT THEM. LOOK AT WHAT THEY DO." I turned to look, and I saw all the women sitting at one table and all the men sitting at another table. I couldn't help but notice, as well, one particular woman whom I'd been eyeing during the lecture. She was stunning. Really stood out from the crowd. The others looked like the Arab equivalent of Hausfraus, but not this chick. She looked like an Arabian princess, like that cartoon character in Disney's *Aladdin* given three dimensions. For a moment I toyed with the idea of approaching her table, snapping my fingers, pointing my index finger directly at her and saying, "Hey, honey, do you want to have my terrorist?" But then I thought better of it....

So I turned back to Red Shirt and said, "Yeah? So?"

He said, "LOOK AT THEM." His fingers were digging into the bench; cracks formed in the table. His voice grew deeper and louder. "THEY'RE FUCKED. THEY'RE *FUCKED!*"

"Excuse me," I said, "I can't remember the name for it right now, but isn't there, like, some Jewish ritual in which men and women are segregated?"

He just stared at me for a moment. He said, "YES... BUT THAT'S DIFFERENT."

"What's different about it?"

He looked at me as if the answer should be obvious. He said, "THEY'RE FUCKED. THEY'RE *FUCKED!*"

My friend said to him, "Saying shit like that isn't going to help anything."

He just stared at her. In his robotic tone he said: "YOU'RE RIGHT. IT WON'T." Then he went back to eating his Chinese salad (sans chicken).

"The only thing that's going to help is communication," she said.

Red Shirt took his time pulling the plastic fork out from between his clenched teeth, strategically scraping his pearly whites on the plastic, thus creating an ear-piercing fingernails-on-chalkboard sound. He pointed the fork at her. "COMMU-NICATION IS DEAD. PEOPLE CAN'T TALK TO EACH OTHER ANYMORE."

"Then who do they talk to?" I said.

"THEIR TELEVISIONS."

Being conversant with the work of media critic Marshall McLuhan and the field of postmodern literary theory that has arisen in his wake, I couldn't help but say, "Nah, I don't think that's quite true. The televisions are actually talking to each other."

He just stared at me again for a long time. At no point in the last five minutes had the slightest trace of a smile distort-ed the stoic expression frozen on his face. He said: "YOU'RE WRONG." Back to his salad. "WE'RE AT WAR."

"You can't think of it as a war," my friend said. "If you think that way, you're just being like Ali."

Red Shirt paused for a long moment while he masticated a piece of iceberg lettuce sprinkled with bits of red onion, then said, "YOU OBVIOUSLY DON'T MAJOR IN PUBLIC RELATIONS."

"No," my friend said, "I'm an art major."

Another long pause. The sour, somber look on his face re-sembled that of a man choking on a lemon peel. "YOU AND I SEE THE WORLD DIFFERENTLY," he said.

253

I couldn't hold it in any longer. I just started laughing. "Hey, are you ticklish?" I said, wiggling my fingers in front of him. "Can I tickle you?"

"NO."

"Have you ever seen any Marx Brothers movies?"

"NOT LATELY."

"I recommend you watch their first seven—*Coconuts, Animal Crackers, Monkey Business, Horse Feathers, Duck Soup, A Night at the Opera,* and *A Day at the Races*—all in a row. It might make you feel better."

He didn't say another word to me after that. Maybe he hates Jewish comedians. Who knows?

At one point or another my friend got up from the table and left me stranded among these madmen. She was gone for a long time. A rabbit turned to me and asked me if he could butter my pocket watch, then Bob Marley thrust his staff out in front of him, nearly taking my head off, and said, "Look!"

I turned. My friend, who's about five foot three with boots on, was standing in front of Ali and about three dozen muscle-bound Muslims. She seemed to be having a conversation with Ali. And he was actually *listening.*

One of the women said, "Look at that. David and Goliath."

Bob Marley laughed and said, "Yeah, and *she's* Goliath."

"Look at her," someone said, "she doesn't look intimidated at all."

"Oh, trust me," I said, "she's not."

A few moments later the conversation ended and the swarm of Muslims buzzed away. My friend approached the table and said, "They agreed to begin the second session with questions and answers."

Everybody was stunned. "He's actually going to allow that?" one woman said. "How is that possible? What did you do?"

"I just *asked* him," she said.

I guess nobody there had ever thought of taking that approach before. Red Shirt, the guy who insisted that communication was dead, didn't bother to comment on the fact that his theory had just been proven wrong. He kept eating his salad, looking more morose than ever before.

Go Ask Ali

We returned to the room in the Student Union where the next session was to begin. While waiting, I saw three protestors studying large glossy photos hanging in the window. The photos apparently depicted various atrocities committed against the Palestinians by Israeli soldiers. One photo depicted an Israeli soldier aiming a gun at an old woman.

One female protestor said, "Look, that was done in Photoshop, you can tell."

"What?" I said. "How do you know?"

"The resolution in the background is different."

"It is? Looks the same to me."

"I work with photographs all the time."

"Okay. Still looks like a real photo."

"It's not. I-It's just impossible."

"Impossible? I don't get it. Are you, like, saying it's against the laws of physics for a soldier to abuse his power or something? I guess that's never happened before, right?"

"No, I'm not saying that. It's just highly unlikely, that's all."

"Why is it unlikely?"

"It just *is*. Have you ever been to Israel?"

"No… but you can cruise around Los Angeles on any random night and watch police officers abusing their power for fun and profit. Why the fuck would it be any different in Israel?"

She didn't respond at first. "It's a fake," she whispered.

Suddenly, I was very glad that Photoshop didn't exist when the first photographs were taken of Holocaust victims in Auschwitz.

The second session began at 4:00 P.M. on the dot. I sat with my friend on the left side of the room. I had my notebook out ready to begin writing. I couldn't help but notice the words on the screen behind Ali: "The Martyrdom of Malcolm X and COINTELPRO." *Huh*, I thought, *now we're finally going to hear something relevant. I wonder if they'll get around to mentioning*

Yakob and his weird laboratory where all my ancestors were created lo these many years ago.

Then I felt a hand on my shoulder. I turned to see one of the mean-looking Muslim dudes staring down at me. "Could you move to the other side of the room?" he said.

I stared at him. "Huh? Why?"

He gestured toward the right. "We need all the men to sit over there, on that side of the room."

I glanced over to the right and saw that nothing but men, mostly Muslim, were sitting there. I glanced back to where I was sitting and realized I was the only man in that section. *Oh,* I thought, *it's another kooky religious thing. Okay. Cool. Whatever. No weirder than having to sing the National Anthem every god damn morning back in freakin' elementary school.* So I immediately got up and sat on the other side of the room. And by "other side of the room," I mean only about five feet away.

Enter: a middle-aged redheaded woman who'd been eating kosher sandwiches in between the cheerleaders and the Bob Marley lookalike during the break. She sat down next to her husband. Muslimdude came over, put his hand on Husband's shoulder, and said, "Could you move to the other side of the room?"

Husband stared at him. "Huh?" he said. "Why?"

"We need all the men to sit over there, on that side of the room."

Husband glanced to his right, saw all of us sitting there, at which point the light of realization dawned in his eyes. He started to get up.

Wife said, "Why does he have to move?"

"It just has to be that way," Muslimdude said.

Wife said, "That's outrageous, I've never heard of such a thing!"

Husband was looking at all of us. It seemed to me like he just wanted to move. Muslimdude was getting more and more exasperated. He just stood there, pointing toward our side of the room.

"You people have no right to force him to move," Wife said.

Bob Marley, who was sitting in the row ahead of me, turned toward Wife and said, "Hey, listen, just tolerate it for now, okay?"

"I *refuse* to tolerate this behavior, why, I—!"

One of Red Shirt's friends, who was sitting right next to me, said to her, "It's just like a _____." (He reeled off the name of that Jewish ceremony where men and women are segregated, I can't remember it right now—and I don't really want to bother looking it up, okay?)

"But that's in a synagogue!" Wife said. "This is a *public* University! They don't own this place. Do they think they can walk into a place and just... just *take it over*?"

I almost laughed at the irony of that statement, but nobody quite seemed to get the humor except for me. I just groaned and put my face in my hands. My friend had done an honorable thing by confronting Ali and politely asking him if he would allow questions and answers before the second session. Ali, to his credit, politely agreed. Now this *momzer* has to waltz in and ruin it for everybody.

This useless distraction delayed the beginning of the meeting by a few minutes. Soon, however, the Muslims got wise and just decided to let this one go. In the end Wife was the one who came off looking like a *schlemihl*, not the Muslims. And Husband... well, I don't know if there's a Yiddish word for pussy-whipped, but if so I would have used it right here (if you're Yiddish, please fill in the blank): _____.

Ali announced that the meeting would begin with questions and answers. "Since the young lady in the front here is the one who requested this, we'll let her begin."

My friend deferred to the woman sitting next to her: "Have you ever been to Israel?"

Ali said, "No. They probably wouldn't let me go over there. They've got check points you have to go through, you know. I don't know if I'd be welcome."

"I'm not surprised you haven't been there. If you had, you wouldn't be saying some of these things that you're saying.

They're just not true. For example, how can you say there are Jew-only roads in Israel?" (This was a comment he'd made during the first session.)

"I don't have to be there to know it's true," Ali said. "But I'd like to go to Israel. I'd like to go just to see the indomitable spirit of the Muslim people managing to survive in an apartheid state. The problem is, a whole lot of Israelis are living in a state of denial. Do you think the Palestinians are an oppressed people?"

With only a brief hesitation, the woman replied, "In many ways they *are.*"

A different woman spoke up and said she felt sorry for what had happened to the Palestinians over the years. She even apologized for it.

Ali replied, "If you're so sorry, why don't you give the land back? Everybody says they're so sorry. Let's forgive and forget. Let's live in peace. Why don't you give the land back?"

The woman replied, "Should the United States give L.A. back to Mexico?"

Ali didn't respond to that question. He continued talking: "If you want to be friends, right the wrongs. Otherwise, there's no reason to talk. Go back to pre-1948 and then we'll talk about it."

I thought that was one of the most revealing quotes of the evening. I mean, anybody who requires the invention of a time machine in order to negotiate a problem is definitely unworkable.

The funniest exchange of the session, however, was when a woman stood up and said, "Do you believe Jesus lived in the same region where Israel is now?"

"Of course," Ali said, "that's something we can both agree on."

I thought it was amazing that the one point both sides could agree on was the only one that was historically in doubt. Nobody knows for sure if Jesus even existed, but *that's* the one point both sides could get behind?

Even if Jesus did exist, the fact is that by now he has become nothing more—and nothing less—than a *metaphor.* But a metaphor for what: Peace or Sacrifice? Either way, a metaphor that martyrs all around the world choose to die for every day. Joseph Campbell was definitely right.

The Q&A began to wind down when Wife felt compelled to ask an eight-minute long question interspersed with irrelevant autobiographical details. Reduced to its essentials, the question was pretty much as follows: "How can you say that the Israelis have no right to live in that region given the fact that the whole world already agreed to give the region away back in 1917 when the League of Nations decided to divide it into separate nation-states?"

I thought to myself, *What do you mean "the whole world"?*

Ali responded, "What do you mean 'the whole world'?"

Wife said, "I mean the League of Nations."

I thought, *The League of Nations isn't the whole world.*

Ali responded, "The League of Nations isn't the whole world. The League of Nations had no right to give away someone else's country."

Wife had little to say to that. I thought, *God damn, these people are some of the worst debaters I've ever seen.* I mean, after a whole ninety minute break you'd think you'd be able to lead off with a better question than, "Have you ever been to Israel?"

Anyone even vaguely schooled in logic and argumentation could immediately point out what's wrong with this approach. There's a reason historians are barred from employing *primary sources* in their scholarly work. Primary sources are colored by emotion and selective perception. The argument "I've been to Israel, you haven't" merely gives Ali another opportunity to make his point again about the Israelis living in a state of denial. If someone firmly believes you're living in a state of denial, it doesn't matter how well-traveled you are. Your word won't mean anything to them.

After the meeting I asked one young woman about Ali's allegation concerning Jew-only roads in Israel. First she told me there weren't any at all. Then she said there were, but they only lead to Jewish settlements. Then she told me she didn't know. She wasn't lying, of course, she was just confused. Despite the fact that she'd been to Israel many times, she had no answer to the question. Does this mean she was mentally defective in some way? No. It simply means that having lived in a country doesn't make you an expert on it.

If someone from another country asked me if there were white-only roads and black-only roads in Los Angeles, I would say, "Yes, there are. But they aren't marked that way on the map. You just have to figure it out, sometimes the hard way."

Now if that same person asked me where the best place was to buy heroin in Los Angeles, I wouldn't be able to tell them. Does that mean I've never lived in Los Angeles? No, it means I've never bought heroin in Los Angeles. Living in Los Angeles doesn't necessarily make me an expert on every aspect of it. Some people can live in Los Angeles their entire lives and never leave their immediate neighborhood. Some people live and die on the same damn block before they even hit the age of eighteen. Those people could tell you a lot about white-only roads in L.A., but they might not be able to tell you about the best place to buy a baguette.

This is why the question "Have you ever been to Israel?" was really a waste of an opportunity. Ali agreed to open the floor to questions, but the chosen questions were ultimately meaningless. Not one of the people who had arrived to debate Ali could source any facts. They hadn't bothered to do any hardcore research. They hid behind their heritage as if it was a "Get Out of Jail Free" Card. Or more specifically, a "I Don't Have To Do Any Research Because I Already Know I'm Right" Card. It's fine to have this attitude, but don't claim to be an effective debater because of it. If you show up to "dialogue" with a Muslim, how about reading the Koran first? Same goes for a Muslim. Read the freakin' Torah? Why not? Will it cause your head to spontaneously combust? Everyone in that room should be forced to take comparative religion classes as soon as possible.

All in all, some of Ali's responses were educational, but not in the way he probably intended them to be. In fact, that could pretty much sum up the whole event. I took a lot out of it, but not quite what either side would have wanted me to.

I did want to stay and hear the lecture about Malcolm X and COINTELPRO. I wanted to know if Ali had ever read John A. Williams' book *The Man Who Cried I Am*, an obscure but important novel set in the late '60s that involves a U.S. government contingency plan to toss thousands of minorities into concentration camps. Though ostensibly fictional, some believe that Williams based the book on actual documents he got his hands on while working as a journalist. The plan, called "King Alfred" in the novel, sounds eerily similar to what's happening on Guantanamo Bay right now. It would have been interesting to hear Ali's take on what might be an important piece of literary history, but instead there was an immediate exodus of protestors out of that room at the end of the Q&A, which I thought was unfortunate. They probably could have learned something from the lecture. Alas, I couldn't stay either. I had an art exhibit to attend. That was the main reason I was there, after all. I hadn't expected this detour into the Twilight Zone.

Nonetheless, I was satisfied with the experience. I've now got all three major religions under my belt. Last October, purely as a sociological experiment, I attended a massive Billy Graham rally at the Rose Bowl in Pasadena. I found it quite invigorating being surrounded by thousands of people who all want the world to end *yesterday*.

Having now shared close quarters with Christians, Jews, and Muslims, I can attempt to answer the key question....

If I had a choice, and I had to be stuck in a room full of fanatical Christians, fanatical Jews, or fanatical Muslims, who would I choose? Though this is definitely a quizzer, I think I'd have to pick the Born Agains. At least you know the hardcore Christians are definitely into twisted, kinky sex. I mean, at least we'd have that much in common. You can't really be assured of that when it comes to the Muslims and the Jews. By the way, perhaps that's why the Christians seem far less angry than the Muslims and the Jews. The immediate after-effect of any perverted sex act usually carries with it a calm, soothing effect. I recommend it. (Allow me yet another brief tangent, fair Shahrazad. Isn't it weird that "sodomy" was named after Sodom and not Gomorrah, when the word "Gomorrah" more accurately reflects what it feels like to be sodomized? Things like that never fail to amuse me. What would the Buddhists say about such zen-like koans? I can't help but recall what Confucius once said to me: "'Tis better to engage in a crazed orgy with a bunch of Christians than spend 1001 nights with your forehead stapled to the floor.")

How To Bring Peace To the Middle East

After having spent an afternoon stuck in the middle of an all-out holy war, you might wonder if I have a prescription for change. I do. Please listen closely, my dearest Shahrazad. I should be allowed to appear on both Israeli and Palestinian television to tell the following story: When I was ten years old I was a fan of a superhero comic book called *The Defenders* written by a fellow named J.M. DeMatteis. The book starred off-beat outsiders and misanthropes like The Hulk, Doctor Strange, The Sub-Mariner, The Silver Surfer, The Valkrie, and something called The Gargoyle. In one issue (hold on a minute while I pull it out of the closet... issue #115, to be exact) four of these characters get sucked into an alternate dimension that resembles a Dr. Seuss book. Except for our main characters, the entire issue is purposely drawn to mimic the good doctor's artistic techniques. Our Heroes get involved in a war between two different races of funny little creatures who speak in rhyme. They've been at war for centuries. At the end of the issue, we learn the reason for the war. One side claims they live in a place called "Here" and the other side lives in a place called "There," while their enemies claim they live "Here" and the other side lives "There." They can't agree which side should lay claim to the name "Here." That's the entire reason for the war.

Now, if I were to go on the *Jim Lehrer Newshour* and repeat that story, it would pretty much just shut down the whole
problem. Everyone in the Middle East would feel so silly, they
would instantly drop their weapons, break into tears, and give
each other great big bear hugs. But until that's allowed to happen, I'm afraid the Middle East is screwed.

(The weird thing is, whenever I tell people this story, I often
leave out the fact that the story is from an obscure comic book
called *The Defenders* because I don't want to bother explaining
what the hell that is. So I just tell them it's an actual Dr. Seuss
book. Invariably, at least one person will say, "Hey, I remember
reading that book!" Of course, they don't remember any such
thing, they just think they do. Which means DeMatteis did his
job rather nicely. Far better than Abdel Malik Ali.)

At the end of the day, Ali didn't come off too well. He was
good at reeling off well-rehearsed slogans that were actually
intended to fire up the Muslims in the room more than sway
the uninitiated. My gut instinct after hearing him speak for
over two hours was that he was the kind of guy who lacks confidence and needs to surround himself with yes-men 24/7, a
pissant martinet who got his fingers stuck between a "Louis
Farrakhan Sings Calypso Hits" eight-track and the top of the
tape deck way back in '78 and never managed to get them out
again. He's the kind of functionary who'd sit behind a desk at
the DMV and screw you over by shifting your appointment
around at the last minute just for the pleasure of hearing the
frustration in your voice and watching the blue vein bulge out
of your right temple, the kind of pain in the backside who wears
an orange coat on the side of the freeway and purposely waves
that little red flag above his head when he doesn't need to just
to see traffic back up for six miles.

One woman in the audience compared Ali to Hitler, but
that's silly. At least Hitler had the capability of converting people to his cause. All Ali can do is couch-surf from campus to
campus collecting spare change donations from hungry students while preparing for the imminent dawn of a Novo Mus-

lim Ordo Seclorum. Well, good luck, Sahib. Maybe you'll treat the world better than the cabal of Zionist Jews who hired me to write this story, but I doubt it.

I have a feeling that all the protestors I spent the afternoon with on Cinco de Mayo would be a little annoyed by this story if they ever read it. After all, I didn't trash Ali for 9,000 words. I actually managed to say some positive things about the man here and there and you're not supposed to do that. You're just supposed to see the world their way and shut the eff up. Fanatics come in many flavors. Some of them are *goyim* and some of them are *infidels*. I prefer orange sherbet myself.

Before I go, let me tell you one last story:

When I was unemployed a few years ago, my friend Wendy said to me, "You should think about getting on S.S.I."

"Huh?" I said. "I don't have a disability."

"Sure you do," she said.

"What're you talking about? What's my disability?"

She paused for a second, and with utter sincerity said, "You see things too clearly."

The sad side effect of this disability is that if I end up dead over this book, you won't know exactly whom to blame.

I say pin it on Whoopi. She needs the publicity.

* * *

Well, that was a delightful little tale, wasn't it, my child? In fact, I believe I shall—oh, my! It seems dear Shahrazad has expired due to a strange mixture of amazement and boredom. I must inform her father. *Vizier!* Take this message down at once: "I'm afraid the bitch is dead. If you have any other daughters, please send them along posthaste. I love nothing more than to hear fantastic stories. Alas, the real world is often stranger and far more tragic. Dear Shahrazad discovered this the hard way. Try not to follow in her delicate footsteps. Let the Supreme God be your True Guide. Praise be to Allah, the Beneficent King, the Creator of the world and man."

Works Cited

Corydon, Bent. *L. Ron Hubbard: Messiah or Madman?* Secaucus, NJ: Lyle Stuart, 1987.

DeMatteis, J.M. and Don Perlin. *The Defenders*. No. 115, Jan. 1983.

Emory, Dave. "The Assassination of Dr. Martin Luther King, Jr. & Malcolm X." Lecture. Foothills College. Palo Alto, 27 Feb. 1993.

Evanzz, Karl. *The Judas Factor: The Plot to Kill Malcolm X.*. New York: Thunder's Mouth Press, 1992.

Haddawy, Husain. *The Arabian Nights*. New York: W. W. Norton, 1990.

Korzybski, Alfred. *Science and Sanity*. Lakeville: International Non-Aristotelian Library, 1948.

Loftus, John and Mark Aarons. *The Secret War Against the Jews*. New York: St. Martin's Press, 1994.

Marrs, Jim. *Crossfire: The Plot That Killed Kennedy*. New York: Carroll & Graf, 1989.

Williams, John A. *The Man Who Cried I Am*. New York: Signet, 1968.

PART FIVE

PUPPETS IN HIGH PLACES

CHAPTER SIXTEEN

FAHRENHEIT 24/7:
THE FURTHER
ADVENTURES OF BUSH & CHENEY
(OR)
WAR ALL DAY EVERY DAY
(OR)
"HAVE FUN AND HAVE FUN
QUICK, KIDS, 'CAUSE RECESS IS
ALMOST OVER!"

11-5-04

My Fellow Americans,
Like you, I've been extremely depressed these past few days, and yet I know this reaction is purely an emotional one. Rationally, I know that the situation in Iraq would not have been altered substantially by John Kerry's presence in the White House. I know that the Democratic and Republican agendas were so similar (on a macroscopic, rather

than microscopic scale) as to be almost indistinguishable from one another.

All evidence indicates that Kerry won the 2004 election, just as Al Gore did in 2000 (read, for example, journalist Greg Palast's report "Kerry Won..." at http://tompaine.com/articles/ kerry won .php). I've suspected since 1994 that the voting system in this country is corrupt from top to bottom; nevertheless, I persist in casting my votes mainly because I've been holding out a thin, ever weakening strand of hope that something like a democracy still exists in this country. I no longer believe this is the case, and strongly suspect that if every single person in this country had refused to vote last Tuesday, the percentages would have been exactly the same. "Tight race, wasn't it? Whew! My, so exciting!" A photo finish always makes for good theatre, and keeps the sheeple entertained.

However, that's beside the point now. The real point is this: Since Tuesday all my "liberal" friends have been in a funk, as have I. (Full disclosure: I voted for Nader, just as I did four years ago.) The truth of the matter is this: My friends would have had just as many reasons to be depressed if Kerry had been elected. But instead, they would have partied all night Tuesday... and on Wednesday morning, fallen right back into a complacent slumber. Content.

I understand this reaction. Like you, I do not wish to see Bush's face on my TV screen ever again. I do not wish to hear his voice or his halting pronouncements, uttered with the confident bravado of a man unhindered by either intelligence or self-reflection. I do not wish his backwards ideology to poison me or my family or my friends or their unborn children or their pets or the clouds overhead or the trees or ticks or stem-cells or the molecules of which they're composed. But this is purely an emotional reaction, not a logical one.

This morning, after teaching my classes, I hunkered down in my office and began writing (what was intended to be) a short piece titled "A Brief History of the United States." I decided to begin writing it after I received an e-mail from a colleague that read, "As a friend recently said, 'At least Bush will be gone in four years. That doesn't always happen in Argentina.'"

Though I know my colleague means well, I think he goes astray by presupposing that Bush is going to be gone in four years. In fact, he's presupposing that Bush ever left in the first place.

The venerable political researcher Dave Emory once said that George Bush Sr. was the first President who had been in office for five terms: Two of Reagan's, one of his own, and two of Clinton's. Of course, Emory said this back in 1999. (So imagine what he would say now!)

What he meant by this statement was not that Clinton was, in actuality, Bush disguising himself inside a fat-suit, but that former members of the Bush administration were covertly influencing the Clinton administration from outside, as well as from within. (Do any of you remember David Gergen?)

I voted for Clinton in '92, not really thinking he would win. I was stunned not only by the pleasant notion that I would no longer have to see Bush's face on my TV screen, but also by the fact that Clinton's *very first act in office* was to allow gays in the military. This was clearly a bold move, and immediately pissed off every fundamentalist Christian in the nation, a worthy endeavor in and of itself. This, of course, was his first error.

From that moment on, there was talk within right-wing conspiracy circles of a "Clinton Death List," referring to the improbable number of close friends and associates of the Clintons who were being picked off like insects. The common interpretation was that Hillary herself was wandering around the backwoods of Arkansas, and through the ornate corridors of D.C. as well, massacring political rivals with a machete like some deranged '90s version of Lady Macbeth. Sorry, fellas, I don't buy that—Pat Robertson's protestations notwithstanding.

Don't get me wrong. There really *was* a Clinton Death List, Vince Foster and Ron Brown being the foremost "bulletpoints" on this list. Clinton's colleagues were croaking every week, as if all of them had just stumbled out of a remake of *The Mummy's*

Curse. It's improbable that so many people could die so mysteriously, all intimately connected to two specific people, as the result of mere "happenstance." If you ever wondered why Clinton made so many bone-headed, right-wing moves during his Presidency (like bombing Iraq to bits in his first term just because of an "alleged" Iraqi plot to assassinate President Bush), just ask yourself: What would *you* do if everybody you knew was getting knocked off every other week? "Gee, I guess it might be a good idea to put my signature on this extremist right-wing bill here (oh, but let's do it at 3:00 A.M. when no one's watching)." More often than not, a gentle little suggestion is far more effective than a bullet to the head. When Hillary went on the *Today Show* and "raved" about a vast right-wing conspiracy, she wasn't blowing smoke up anybody's skirt.

"But, wait a minute, you write for that conspiracy rag, don't you? Aren't you one of them wingnuts who thinks 'they're all in on it' together? Aren't you contradicting yourself?" No, not really. They *are* all in on it together, just like the Mafia—but remember, the Mafia also kills its *own*. And gang warfare still runs rampant in the streets, though it may seem somewhat subtler nowadays (more so than Al Pacino whipping out a pistol in a restaurant in New York to avenge a brutal attack on Marlon Brando).

Ever heard of Roberto Calvi? He was the former president of Banco Ambrosiano and one of the principle managers of the Vatican's financial affairs—that is, before he was found hanging from the Blackfriars Bridge in London in 1982. According to journalist David Yallop in his book *In God's Name*, Roberto Calvi once said that if you wanted to understand "how the world is really run," you need to read only one book: not the Bible, not *The Art of War* by Sun Tzu, not *The Prince* by Machiavelli, but—drum roll, please—*The Godfather* by Mario Puzo.

American politicians alternately snipe at one another and protect one another as well, just like the Mafia. An example: In 2003 President Bush blocked the investigation into Clinton's last-minute pardons (known to some as "pardongate"). The

U.S. attorney for the Southern District of New York didn't even issue a report, despite the fact that it was a legitimate criminal investigation already three years old. When a writer for World-NetDaily asked Ari Fleischer, the presidential press secretary, if Bush was "going to just drop it," Fleischer replied, "The president is looking forwards, not backwards, and I would highly recommend that to you as well." Yes, indeed. A most interesting little game is being played here, is it not?

As a result of my colleague's e-mail, I decided to start writing "A Brief History of the United States" because I suddenly realized that a lot of well-meaning people are completely in the dark as to what's going on here, though the overall scenario seems so clear from an outsider's perspective. As you no doubt already know, if you want accurate news about America, refer to foreign sources. It's not an accident that the French were onto the 9/11 fraud before any American journalist.

Speaking of 9/11, this is an important point: On September 11, 1994, at 1:55 P.M., a "lone nut" named Frank Corden stole a single-engine Cessna from Aldino Airport in Churchville, Maryland. Eleven hours later he rammed it into the Executive Mansion of the White House where the President and the First Family would normally be sleeping; however, on that particular evening they were staying elsewhere due to the fact that the Mansion was undergoing renovations. (Those gentle little "suggestions" can get pretty serious, can't they?) The image of that Cessna flying into the White House was the very first image that entered my mind exactly seven years later on September 11, 2001. "Why, we never *dreamed* that somebody would use a plane as a weapon. Not even a science fiction writer could have predicted something as improbable as that!" Huh? Some freakin' "nut" rammed a *plane* into the fucking White House in 1994 and you're telling me you never "dreamed" it could happen in 2001? How stupid do you think I am? (Wait, don't answer that.) Those planes were *allowed* to fly into the World Trade Center in order to kick-start this war, a war we now know Dick Cheney already had planned months before 9/11/01. According to Eric Hufschmid, creator of the documentary *Painful Deceptions* (readily available for purchase at www.erichufschmid. net), no plane flew into the Pentagon on September 11, 2001. Hufschmid insists it was, instead, a missile or a predator drone. He contends that the truth of his claims can be determined through, among many other means, analyzing the color of the Pentagon explosion caught on tape (the chemical components of an explosion resulting from a crashing 757 are significantly different from what one would find in a missile explosion), footage that can be seen in Hufschmid's documentary.

The roots of the 9/11 plot can be found in the Operation Northwoods document, an actual plan prepared by the Chairman of the Joint Chiefs of Staff in the 1960s to hijack jet airliners, blow up U.S. military bases, and use paramilitary sniper teams to shoot at American civilians in the streets of Washington, D.C. and Miami in order to precipitate a war with Cuba. Read about it more fully at: www.infowars.com/northwoods.htm and view the actual documents at: http://elfis.net/parapolitics/northwoodsdoc1.pdf.

Of course, this kind of operation can be traced back much farther. FOIA documents now prove that President Roosevelt allowed the invasion of Pearl Harbor to occur in order to draw an isolationist country into a war it did not want. This incontrovertible proof can be found in the recent book *Day of Deceit* by Robert Stinnett (who, oddly enough, served in the U.S. Navy under Lt. George Bush from 1942 to 1946). The events of 9/11/01 were no different. In fact, I can't think of a major 20th century "conflict" that didn't begin in a similar manner, including the Spanish Civil War, WWI, the Korean War, and Vietnam.

In 1961, in his farewell speech to the nation, President Eisenhower warned of the growing influence of the "military industrial complex." He knew full well that monolithic corporations with ties to the U.S. military were using campaign contributions to exert more and more control over politicians, who in turn were enacting restrictive laws to mold the population into fearful automatons who soon came to believe they had only two choices left to them: volunteer to give up more and more of their rights, or get killed by Communists, terrorists, drug dealers, or fatal plagues. President Eisenhower was saying, in essence, "Have fun and have fun quick, kids, 'cause recess is almost over!"

Only two years after this speech, a barrage of bullets blow open the skull of President John F. Kennedy, at which point a group of schoolyard thugs took over the United States and reversed Kennedy's decision to pull the troops out of Vietnam. (For proof that Kennedy did indeed plan to withdraw from Vietnam, read *JFK and Vietnam* by John Newman, and *JFK: The CIA, Vietnam and the Plot to Assassinate John F. Kennedy* by former Kennedy advisor Col. L. Fletcher Prouty). Nobody can know for certain if Vice-President Lyndon Johnson was in on the plot, but in the final analysis it doesn't matter. He didn't need to be. As Jim Garrison has pointed out, at one time Lyndon Johnson was known as "The Senator from the Pentagon." He was in the pockets of the military from day one. If he was told to do something, he did it. No matter how many ways you parse the issue, the escalation of the Vietnam War was Johnson's responsibility. And as a result, a relatively small group of Texas oil men got rich and tens of thousands of American soldiers were blasted into confetti-meat in Southeast Asia. George Bush Sr. was most likely a member of this Texas cabal; other possible suspects include H. L. Hunt, Clint Murchison, Herman Brown of the law firm Brown & Root, George de Mohrenschildt, James Baker, Vito Genovese, John J. McCloy, Clyde Tolson, and J. Edgar Hoover. All of these gentlemen were either rich Texan industrialists or major stock holders in companies owned by rich Texan industrialists; all of them stood to gain financially by a dead Kennedy and a protracted war in Southeast Asia.

Let's not forget that Bush Sr.'s father, Prescott (a member of the Yale secret society Skull & Bones—just like Dubya and Kerry), was convicted in 1942 under the Trading With the Enemy Act for aiding the Nazis financially in time of war. I refer you to the 1994 book *The Secret War Against the Jews* by John Loftus and Mark Aarons for more details on this matter. In fact, this particular book is one of the most comprehensive and informative histories of the decades-old war for oil in the Middle East, focusing heavily on the criminal dealings of the Bush Family.

A load of evidence suggests that the same gang responsible for the murder of JFK were also responsible for the assassinations of Bobby Kennedy (see *The Assassination of Robert Kennedy* by William Turner and Jonn Christian), Martin Luther King (see *Orders To Kill* by William Pepper), and the attempted assassinations of both George Wallace and Ronald Reagan. This shouldn't be surprising. These creeps are not bound by party lines. They are not bound by national borders. They're out to drain as much power and money from the sheeple as inhumanly possible, pure and simple. They don't even think of this as "betraying their country." Countries don't exist to them, and "citizens" are mere fleshy receptacles standing in the way of the greater goal: owning the air and the hemisphere and the stars themselves.

If they have to axe one of their own in the night to attain their goals, as with the political assassination of Richard Nixon (see *Silent Coup* by Len Colodny and Robert Gettlin), they will do so with little hesitation. Eventually these fairweather warriors pulled out of Vietnam, not because "hippies" politely requested they do so, but because they had made as much money out of the situation as they possibly could and decided it was time to go poolside for awhile. (My Lai Mai-Tai, anyone?)

These same thugs were responsible for unnecessary military adventures in Chile, El Salvador, Guatemala, Columbia, Nicaragua, Panama and Iraq. They're still in Afghanistan sinking their fangs through a waist-high carpet of dead bodies to suck the oil directly out of the earth like giant vampires. How much blood is on the hands of these monsters? Check out Michael Ruppert's book *Crossing the Rubicon: The Decline of the Ameri-*

can Empire at the End of the Age of Oil for the answers to that cheery subject. Ruppert used to work with the CIA when he was an LAPD narcotics detective, so he knows what he's talking about. You can get this extremely well-documented tome from www.copvcia.com. Makes a great Christmas present for your loved ones. "I bought this for you, dear. Here's a razor blade to go with it."

Liberals have the tendency to think that these war hound scum are Christians. George W. Bush is as much a Christian as the Marquis de Sade was a day spa masseuse. True Christians are just as angry about their demonic shenanigans as Liberals are. It's time Liberals and Christians (and Muslims and Jews and Buddhists and Labor Unions and socialists and anarchists and even those wacky Libertarians) ban together to put a stake through the heart of the real enemy. Alex Jones has produced a video called *Dark Secrets Inside Bohemian Grove* that presents a small glimpse of what the enemy's peculiar predilections truly are, and they sure ain't "Christian." Dubya may claim he's a Christian, but then again Hitler enthusiastically promoted what he called "positive Christianity." Meanwhile, after hours he was practicing Black Magic in the Castle of Wewelsburg with Himmler and those other delusional occultists (see the well-documented book *Unholy Alliance: A History of Nazi Involvement with the Occult* by Peter Levenda—which includes an illuminating introduction by Norman Mailer, a fascinating read).

The only weapon capable of destroying these fiends is sunlight. Despite the fact that they can't see themselves in mirrors, they're obsessed with appearances—obsessed with the mercurial whims of public opinion. It's the only thing they fear. It's why they spend so much money trying to alter it. They know Dr. Moreau was murdered by his own genetically-engineered slaves—hell, they should; the story was written by one of their own.

The cryptocrats often need to invite people into the fold simply for the purpose of sacrificing them, to assuage the public's need for blood, just like the end of that twisted Christopher Lee film *The Wicker Man* (recommended viewing). This is what happened to Nixon. Despite his aspirations, Nixon was an outsider. He was not a Blueblood, not like Bush, not like Kerry (who are related to each other, 16th cousins three times removed, in a genealogical line that traces all the way back to Vlad the Impaler, the historical inspiration for Bram Stoker's Dracula—and if you don't believe me, check out this AP news story at: www.infowars.com/print/Secret_societies/vladtree. htm.)

Nixon was a poor kid from Yorba Linda who clawed his way to the top, like that psychotic politician in Stephen King's *The Dead Zone*. He served his purpose for a while, was allowed to hang around the grounds and puke on the exotic landscaping, then he was summarily ejected from the premises like an uncouth party crasher. You probably don't realize this, but George Bush Sr. was the man who unofficially "fired" Nixon's ass when he got "too bad for business," as it were. See Chapter 16 of *The Secret War Against the Jews* for a more involved account of these events. (Ironically, George Bush Sr. would become *almost* as bad for business by the time 1992 rolled around. Ah, the wheel turns, my friend, the wheel turns.)

In his article "The Kennedy Assassination: The Nixon-Bush Connection," originally published in Paul Krassner's *The Realist*, available for viewing at http://truedemocracy.net/td2_3/56_nixon-bush.html, Paul Kangas writes:

> According to a biography of Richard Nixon, his close personal and political ties with the Bush family go back to 1941 when Nixon claims he read an ad in an L A. newspaper, placed by a wealthy group of businessmen, led by Prescott Bush, the father of George Bush. They wanted a young, malleable candidate to run for Congress. Nixon applied for the position and won the job. Nixon became a mouthpiece for the Bush group. In fact, Prescott Bush is credited with creating the winning ticket of Eisenhower-Nixon in 1952.

Unfortunately for Nixon, Kennedy came along and whooped his butt in the 1960 Presidential election (admittedly with the help of some dead people voting in Chicago.) Now, how many of you are aware of the fact that Jack Ruby, the very same man who murdered Lee Harvey Oswald, worked as a spy for Nixon in 1947? A FOIA document released by the FBI proves this fact. (See p. 269 of Jim Marrs' book *Crossfire*.) Like Oswald, Ruby himself later ended up dead under rather mysterious circumstances, but not before writing a lengthy letter to a fellow prisoner in which he stated:

> I know that my time is running out... they plan on doing away with [me].... As soon as you get out you must read Texan looks at Lyndon [*A Texan Looks at Lyndon: A Study in Illegitimate Power* by J. Evetts Haley] and it might open your eyes to a lot of things. This man [Johnson] is a Nazi in the worst order. For over a year now they have been doing away with my people....

Later, he told his psychiatrist that the assassination was "an act of overthrowing the government" and that he knew "who had President Kennedy killed.... I am doomed. I do not want to die. But I am not insane. I was framed to kill Oswald." (For these quotes, see the aforementioned *Crossfire* pp. 430-31.) Ruby died in '67, at the age of fifty-six, less than two years before Nixon finally took the Presidency.

After the public debacle of Watergate destroyed Nixon, the cryptocrats needed someone warm and cuddly like Jimmy Carter to change the tide, to give everybody a false sense of security before they had the real whammy laid on them in the form of Ronald Reagan. Ah, I find myself growing more and more nostalgic for the '80s every day. When you have a president like Reagan, who needs terrorists? Reagan revealed the true sympathies of his masters on May 5, 1985, when he kneeled down in front of those Nazi graves in Bitburg, Germany, clutching a wreath in his arthritic hands, and muttered prayers in honor of a cemetery packed with the corpses of Waffen S.S. death squad soldiers, later explaining away his actions by saying the Nazis were "victims just as surely as the victims in the concentration camps." I choose to interpret this act as Reagan's symbolic surrender of the United States to the Sixth Reich.

People say, "Oh, how can anyone keep such a huge conspiracy secret all these years?" Well, the simple answer to that question is: They didn't keep it a secret. That's how I'm able to tell *you* about it. Most of these conclusions can be drawn from reading the newspaper and accessing available government documents. To tell you the truth, it's not necessary to call it a "conspiracy." You could just as easily call it, "Business As Usual."

Is there hope for change? Of course there's hope. As Marshall McLuhan once said, "There is absolutely no inevitability as long as there is a willingness to contemplate what is happening." Or as Buckminster Fuller said, "Human beings always do the intelligent thing, after they've exhausted all the stupid alternatives." Unfortunately, stupidity isn't as scarce as oil.

Thank you for your time, my friends, and God bless the United States of America.

But then, doesn't He always?

Yours sincerely,
Robert Guffey, 32°

CHAPTER SEVENTEEN

GEORGE W. BUSH IS NOT
A CHRISTIAN

So one day Jesus Christ (Our Lord and Savior) and Leo Strauss stroll into the Oval Office....

It could be the beginning of a joke. Instead it represents the beginning of the systematic massacre of the First Amendment of the U.S. Constitution, the rollback of civil rights, and the violent rape of the high ideals of the signers of the U.S. Constitution. Blues.

We all know Jesus Christ (if not personally, then by reputation), but many fewer of you know the name Leo Strauss. Strauss' influence on recent U.S. foreign policy is slowly coming to light. A number of neoconservatives, who have molded U.S. foreign policy in the first decade of the new millennium to apocalyptic effect, were either former students of Strauss or devotees of his philosophy. Foremost among these "neocons" are Paul Wolfowitz, the Deputy Secretary of Defense, Richard Perle, former Chairman of George W. Bush's Defense Policy Board, Vice-President Dick Cheney, Irving Kristol, who popularized the term "Neoconservative" in his 1983 book *Reflections of a Neoconservative*, and Irving's son William, founder of the influential think tank Project for a New American Century.

During a 2006 interview on CNN, Alexander Haig, former Secretary of State for the Reagan administration, accused the neocons of having "hijacked" the Republican Party. Of the Iraq War he said, "This is a conflict that's essentially political. It's not just purely military. It's political and religious and ideological. And it was driven by the so-called neocons that hijacked my party, the Republican Party." (The full transcript of this interview can be found here: http://edition.cnn.com/TRAN-SCRIPTS/0610/22/le.01.html.) The "hijackers" Haig named specifically were Dick Cheney, Paul Wolfowitz, and Richard Perle. These three men have in common an adherence to the teachings of Leo Strauss.

When discussing Strauss' influence on their way of thinking, the neocons inexplicably revert to a kind of rhapsodic enthusiasm, near-orgasmic joy rarely seen in their writing even when they're speaking of subjects close to their heart, like killing thousands of innocent people in the Middle East merely to line their pockets with more cash. Irving Kristol writes, "Encountering Strauss' work produced the kind of intellectual shock that is a once-in-a-lifetime experience. He turned one's intellectual universe upside down" (7). Kristol elaborates:

> [I]n the United States... the writings of Leo Strauss have been extraordinarily influential. Strauss' critique of the destructive elements within modern liberalism, an analysis that was popularized by his students... has altered the very tone of public discourse in the United States.... To bring contemporary liberalism into disrepute... is no small achievement. (379-80)

Strauss' central beliefs are crucial to understand if one wishes to penetrate to the heartmeat core of the neocons' duplicitous policies. Essentially, Strauss believed the vast majority of the human race was so unequipped to handle the disturbing truths of the universe that they needed to be spoonfed pretty lies in order to endure their inferior existences. On the other hand, what he called "the philosophers" (i.e., Strauss and his academic cronies) represent that rare breed of individual who can face the truth "that there is no God, that the universe cares nothing for men or mankind, and that all of human history is nothing more than an insignificant speck in the cosmos, which no sooner began, than it will vanish forever without a trace. There is no morality, no good or evil..." (Papert 52). According to Strauss these philosophers must feed the ignorant with the "religious, moral and other beliefs they require" in order to survive. But they do this not out of benevolence. No, Strauss is clear on this point: The duty of the "philosopher" is to use his superior intellect to manufacture falsehoods "to shape society in the interest of [the] 'philosophers' themselves" (Papert 52). This is the only route to take, Strauss believed, if truth was to survive.

Irving Kristol comments on this facet of Strauss' philosophy:

> What made him so controversial with the academic community was his disbelief in the Enlightenment dogma that "the truth will make men free." He was an intellectual aristocrat who thought that the truth could make *some* minds free, but he was convinced that there was an inherent conflict between philosophic truth and the political order, and that the popularization and vulgarization of these truths might import unease, turmoil and the release of popular passions hitherto held in check by tradition and religion. (8)

Allow me to translate. What Kristol is really saying is this: "If us rulers were to openly admit to the masses, 'You're all a bunch of sheep and you're here to serve us, because we're better than you, so kiss my butt,' the masses might get a bit riled by such a comment and actually rise up and hang all of us assholes from lampposts." Needless to say, the neocons don't wish this to happen. In order to prevent it, therefore, dissimulation is absolutely necessary.

Strauss believed the philosopher must write his books in such a dense, esoteric style that its true secrets would be clear only to the initiated. Since the truth is so dangerous, it can't be put in the hands of the naïve and the profane. The style of the book must be doubly-coded in such a way that the few novices who even attempt to understand it would merely come away from the book shaking their heads in bewilderment and bored dismay. As Strauss himself once wrote, in a rare and paradoxi-cal moment of clarity, "[A]n author who wishes to address only thoughtful men has but to write in such a way that only a very careful reader can detect the meaning of his book" (*Persecu-tion and the Art of Writing* 25).

Strauss believed government policies should be designed in this manner. Just as Strauss' texts were doubly-coded, the exec-utive branch must operate in a similarly kabbalistic fashion if it is to do what is necessary for the stability of political life. While the masses are treated to the amusing and mundane caperings of an exoteric dog-and-pony show, beneath the surface oper-ate the esoteric centers of power: the philosophers themselves. These "wise men" represent government's esoteric underside. The exoteric side, meanwhile, is represented by what he called "the gentlemen."

> ...[T]he philosophers require various sorts of people to serve them, including the "gentlemen".... Rather than the "esoteric," or secret teachings, the future "gentlemen" are indoctrinated in the "exoteric," or public teachings. They are taught to believe in religion, morality, patrio-tism, and public service, and some go into government.... Of course, along with these traditional virtues, they also believe in the "philosophers" who have taught them all these good things.
>
> Those "gentlemen" who become statesmen... continue to take the advice of the philosophers. This rule of the philosophers through their front-men in government, is what Strauss calls "the secret kingdom" of the philoso-phers, a "secret kingdom" which is the life's objective of many of Strauss' esoteric students. (Papert 52-53)

Which, of course, brings us to George W. Bush and to Jesus Christ.

According to Strauss, philosophy has disproved the tenets of Christianity and all other religions. Nonetheless, he recognized these religions had many uses. "[C]ivil government," he wrote, "is not in itself sufficient for orderly corporate life within society.

Religion is a regulator of order in social life.... It is... a code of law prescribed for the many by higher intelligences" (*Spinoza's Critique of Religion* 47). The "gentleman" would have to be someone schooled in the basic tenets of religious teachings, someone with the ability to rattle off dogma for rhetorical purposes while functioning as the mouth piece of the wise men.

Professor Hugh Urban of Ohio State University has recently published a brilliant analysis of Strauss' influence on the Bush regime titled "Religion and Secrecy in the Bush Administration: The Gentleman, the Prince, and the Simulacrum" in which he offers a concise summary of the overlapping ideologies of Strauss and the neocon movement:

> His appeal [for the neocons], I think, centers around four main ideas: 1) his sense that the modern Western world is in a state of intense "crisis," which is due in large part to the dangerous weaknesses within modern liberal democracy; 2) his emphasis on secrecy and esotericism, or the art of writing and reading between the lines; 3) his belief that religion is necessary for the coherence and stability of society, even though the philosopher or wise man has transcended such "noble lies"; and 4) his description of the "gentleman," the public figure or politician who embodies the ideals of religious faith and virtue, and so serves as the liaison between the wise men and the common populace. (14)

Urban suggests that George W. Bush was tapped by the neocons for the express purpose of serving as this "liaison." Bush, himself, need not understand a single word of Strauss to function in this specialized capacity, and Bush knows this. Bush is well aware of his severe intellectual limitations and never even believed he could win public office. His good friend and Yale classmate, Roland Betts, once quoted Bush as saying: "You know, I could run for governor but I'm basically a media creation. I've never done anything. I've worked for my dad. I worked in the oil business. But that's not the kind of profile you have to have to get elected to public office" (Hatfield 95). What Bush saw as a limitation became his strength in the eyes of the Straussian neocons. When Strauss defines his conception of the "gentleman," he's essentially talking about a media creation: "The gentleman... is the political reflection or imitation of the wise man" (*Natural Rights and History* 142)—an imitation that is easily manipulated from behind the scenes.

Of course, numerous commentators have accused Vice-President Cheney of being the prime manipulator of the President's actions since before Bush was even elected. When directly asked about this by a reporter from *USA Today*, Cheney replied, "Am I the evil genius in the corner that nobody ever sees come out of his hole? It's a nice way to operate, actually" (Engelhardt). Apparently, the Straussians are well aware of the simple fact that sometimes telling the truth can be far more effective than prevaricating.

If the administration's collaboration with the evangelical Christian movement is merely a false front, is it then logical to assume that these religious leaders are having little or no effect on Bush's actual policies? Absolutely not, for the neocons are skillfully manipulating the evangelical community to accomplish a very specific goal—and vice versa. The evangelicals have always had a perverse desire to witness Christ's return to the Holy Land in their lifetime, preferably in the form of an apocalyptic showdown between the forces of God and Satan (or Good and Evil, concepts the Straussians claim don't even exist) in the cradle of civilization. The neocons certainly know this, and have manipulated the religious obsessions of these evangelicals to push their selected "gentleman" into the Oval Office, a "gentleman" with the power to conjure forth an insane foreign policy in "the Holy Land" for the express purpose of extracting what the neocons want most out of the Middle East: total domination over the region's oil. As per Leo Strauss' dictums set forth decades ago, they have utilized the religious delusions of the masses to attain the secret desires of the "philosophers"—the hermetic goals of the so-called "wise men" lurking just behind the throne.

Near the end of Dubya's last term in office, more and more Christians began to wake up to the fact that President Bush is an impostor dragging the name of their Savior through the mud. A number of books written by Christians have taken Bush to task for his egregious duplicity, one of the best being *Christian Words, Unchristian Actions* by John Stoddard Klar. If you know any Christians in desperate need of the truth, you might want to give them a copy of this book which is filled with any number of cogent analyses of the Iraq War from a *genuinely* Christian perspective. Here's an example:

> The War in Iraq desecrates Jesus Christ because it has been undertaken by a president and nation who call themselves Christian, while the violence and injustice of that war are akin to the actions of Christ's oppressors— Jesus abhorred violence, and never endorsed its use, even in his own defense. The doctrine of just war is also violated by our country's actions in Iraq. President Bush's Iraq War smacks strongly of unchristian vengeance, was planned from before Bush came into office (the evidence is overwhelming to the willfully-informed), and had no supportable connection to 9/11, weapons of mass destruction, terrorism, or humanitarian liberation. This tremendous waste of life, resources, opportunity (to actually combat terrorism rather than incite it), and American goodwill is demonstrably unchristian, and need not await an outcome in Iraq to be judged accordingly. For under Christ's and God's law, the end does not justify the means. If things deteriorate completely out of control in Iraq, that would not make Christian effort sinful: neither does "success" (however that is measured) bestow God's blessings on an unchristian action. (304-05)

To hear reasoned criticism such as this coming from the mouth of a Christian is refreshing... but also a little shocking these days, for just as the Republican Party has been "hijacked" by the neocons, the entire Christian religion has been hijacked by the fundamentalist evangelicals who believe they have the

God-given right to steamroll over any viewpoint not shared by Pat Robertson's myopic interpretation of the Old Testament. So loud, so obnoxious, so authoritarian are these little crypto-Christian martinets that they have now come to represent the entire religion in many people's minds. And when one dares suggests this to a Christian acquaintance, said individual will invariably reply, "I despise those fundamentalists as much as you do. I think they're embarrassing." And yet said individuals hardly ever speak up in public about their feelings, never refute the hate-mongering words of such philistines as Oral Roberts, Jerry Falwell, George W. Bush and Dick Cheney... the same Dick Cheney who, in December of 2003, mailed out a personalized Christmas card to close friends and colleagues that read, "If a sparrow cannot fall to the ground without His notice, is it probable that an empire can rise without His aid?" (Urban 25).

Of course, the honorable Mr. Cheney does not stop to consider the slippery slope of his analogy, the fact that the term "empire" does not only pertain to the twenty-first century *American* empire, but to all empires of the past... including the Roman empire, the very same one that Jesus and his disciples resisted with all the resources at their disposal.

Cheney's perverse definition of Christianity, one he has carefully molded to fit his imperialist agenda, should be a source of disgust for all Christians, and yet only a few of them have stood up to voice their outrage. Since it's *their* religion that's being manipulated and desecrated, it is *their* job above all others to stand up against these authoritarian warmongers. David Ray Griffin, professor emeritus at the Claremont School of Theology and author of the 2006 book *Christian Faith and the Truth Behind 9/11*, called for his fellow Christians to band together and resist the christo-fascist Bush regime, just as genuine Christians were forced to do in Nazi Germany when Hitler justified his worst actions by claiming he was fighting to restore what he called "positive Christianity" to his homeland (Shirer 234). The number of such Christian resisters grows every day as the fragile lies that led to the Iraq War deteriorate further and further, the outrageous cover stories and propaganda techniques growing so brazen that even the most naïve, flag-waving patriot in Orange County, California is beginning to see through the scam. But these numbers are not enough. They need to evolve, as swiftly as possible, into a mass resistance strong enough to overcome these philosophers manqués, these High Priests of chaos, who have sacrificed thousands of innocent lives in the pursuit of some misguided notion of attaining godhood here on earth in the form of unlimited wealth and power.

Though such a dramatic revolution cannot occur overnight, nonetheless there are other, more modest, ways of combating this wave of christo-fascist terrorism being committed against us continually on the home front. The answer is to stand up to it whenever you encounter it. Don't be afraid of these people. What is there to fear? After all, their own god isn't even on their side.

Works Cited

Engelhardt, Tom. "Flushing Cheney." MotherJones.com. 2 Feb. 2004. www.motherjones.com/news/dailymojo/2004/02/02_500.html.

Hatfield, J.H. *Fortunate Son: George W. Bush and the Making of an American President*. New York: Soft Skull Press, 2001.

Klar, John Stoddard. *Christian Words, Unchristian Actions*. Irasburg, Vermont: RevElation Press, 2006.

Kristol, Irving. *Neoconservatism: The Autobiography of an Idea*. New York: Free Press, 1995.

Papert, Tony. "The Secret Kingdom of Leo Strauss." *Children of Satan*. Ed. Lyndon LaRouche PAC. Leesburg: Lyndon LaRouche PAC, 2004. 47-57.

Shirer, William. *The Rise and Fall of the Third Reich*. New York: Simon & Schuster, 1960.

Strauss, Leo. *Natural Rights and History*. Chicago: University of Chicago Press, 1953.

---. *Persecution and the Art of Writing*. Westport: Greenwood Press, 1973.

---. *Spinoza's Critique of Religion*. New York: Schocken Books, 1965.

Urban, Hugh. "Religion and Secrecy in the Bush Administration: The Gentleman, the Prince, and the Simulacrum." www.esoteric.msu.edu/VolumeVII/Secrecy.htm.

CHAPTER EIGHTEEN

JESUS IS A ROBOT FROM OUTER SPACE (A STRANGE & PORTENTOUS CASE STUDY IN CREEPING CHRISTO-FASCISM)

I teach English at California State University at Long Beach, and I've been doing so since 2002. After teaching hundreds and hundreds of students over the course of those years, I've finally received *one* complaint. However, this wasn't a complaint from a student. This was a complaint from the *father* of a student, a surprising incident on a campus where the students are adults. This is not high school. And yet apparently somebody, a Jesus freak with a rather limited view of the word "education," decided to take it upon himself to write a letter of complaint directly to the President of the University upon hearing from his daughter that I had said, on the very first day of class, that Jesus was a robot from outer space.

Now, apparently it didn't matter to this individual that I never said such a thing. Nor did it matter to the President of the University. Nor did it matter to the Dean of the English Department. Nor did it matter to the Associate Dean for Curriculum and Personnel. Not one of these people went to the trouble of simply *asking* me what I had actually said.

This is what I said: I visited the Crystal Cathedral in Anaheim, California (also the home of Disneyland, the Happiest Place on Earth) in the company of a friend from New York, the novelist Jack Womack, where we saw a statue of the baby Jesus that was perfectly smooth and silver and reflected sunlight like a mirror. It resembled a robot. I offhandedly mentioned this observation on the first day of school. This comment took up about thirty seconds of class time.

Nobody asked for clarification. Every single one of my "superiors" assumed—because after all, my exact words were quoted secondhand in the letter, weren't they?—that I had authoritatively stated that Jesus Christ was a robot from outer space. Nobody likes being accused of doing something they didn't do, but it's particularly offensive when you're accused of doing something that's A) utterly absurd and B) even if it were true, protected by my rights as a citizen of the United States of America under the First Amendment of the Constitution. Every single functionary I was forced to deal with during the course of this madness acted as if they had never heard of such a document. When I called what is ostensibly my union to ask them what my rights were under these circumstances, I received this response: "We have the utmost respect for the freedom of speech... but you have to watch what you say."

To educate my readers in countries outside the U.S., the First Amendment of the Constitution reads as follows: "Congress shall make no law respecting an establishment of religion, or prohibiting the free exercise thereof; or abridging the freedom of speech, or of the press; or the right of the people peaceably to assemble, and to petition the Government for a redress of grievances." Note the fact that it doesn't say, "Congress shall make no law respecting an establishment of religion, or prohibiting the free exercise thereof; or abridging the freedom of speech, or of the press (but you have to watch what you say.)" Note the fact that it doesn't say, "Congress shall make no law respecting an establishment of religion, or prohibiting the free exercise thereof; or abridging the freedom of speech, or of the press (but you can't say anything negative about Christianity)." Note the fact that it doesn't say, "Congress shall make no law respecting an establishment of religion, or prohibiting the free exercise thereof; or abridging the freedom of speech, or of the press (oh, but you can't say Jesus was a robot from outer space)." It says none of that. I should know because I've become intimately familiar with the First Amendment over the past few months. In fact, I keep a copy on me at all times now, because after all you never know when you might find yourself in a situation where it *won't* come in handy. Like this one.

The reaction of one of my colleagues to this entire incident was illuminating. When I confided in another teacher, a woman who's almost retirement age, her immediate response was to compare me to Adolf Hitler. I found this to be an extreme comparison. With a straight face she told me, "Robots are *below* Man. The last time I looked, Jesus was *above* Man!" [Insert Twilight Zone music here.]

Almost everybody around me told me to act as if none of this had ever happened, to just forget about it... but I couldn't do that. Every attempt to suppress freedom of expression must be challenged. How could I teach my class knowing there was one person in the room who might go home, repeat whatever "objectionable" remark I had made that day, and start the whole nasty process all over again? Such psychological terrorism creates a chilling effect that compels you to second guess every word that comes out of your mouth. You begin contemplating avoiding certain subjects simply because you don't want to embroil the entire school in another controversy. But you can't allow this chilling effect to set in. You must combat it.

After contemplating the situation for some time, I managed to think my way out of the dilemma. I passed out a copy of the First Amendment in class and we analyzed it word for word, just as we would any other piece of writing. I discussed the incident with them, rather than ignoring it, and tied it in with the many attempts to ban Kurt Vonnegut's *Slaughterhouse-Five* (the novel we were reading at that time). I taught them the difference between the signifier and the signified... that the map is not the territory... that icons are not people... that statues are not the same as the figures they're intended to represent. Indeed, I said, if people began to lose sight of the difference, this could very well lead to something called *idolatry*. The last time I looked, the Old Testament had some rather nasty things to say about *idolatry*.

The point seemed to get through to them. And, by extension, to Daddy Dearest. I have no way of knowing what dark thoughts are brewing in the cellars of that gentleman's mind, but nonetheless I haven't received any further complaints since then. Of course, that could change at any moment because, ultimately, I decided not to alter the way I taught the class, despite the fact that my "superiors" strongly advised me to watch my every step. But to do so would be a living death. To do so would be giving the christo-fascists exactly what they want. And if you let these people win without even attempting to fight, then what is the use of the First Amendment? If the First Amendment has no use, if there really is "no more academic freedom," then what use is a university at all? Why are we teaching? To collect a paycheck and eventually retire to a little cabin in the hills outside Apple Valley? Or is it to teach students viewpoints they wouldn't be exposed to otherwise? If we're not going to make even the slightest attempt, at the most microcosmic level, to defend our right to say what we want and teach in the way we think is most beneficial to the students, why don't we just burn down the university and build a prison in its place? If the christo-fascists are allowed to have their way, nobody would even notice the difference.

It's so easy to say nothing. It's so easy to do nothing. And yet the sad irony is that the vast majority of human beings on this planet do not agree with the authoritarian views of the neocons and the christo-fascists. Almost all of my students were shocked that someone had been offended by my offhand comment. Every one of my students agreed that I had not said what I had been accused of saying. One student even came up to me after class and said, "Hey, I'm a Christian and I wasn't offended." But that guy's not going to write a letter to the President of the University praising my teaching methods. Only the christo-fascists seem to exercise their power to speak, their power to vote, their power to change the world around them. They know that action is required to change the world. They are radicals, *true* radicals, and they will stop at nothing until every single person on the planet is either converted to their way of thinking or bombed into tiny, jagged, bloody pieces.

Lebanon and Iraq are being bombed for real, but the United States is no less under attack. It's not Muslim terrorists who pose the greatest threat to America's freedom, but the wolves in *wolves'* clothing who are now stalking the corridors of power, on the hunt for their next prey. And when they've finished gutting the Middle East, don't think for a moment their appetite will have been satiated. Inevitably, they will turn their sights *inward*. And their appetites will have grown much heartier by that point. What is now limited to threats and intimidation and Madison-Avenue-style psychological warfare will evolve into full-fledged, jackbooted parades down the streets of our cities: young, baby-faced soldiers waving the white flag while hefting the severed heads of Muslims into the sky... proclaiming victory in the name of the Prince of Peace while constructing wooden gibbets for the profane and the unholy and the just plain *difficult*... bragging to other countries about the superior freedoms of the West while broadcasting swift executions of dissidents on a Fox Television reality TV show titled "Salvation Through Transmigration" in which unwilling contestants gain the reward of eternal peace by first proclaiming their loyalty to the Lord right before having their heads chopped off by a golden axe held aloft by a priest from Anaheim with a personal computer and a stylized letterhead and a panic-stricken, doting daughter waiting for him in the dungeon at home. Hell, all them letters really paid off, the priest will think, elated by his brand new title, "Homeland Security Theological Grand Inquisitor."

He will intone the final rites for the Accused in the original Latin, then bring the blade down on his neck with an anticlimactic *thunk*....

"No need to be concerned, ladies and gentlemen. These transmigrations are not intended to be punishments. They are rewards. We televise these special events to give you hope for the future, not to instill *fear*. These transmigrations are by no means meant to be interpreted as *threats*. This administration respects the right of freedom of speech as much as any other administration. Yet this is a new world. Times have changed, as I'm sure you'll agree. You have the freedom of speech. You always will.

"But watch what you say.

"And now, ladies and gentlemen, for our next contestant this evening...! Just put your head down right there and confess your sins, beginning with early childhood...."

An exaggeration? Perhaps. But as the Patriot Act is strengthened and the writ of habeas corpus stripped from the Constitution, as the U.S. Senate officially approves torture and black Homeland Security buses with barred windows cruise the streets of my own neighborhood in Long Beach, CA, I really have to wonder if one's worst nightmares are all that far out of reach.

Which is why it's so important to remain steadfast in our opposition to the nightmare by fighting the authoritarian bastards at every level, no matter how small or insignificant or absurd the battle may seem at the time.

Keep a stiff upper lip, chum. The truth will out. As Jesus Christ himself once said (and he said it in red ink, so it must be true), "Nothing is secret that shall not be made manifest" (*Luke* 8:17).

CHAPTER NINETEEN

The Mass Psychology of Fascism in the United States: Wilhem Reich, Adolf Hitler, and the Parallels of Propaganda Between Nazi Germany and Recent U.S. History

"The gun is good, the penis is evil."

—Zardoz, 1973

In 1933 Dr. Wilhelm Reich fled Germany due to the storm of controversy caused by the publication of his book, *The Mass Psychology of Fascism* (Boadella 90). The Nazis decried the book and its author as a threat to the security of Hitler's Germany. This was an accurate statement, for the book studied aspects of the hidden core of German mass psychology that, according to Reich, had helped the National Socialist Party develop. In the book, Reich applies his sex-economic theory to the rise of fascism in Germany. Reich was well aware that this theory was directly opposed to that of Sigmund Freud, who believed economic considerations were completely irrelevant to studies of sexuality and mass psychology (Freud 67). Reich, on the other hand, viewed fascism as the end result of a society whose sexual needs have been stamped out beneath the collective boot of Church and Family. Ironically, Reich's books were later burned *en masse* by the very same nation in which he sought refuge, i.e., the United States of America, another country well known for its hypocritical, and often contradictory, sexual taboos.[1]

Many schools of psychology and philosophy, such as those promoted by intellectual luminaries like Sigmund Freud, Herbert Marcuse and others, theorize that sexual repression inevitably causes a highly regulated, patriarchal society. Reich maintained that sexual repression is the result of such restrictions. What Freud would have attributed to a death instinct in the Germans, Reich attributed to outside repressive forces working in tandem with the fascist ideologies imposed upon the German people by both a male-dominated family structure as well as a religion that draws its most "holy" of inspirations from the image of an innocent man bleeding on a cross. With an icon like that, it's no mystery why Hitler was such a rabidly enthusiastic supporter of "positive" Christianity (Shirer 234).

Recently, modern historians and psychologists have reevaluated both the positions of Wilhelm Reich and traditional psychoanalysis on the subject of fascism. Writers like Janine Chasseguet-Smirgel and Béla Grunberger have supported some of Reich's conclusions about fascism, but take umbrage with his anti-Freudianism stance. They imply that Freud is a destroyer of illusions, a realist, whereas the people who support Reich are merely idealists with their heads in the clouds. Meanwhile, a behaviorist might claim that Freud's theories are equally fanciful considering the fact that the "id," the "ego," and the "super-

---

1   See Chapter 31 of Myron Sharaf's biography *Fury On Earth* for further details on the burning of Reich's books in the United States.

ego" are theoretical constructs that cannot be traced back to the central nervous system. Such arguments are virtually endless, and will no doubt continue for a long time. However, it should be pointed out that Reich is not as idealistic or "illusionary" as Chasseguet-Smirgel and Grunberger seem to believe. His theories of fascism do not lay the blame of Nazism solely on Hitler's shoulders. He does not claim that Hitler waved a magic wand and hypnotized the German people into following his every order; far from it. He decries those who would use the term "Nazi-psychosis" to explain the horrors of World War II.

Reich claims that the success of a fuhrer can only be possible if his point of view, his ideology, strikes a responsive chord in the middle class. Obviously, if a broad category of individuals find someone like Hitler repugnant, then that potential fuhrer will simply wither on the vine, never reaching his full bloom. In 1982 Ira H. Cohen published a re-evaluation of both Reich and Freud, called *Ideology and Unconsciousness*, in which he agreed with Reich's unique observation that the middle class is usually the least likely to resist the authority of dictators (who attempt to exploit all classes, but definitely some more than others). In a capitalist society, Reich said, division of labor requires a certain amount of cooperation among workers, whereas middle class employees are more separated from each other, alienated in their high-security, gingerbread houses, and thus develop a far more rigid personality, one that almost yearns for an authoritarian figure like Hitler to draw it out of isolation from behind a cocoon of fear and hatred shielding it against the "taint" of anyone who does not fit the status quo.

This status quo often includes a neurotic repression of sexuality, and Reich went so far as to blame the rise of fascism on this repression. The Freudian psychoanalyst Herbert Marcuse believed Reich was correct in linking the growth of fascism with instinctual, mass repression; however, he disagreed with Reich's claim that the defeat of fascism could be brought about through sexual liberation (Marcuse 130). Marcuse countered that an authoritarian society could advance a great deal with a sexually liberated populace; indeed, it could feed on it quite effectively. Unfortunately for Marcuse, he makes a rather unbelievable leap of faith in comparing authoritarian capitalism with fascism. Perhaps Marcuse is correct in this comparison, but since Reich didn't see it that way, it has no place in his evaluation of Reich's work. Reich was more interested in the psychological contradictions that arise out of a capitalist economic crisis and the dominance of one culture over another in that same system. As Cohen points out, Marcuse's interpretation of Reich's theories—particularly those concerning fascism—falters somewhat when he says that Reich found the *root* of fascism in mass repression. With this statement, Marcuse seems to be attempting to reign in Reich's theories in order to force them into his pre-existing, Freudian model. Reich believed this repression was a precondition for the average middle class individual to identify with a fascist fuhrer, not the *root* of it.

Marcuse further says that the freeing of sexual inhibitions, as Reich spoke of it, could just as easily work *for* the status quo rather than against it. He based this idea on the fact that behaviors that are at one time considered sinful can then become acceptable as long as enough people start engaging in the activity. After all, that's how lynch mobs are formed. If pleasure can be manipulated by the people in power, Marcuse said, it can encourage submissiveness among the middle class just as easily as repression of pleasure. Aldous Huxley presented the same concept in his 1932 dystopian novel *Brave New World*, in which a sexual game called Centrifugal Bumplepuppy is used to control children beginning in early adolescence. Marcuse admits that sexuality can be a revolutionary force, but he doesn't go as far as Reich, whose basic conclusion about fascism is that it cannot exist in a matriarchal society unhindered by sexual repression. Unlike Marcuse, Reich's views are echoed by novelists who weren't even born when he first published his study on fascism. In 1975 the acclaimed feminist writer Joanna Russ published a utopian novel titled *The Female Man*, in which a society of women reproduce without the help of men;

not coincidentally, there is no war in this hypothetical society. Perhaps this is a vindicatory sign, showing that Reich's controversial theories were not "insane," as Paul A. Robinson claimed in his 1969 study *The Freudian Left*, but merely forty-two years ahead of their time.

Robinson is not alone in his opinion of Reich, however. In a 1995 review of *Beyond Psychology*, a collection of Reich's letters, Rosemary Dinnage referred to him as "an interesting lunatic" (Dinnage 13). A similar view was held by Richard Morrock in a 1992 article for the international journal *The Skeptical Inquirer* (Morrock 237-9). *Psychology Today*, in a kindlier mood, simply referred to him as "troubled" (Simon 70-1). Not surprisingly, after scouring through more than a dozen recent reviews, the few publications that gave Reich any serious attention at all were David Jones' *New Dawn*, Jim Martin's *Flatland*, and Kenn Thomas' *Steamshovel Press*, magazines that have all been accused of being outlandish "conspiracy tabloids" by the mainstream press.

For proof that Reich was not "insane"—or even "troubled"—when he identified sexual repression as a significant factor in the rise of fascism, a mere cursory study of the propaganda used during World War II will suffice. Sexual overtones were evident in the propaganda used by the Axis powers as well as by the Allies. Reich never limited his criticism to just Germany. He found the patriarchal paradigm in most of the "civilized" world. Reich believed that fascism was possible anywhere. Perhaps this was his most important message, the one that perplexed his critics above all others. He was not willing to condemn the German people as uniquely "sick," nor did he relieve them of their guilt by claiming they were victims of Nazi propaganda. The fact that the propaganda techniques used by the Nazis were essentially no different from those used by the Americans shows that Reich was correct. As Walt Kelly once wrote, "We have met the enemy, and he is us." So let's peer into the face of the enemy....

You're an American GI and you're stationed far from home. You haven't eaten a decent meal in months. Off in the distance, enemy artillery shells pierce the night with the obnoxious abruptness of crude machinery. You're crouched in a foxhole and the taste of dust coats your mouth. Beside you lay the bodies of men no older than yourself. They were living and breathing only moments ago. Though you really don't want to, something forces you to glance at your fallen compatriots out of the corner of your eye. What you see are empty sacks of flesh stained with the slick brightness of blood. What's all this for? you think. What the hell is all this for? You want to be far away from here. For a moment you close your eyes and try—try so *hard*—to imagine that you're flying far, far away from this place… but a loud concussion nearby jerks you out of your reverie, as if you were a puppet pulled to a fighting stance by flimsy strings. In this case, the strings are called fear and patriotism. If you've been properly indoctrinated by the propaganda of your country, you will not run away from that foxhole—you will not fly away—no, you'll stay there and fight to the death for "God and country." That is, if the patriotism overrides your fear; if the strings have been sufficiently tightened around your joints… tightened ever so slowly since the day of your birth.

How does the state ensure the tightness of your strings? Through propaganda, of course. As William Burroughs stated in his 1959 novel *Naked Lunch*, whoever controls the Reality Studio controls the perceptions of the masses. During wartime, the operators in the Reality Studio must begin working overtime. Reality is reduced to its most primal level; it's transformed into an ideological stance between binary opposites. White is Us and black is Them and there is no room for discussion, because discussion might lead to reason and reason might lead to a joining of forces and a mass raid on the Reality Studio. That's the last thing the operators of the Studio want. So they furtively push their buttons and crank their levers and churn out juicy material like—

This: You're an American GI staring at a full color painting reduced to the size of a small flyer. It depicts an Anglo female staring up at the heavens with woeful, imploring, doe-like eyes. Her hands are tied behind her back. Her Nazi captors are marching in the background. Behind *them* stand more females, all of whom are completely naked and huddled together behind a wire fence like cattle. However, the most eye-catching aspect of the painting is the fact that the rope-strewn woman in the foreground possesses an improbably large pair of milk-producing glands that defy all the laws of gravity and probably a number of other laws not under discussion at the moment. These glands are strategically hanging out of her torn blouse (presumably after having undergone the brute attentions of the Nazi soldiers behind her) and are pointing downward at four bold-faced words: DELIVER US FROM EVIL.

As author Sam Keen has pointed out, the most ironic aspects of this flyer are its psychological contradictions. On one hand its intended viewer (a U.S. soldier) is supposed to feel disgust and anger toward the violent and prurient activities of the German soldiers depicted in the flyer, and yet on the other hand they are also supposed to be drawn to its message by the pornographic "bait" of the half-dressed woman waiting for ol' G. I. Joe to "deliver" her from the German rapists. Fear and patriotism are effective and binding puppet strings. The operators of the Reality Studio know that sex must be entwined about these strings in order to enforce their hold on the subject, which any successful advertiser of the modern age could tell you—as could Wilhelm Reich.

Of course, one might accurately point out that since this is ostensibly a study of German propaganda, the preceding example—a product of fine, star-spangled, "Amurican" minds—could be considered slightly off-base and irrelevant. However, it could just as easily be said that studying German propaganda while ignoring its American counterpart would be tantamount to separating inextricably linked forces like yin and yang, good and evil, fire and water, King Kong and Fay Wray. Even little kids playing "Cowboys and Indians" know that the act of choosing sides is merely an arbitrary gesture, a necessary ritual that precedes the *real* game.

Which brings us to two pivotal events of propaganda in Hitler's Germany. What follows are archetypal examples of provocation that transcend national boundaries. These methods did not die with Nazi Germany. If the reader manages to draw any point at all from this chapter, it should be the eight words that preceded this sentence. What advertisers know better than anything else is that if something works, plow it into the ground; the public won't ever grow tired of it. Propaganda (or "international communications," as the cryptocrats like to call it) techniques never go out of style. They've changed little, if at all, since 1933 when Hitler was furiously attempting to push the Weimar Republic into fascism.

In 1933 the National Socialist Party manipulated the paranoid fear the German aristocratic establishment had of the Communist threat, persuading them to hop in bed with Uncle Hitler, who was quickly handed the chancellorship that he needed in order to retain the devotion of his followers. No doubt, when the royalists agreed to make Hitler the Chancellor, they were probably already looking ahead to some indefinite point in the future when they could oust this rapscallion with the funny moustache and replace him with someone who would be far less troublesome. Unfortunately, the royalists were unable to see the Reichstag fire looming in their future.

On the evening of February 27, 1933, the Reichstag (the Weimar Republic Seat of government) exploded into flames with the generous help of the Nazis. The building was devastated within a matter of hours. Hitler blamed a Communist sympathizer who quickly "confessed" after being subjected to the gallant and cavalier questioning methods of the Nazis. Hitler then used the fire to persuade the panicked members of the Reichstag to pass a series of laws that suspended all Constitutional protections. Soon after, on March 23, 1933, the Reichstag voted itself out of existence, thus transferring all political power into the hands of the Fuhrer (Harris Lecture).

The Reichstag fire was a brilliant act of provocation, not unlike the Nazis' subsequent Operation Canned Meat. Under this operation one hell of an unlucky group of concentration camp inmates were clothed in Polish military uniforms and marched to a town bordering Poland where they met a bloody fate at the hands of their S.S. guards, some of whom (appropriately enough) were then shot by *other* guards in order to create the illusion that Poland had attacked Germany. German radio announced this brash act of "Polish barbarism," following which the Nazis—no doubt with brassy Wagnerian strains echoing between their Aryan skulls—Valkyried into the "invading" country and wiped out the imaginary perpetrators of an imaginary crime (Emory). Clearly, this is the archetypal example of false terrorist provocation/propaganda used to justify imperialistic expansionism.

The reason Hitler was able to successfully pull off an act of psychological warfare like Operation Canned Meat was because the German people had essentially allowed him to burn down the Reichstag. The lies of propaganda tend to support each other in intricate ways that are, perhaps, often not even originally intended by the perpetrators. The propaganda somehow takes on a life of its own.

The most puzzling aspect of these operations is how the German people—or any population, for that matter—could allow themselves to be deceived by such obvious acts of psychological warfare. Inadequate is Hitler's famous dictum, later adapted by Goebbels, that the bigger the lie, the easier it will be believed. It doesn't matter if this comment is valid or not, for if the people had simply asked themselves the time-honored question memorized by any political scientist, "*Cui bono?*"(i.e., "Who benefits?") they surely would have arrived at the core truth hiding behind both the Reichstag fire and Operation Canned Meat. Unfortunately, most of them never even allowed themselves to ask such a question. A fascist government has total, final power when it can control not the answers, but the *questions*.

According to Reich, it's not enough to say that Hitler had excellent propaganda and therefore the essentially Pollyanna-like populace fell for Hitler's illusions like a tourist losing cash to a street corner card shark. After all, there's no such beast as a victim who doesn't play a part in his own victimization. It is easy for someone who was not alive during World War II to sit back, lift his feet up onto his mahogany desk, plant his hands behind his head and say wonderingly, "Gee, I can't figure out how those stupid Germans allowed themselves to be fooled by that monster, Adolf Hitler. What a terrible aberration in human history. Hmm, I wonder what's on CNN tonight." The propaganda techniques that Hitler used, all of which were masterfully constructed to appeal to the same repressive elements that Reich correctly identified in his study, have changed very little since 1933. The rhetoric, the costumes, the lights, the parades, the sound and the fury, are all standard elements of any political rally found in the world today. The hateful rhetoric has been stripped down, of course, but not by much.

Examples are abundant. You can simply dip your hands into a pile of headlines and come up with a number of eerie parallels between the Weimar Republic of 1933 and the recent history of the United States. Just the phrase "Homeland Security" alone is enough to dredge up nightmarish, genetic memories of Dachau and Belsen pumping black smoke into an overcast German sky. The architects of the Patriot Act have used the events of 9/11 as an excuse to repeal America's most basic civil rights. In 2003 Hollywood producer Ed Gernon was fired by CBS because he dared to compare the climate of paranoia in the final days of the Weimar Republic—a climate that helped propel Hitler to power—with the paranoia running rampant in George W. Bush's post-9/11 America. Appropriately enough, Gernon had just completed a drama for CBS about Hitler's rise to power when he made this statement (*Los Angeles Times* 4-14-03). In 1988 Presidential candidate George Herbert Walker Bush used almost identical language to Hitler when he tried to stir up a cacophony of nationalism around the flag-burning debate.

The scapegoating of illegal immigrants under Prop. 187 during Pete Wilson's reign as the Governor of California was a mirror reflection of Hitler's tirades against gypsies and Jews. (Given this fact, is it any mystery why Wilson was one of the main "advisors" to Governor Arnold Schwarzenegger?) The targeting of welfare programs by both Republicans and Democrats incorporates Hitler's concept of "useless eaters" into their "bipartisan," "cooperative" agenda. The *New York Times* bestseller *The Bell Curve* resurrected the notion that blacks are naturally inferior to whites. Even more disturbing is the fact that the average "uneducated" blue collar worker wasn't buying *The Bell Curve*; the book's readers were professors, business executives, and no doubt members of Mensa, a society consisting of people with high I.Q.s, whose official journal recently advocated the idea of engineering a "master race" (Saunders). This racist idea is not new to America. After all, Hitler derived his T-4 program—which led directly to the Final Solution—from America's own sterilization and euthanasia laws advocated by infinitely wise and oh-so-learned social scientists who were the darlings of the American intellectual establishment at that time (Kuhl). Compounded with that sad fact is the U.S. military's infamous research into the development of chemical-biological weaponry targeted toward specific ethnic groups (Larson 3-11).

With racist programs like these inextricably woven into the social fabric of the United States, it doesn't take a Nazi rocket scientist to deduce the true roots of the hate crimes against Blacks, Jews and homosexuals that rose dramatically in L.A. county during the Bush regime (*Los Angeles Times* 8-24-01). Nor does it take a tenured psychologist to diagnose the pathological masochism that led the people of California—the state graced with the largest population in the U.S.—to elect the imported progeny of an Austrian Nazi to "govern" them with a gentle but firm fist; to take each of them by their trembling hand and lead them out of a downward-spiraling recession by eliminating funding for education and any social programs intended to help that vast section of the populace known as the "working poor," many of whom willingly voted for a mediocre actor whose primary goal is to make life as difficult as possible for them. Finally, is it any surprise that the same country which recruited hundreds of Nazis into its Office of Strategic Services after World War II for purposes of supplying the Pentagon with intelligence on the Soviet Union (Simpson, *Blowback*) should also become increasingly obsessed with militarizing every aspect of its civilian life, whether it be "The War On Drugs" or "The War On Cancer" or "The War On Domestic Violence" or "The War On Guns" or "The War On Terrorism?" No doubt "The War On War" is next on the agenda. As Peter Drucker has pointed out in his book *The End of Economic Man*, the rise of fascism in Germany was preceded by similar social trends.

The most notorious recent example of the sadomasochistic pathology that can result from allowing oneself to become ossified mentally by an authoritarian regime is the tragedy of Abu Ghraib. Interrogators trained by Army officers and the CIA have tortured "suspected terrorists" at Abu Ghraib prison in Iraq in ways that can only be described as blatantly psycho-sexual in nature. (I refer you to Kurt Nimmo's 2004 article "Inside the Cells of Abu Ghraib: The CIA Privatized Torture"—available at www. counterpunch.org—for in-depth reportage on how far the CIA is willing to go to wrench unreliable, worthless information from its detainees.) One need only see the photographs of prisoners being led around on leashes like dogs by government-funded dominatrices to realize that Reich's theories were a lot closer to the truth than his peers in the psychiatric community wished to admit while he was still alive.

One should never dismiss the theories of Freud entirely, however. Listen to this classic Freudian slip by the Commander-in-Chief himself. Asked on 5-13-04 to comment on the revelations regarding the "Baghdad Correctional Facility," the President said: "Like you, I have been disgraced about what I've seen on TV that took place in prison." Of course, he meant to say "disgusted," not "disgraced," but the latter word more accurately describes the President's knowledge of what was really happening in Baghdad.

Sadly, we could go on with such sad and silly examples all day. Why don't we just stop now and forget all this? Let's bury our heads in the oil-soaked sands of Iraq instead.... Ah, that's much more comfortable.

So. Looks like we've reached the end together, haven't we? The moral of this peripatetic treatise is as follows: Any historical analysis of the mass psychology of Nazi Germany must obviously be viewed In terms of the mass psychology and propaganda of the society in which the historian finds herself. If not, she will become blind to the true significance of the information she is gathering. Or as William Faulkner once wrote, "The past is never dead and buried. In fact, it's never even past."

Then again, why not just ignore the depressing lessons of the past and focus entirely on the present (on that $6 creamy chocolate latté sitting in front of you right now; or that brand new sports car you're planning to snap up at a steal; or the mortgage payment that's due at the beginning of next month; or the expensive surgery your pet dachshund needs; or on the pregnancy test your girlfriend just got back from the clinic—the only clinic in the United States that hasn't yet been blown away by The Massachusetts Citizens For Life, that is)? Hey, don't worry about it. The past is past, right? Nothing you can do about it. Just be here now. You'll get along fine. There are plenty of TV shows and entertaining advertisements on the air to occupy your attention, so you certainly won't be bored. After all, as Reich himself might have said if he'd been brilliant enough to think of it: You're never bored when you're a masochist.

Works Cited

Boadella, David. *Wilhelm Reich: The Evolution of His Work*. New York: Dell, 1973.

Burroughs, William. *Naked Lunch*. New York: Grove Weidenfeld, 1959.

Chasseguet-Smirgel, Janine and Béla Grunberger. *Freud or Reich?: Psychoanalysis and Illusion*. New Haven: Yale University Press, 1986.

Cohen, Ira. *Ideology and Unconsciousness*. New York: New York University Press, 1982.

Dinnage, Rosemary. "Sex Was Everything." *The New York Times Book Review*. 25 Jan. 1995: 13-14.

Drucker, Peter. *The End of Economic Man*. New York: The John Day Co., 1939.

Emory, David. *One Step Beyond*. FYI Radio. KFJC, Los Altos Hills. 19 Feb. 1995.

Freud, Sigmund. New Introductory Lectures on Psychoanalysis. New York: W.W. Norton, 1965.

Harris, Suzanne. "The Secret Side of G.A.T.T." Pacifica Radio. KPFK, Los Angeles. 24 Nov. 1994.

Huxley, Aldous. *Brave New World*. New York: Harper & Row, 1932.

Keen, Sam. *Faces of the Enemy: Reflections of the Hostile Imagination*. New York: Harper & Row, 1988.

Kuhl, Stephan. *The Nazi Connection: Eugenics, American Racism, and German National Socialism*. Oxford University Press, 1994.

Larson, Carl A. "Ethnic Weapons." *Military Review*. Vol. L, No. 11, Nov. 1970.

Marcuse, Herbert. *Counterrevolution and Revolt*. Boston: Beacon Press, 1972.

Morrock, Richard. "Orgonomists Meet in Princeton." *The Skeptical Inquirer*. Vol. 16 (1992): 237-9.

Reich, Wilhelm. *The Mass Psychology of Fascism*. New York: Farrar, Straus & Giroux, 1971.

Robinson, Paul. *The Freudian Left*. New York: Harper & Row, 1969.

Russ, Joanna. *The Female Man*. New York: Bantam, 1975.

Saunders, Deborah. "Death Instead of Taxes." *The San Francisco Chronicle*. 13 Jan. 1995.

Sharaf, Myron. *Fury On Earth: A Biography of Wilhelm Reich*. New York: Da Capo P, 1994.

Shirer, William. *The Rise and Fall of the Third Reich*. New York: Simon & Schuster, 1960.

Simon, Linda. "Hot-blooded Wilhelm Reich." *Psychology Today*. Vol. 23 (1989): 70-1.

Simpson, Christopher. *Blowback*. New York: Weidenfeld & Nicolson, 1988.

Zardoz. Dir. John Boorman. TCF/John Boorman, 1973.

CHAPTER TWENTY

THE END OF HISTORY
AND THE
CLASH OF CIVILIZATIONS

Tony Alamo, the Prophet of Hollywood Blvd.

On December 17, 2007, I was standing on the corner of Hollywood and Cahuenga Blvd., waiting for a bus and thinking about the coming new year—about prophecies and predictions, about nonexistent catastrophes foretold by visionaries whose neurons were plugged into the Godhead— when an old man hobbled right up to me and handed me a flyer titled "Tony Alamo Christian Ministries World Newsletter." The flyer is subtitled "New Jerusalem Churches Worldwide." Beneath the subtitle is a color photograph of famed country-western singer and unrepentant marijuana connoisseur Willie Nelson chatting it up with Pastor Tony Alamo backstage at the Grand Ole Opry in Nashville, Tennessee. Mr. Alamo is wearing a pair of dark glasses. Perhaps to hide the stoned twinkle in his eye? One wouldn't want to speculate about such matters any further. Beside the photograph is the beginning of the pastor's article titled "Brace Yourselves." The article begins, as follows:

> Any time now, a worldquake and a series of prophesied catastrophes will shockingly awaken the entire global population to a horrible, God-sent, unparalleled nightmare.

Shortly after this event, two more disasters in the form of two large meteorites will follow, causing more destruction than many hydrogen bombs. One will smash into the ocean, destroying a third of it, including the life therein. It will actually turn the water to blood and, of course, destroy all life and every ship within its realm. The second meteorite will barrel into and flatten a great part of an entire continent, polluting a third of the rivers and fountains, making them poisonous (wormwood). Many men will die of these waters. Following this, an estimated two billion people, one-third of the earth's population, will be killed by fire, smoke, and lava-like brimstone.

Once these plagues begin, life will never again be lived as we know it today. Just before this incredible, unspeakable, several-month-long nightmare, most people will be on their boring, everyday treadmill of work, school, and housecleaning. Some will be going to their social or political activities, looking for new forms of entertainment, buying, selling, planning, etc. Some will be planning or pursuing their routine of daily or nightly promiscuities, or making their usual plans to foolishly spend their paychecks on Friday and Saturday....

Then, to the woe and dismay of everyone in the world, Jesus, who is commonly and falsely today known as "sweet Jesus," will abruptly, without notice, turn the world upside down in a moment and literally tear it to pieces. Again, one-third of this world's population will be annihilated, then millions upon millions more will be killed in the most dreadful ways, ways that could never be imagined or dreamed of by the human mind.

For the sake of convenience I've taken the liberty of eliminating the footnotes citing the exact passages in the Bible that supposedly back up every one of the pastor's proclamations. If you really need to see them, however, I'm sure you can get hold of a copy of the pamphlet in question by calling the pastor's twenty-four hour prayer and information line: 479-782-7370. You can call it collect, or at least that's what it says here.

The good pastor goes on to state, "All of the world conditions are in the exact position that the Bible stated they would be in when these events would take place." It's important to note that the Rapture-obsessed bestselling author Hal Lindsey said almost the same thing way back in 1970 when he published *The Late Great Planet Earth*. Of course, Lindsey also mentioned in one of his '70s grimoires that the Xerox machine was an invention of the Devil. There's no word yet on his opinion regarding email or mapquest.

Needless to say, the world's been coming to an end for quite a long time. It's very easy to poke fun at people who are clearly insane. There's no trick to that. But what about people who don't appear to be insane? What about people who possess Ph.D.s and official titles and wrap their hateful, apocalyptic scenarios in the language of political science?

Let's set aside the predictions of seers and mountebanks for a moment and focus instead on the predictions of those who actually pull the strings in this global village of ours. While the perceptions of the crowd are manipulated daily by the mad magicians of Madison Avenue and Wall Street, the perceptions of Those At the Top are just as easily shaped by their own form of idle entertainment: the white papers and treatises and manifestoes of dark geniuses who milk the string of nonsensical letters trailing behind their names to gain an eager and gullible audience at which they fling their pronouncements about the future of world affairs while lurking behind mahogany desks located in the cramped offices of major universities and the basement rooms of influential think tanks like the Rand Institute.

If this sounds paranoid, consider the irony: The *true* paranoia is more often exhibited by Those In Power who choose to listen to the pronouncements of academics and glorified bureaucrats wholly cut off from the real world except in the most abstract sense, who blindly base crucial geopolitical decisions on the guesswork of these overpaid, Ivy League Tony Alamos. Allow me to introduce you to the significant contributions of three such paragons of prescience and logic and humanitarianism at its finest....

Anyone familiar with the key movers and shakers of geo-political affairs of the past three decades will be familiar with Samuel Huntington, Zbigniew Brzezinski and Francis Fuku-yama. These three men and their work represent a triangle of disparate philosophical attitudes toward how the future of America—and, by extension, the future of the world—should be wet nursed and/or managed.

Francis Fukuyama, the Oracle of History's End

In June of 1989 Francis Fukuyama published a now famous article titled "The End of History?" in *The National Interest*, a venerable American conservative journal. In that article, later expanded into a book that bears a similar title (*The End of History and the Last Man*), Fukuyama made a carefully reasoned argument that the Cold War had postponed the progress of civilization. He accurately predicted the fall of the Soviet Union a full year before it happened and insisted that once this inevitable collapse occurred, the world's leaders would have to sit down at the same table and figure out how to get along in a post-communist world in which there was no Great Enemy to blame for our failure to progress beyond the building of better weapons. The concept of civilization itself, Fukuyama claimed, brought with it a series of promises that had gone unfulfilled due to the distraction of fighting this protracted war of con-flicting ideologies. These world leaders would, according to Fukuyama, have to identify the promises that had gone unful-filled and work together to implement "the twin principles of liberty and equality on which modern democracy is founded" (Fukuyama xi) and once that goal had been completed, we would be faced with "the end of history." This, in Fukuyama's eyes, would not be a bad state of affairs at all. As he writes in the introduction to his book:

> This did not mean that the natural cycle of birth, life, and
> death would end, that important events would no longer
> happen, or that newspapers reporting them would cease

to be published. It meant, rather, that there would be no further progress in the development of underlying principles and institutions, because all of the really big questions had been settled. (xii)

Though certainly infused with an odd naïveté that will no doubt appear almost child-like a hundred (or even twenty) years from now, Fukuyama's propositions appear on the surface to be essentially noble ones. He wants civilization to get on with the task of scientific progress and humanitarian endeavors as opposed to the endless bloodshed of needless wars followed by needless wars.

Fukuyama's essay was met with great derision from conservative quarters when the initial article was published. After all, in that optimistic era of Ronald Reagan and Margaret Thatcher everybody knew the Soviet Union was nowhere near collapsing.

Then, on the 7th of February, 1990, the Soviet Union collapsed. Fukuyama had been proven right, at least partly.

Zbigniew Brzezinski, Shaman of the Global Village

In June of 1992 Zbigniew Brzezinski, who was President Jimmy Carter's National Security Advisor from 1977 to 1981 and Barack Obama's senior foreign policy advisor throughout the 2008 Presidential campaign, wrote a response to Fukuyama's treatise in the form of a white paper titled "Out of Control" in which he laid out a slightly different vision for the future of world politics. He claimed that the major concern facing the world, now that the Soviet Union had collapsed, was the potentiality of complete and utter chaos breaking out in what he called "the Eurasian oblong." He predicted a flurry of civil wars between small nation-states whose petty little hatreds had been held in check only by the strong hand of the Soviet Union. The temptation for the United States, Brzezinski claimed, would be to move in and solve these conflicts, either through force or by other means. In "Out of Control" Brzezinski urged the United States to stand by and do nothing, to allow this chaos to build as much as possible until the U.S. would finally be asked to intervene by the countries themselves. This way the U.S. could not be perceived as being invasive or dictatorial meddlers. The foreign policy of the Clinton Administration essentially reflected Brzezinski's proposals.

Brzezinski went on to propose a "New Confederation of States" that would differ from the United Nations in the sense that the U.S. would be its undisputed leader. However, he argued that the U.S. would not be able to hold onto its position as leader of the world through military might, but only through moral leadership. He further proposed that the central purpose of this confederation would be to gather together and identify a common set of ethical principles the world community would voluntarily follow.

Samuel P. Huntington, the Wizard of War

Fukuyama's notion of the "End of History" and Brzezinski's quasi-Utopian vision inevitably prompted a response from the extreme rightwing contingent of U.S. politics. This appeared in the form of Samuel P. Huntington's 1993 article "The Clash of Civilizations?" which was published in the pages of *Foreign Affairs*, a conservative journal published by the Council on Foreign Relations. Three years later the article grew into a national bestseller with a longer and more ominous title: *The Clash of Civilizations and the Remaking of World Order*. A professor at Harvard University, a respected scholar of political science, former director of security planning for the National Security Council in the 1970s, and the founder of the rightwing journal *Foreign Policy*, Huntington was in the perfect position to take Fukuyama to task for his premature declaration of the end of history. After all, every good political scientist at Harvard knows that the entire history of civilization is the history of warfare. Why put an end to warfare when we've barely even perfected it? There's so much more to do, so many methods and techniques for bloodshed and torture we haven't even bothered to try yet.

Water boarding is becoming so passé in this September 12th world of ours. Pretty soon we'll have nanotechnology devices that rip the human body apart molecule by molecule and plasma beam weapons that wipe out the populace of whole cities in the blink of a cybernetic eye while keeping the real estate intact and devoid of lingering and unseemly radioactivity. Why throw the baby out with the bathwater? Why stop when we're just getting off the ground?

Over the course of 367 pages, Huntington lays out the Manifest Destiny for the world of foreign affairs in a twenty-first century that could only be led by a Republican automaton controlled by other Republican automatons, a future in which the central problem for Western Civilization would not be implementing "the twin principles of liberty and equality" or creating a "New Confederation of States," but an all-out world war with the entire culture of Islam itself, immediately followed by a second war with the civilization of Asia in the form of the rising Chinese Empire.

One of Huntington's prescriptions for this imminent clash of civilizations, as laid out in precise detail in his book, is to figuratively draw boundaries around Western civilization, identify what makes Us (the West) superior to Them (the East), to hunker down and enforce those values here at home, throw out this whole misguided and doomed notion of multiculturalism that's been rotting away at White Christian Culture for so long, call upon other nations to isolate the Islamic world, and empower ourselves for the ultimate conflict, first with Islam, and then with China.

Huntington's book was like a breath of fresh air for an *ennui*-afflicted world lacking a clear cut enemy. Here now was a vision of the future with promise. Now we could go back to the good old days of inflated military budgets and messy foreign wars in countries most Americans couldn't identify on a map (no, not even with the help of mapquest). But that wouldn't stop the people from hating them, if they were given the right motivation.

317

Samuel Huntington's book was embraced by many neo-conservatives, and its militaristic vision used by the Dubya administration as a blueprint for both domestic and foreign affairs. In chapter 12 of his book, Huntington states that:

> The central issue for the West is whether, quite apart from any external challenges, it is capable of stopping and reversing the internal processes of decay. Can the West renew itself or will sustained internal rot simply accelerate its end and/or subordination to other economically and demographically more dynamic civilizations? [...] Far more significant than economics and demography are problems of moral decline, cultural suicide, and political disunity in the West. (303-04)

Huntington identifies these "problems" as increased antisocial behavior, family decay, a decline in membership in voluntary associations, a weakening of the work ethic, lower levels of scholastic achievement, "immigrants from other civilizations who reject assimilation," and "the weakening of [Western civilization's] central component, Christianity" (304-05).

Huntington then goes on to warn us that:

> A more immediate and dangerous challenge exists in the United States. Historically American national identity has been defined culturally by the heritage of Western civilization and politically by the principles of the American Creed on which Americans overwhelmingly agree: liberty, democracy, individualism, equality before the law, constitutionalism, private property. In the late twentieth century both components of American identity have come under concentrated and sustained onslaught from a small but influential number of intellectuals and publicists. In the name of multiculturalism they have attacked the identification of the United States with Western civilization, denied the existence of a common American culture, and promoted racial, ethnic, and other subnational cultural identities and groupings. (305)

Apparently, according to Huntington, the basic foundations of the United States as set forth by the Founding Fathers are being eroded—not by theocratic philistines listening intently to invisible deities hovering over the Oval Office; nor by out-of-control black-pajama-boy mercenary teams "disappearing" innocent dissenters who are merely exercising their Constitutional rights to protest an illegal war being waged in a foreign desert for the express purpose of making a very small group of elitists incredibly more wealthy than they already are; nor by a weak and compliant Congress robotically doing the bidding of multinational corporations whose economic interests favor an American government so blatantly fascist that the people trapped within it have accepted their gradual loss of basic freedoms as being the result of an archaic democracy crippled by its own principles of liberty and equality, leading to the mistaken but prevalent belief that the central problem with the United States is that its citizens are *too* free.

No, none of these factors are endangering American principles, says Samuel P. Huntington. What's endangering American principles is the fact that Little Johnny is smoking pot in the school bathroom while he should be putting his nose to the grindstone in one of those enervating Job Placement classes; that Ma and Pa Kettle are no longer encouraged to smash their kid's face in with a lead-lined copy of the King James Bible; that fewer and fewer young men are running out to join the Elks and the Freemasons; that Scam-Tron SAT test scores are down in the dumps due to the fact that they measure little more than one's facility at succeeding as a Middleclass Caucasian Accountant; that Muslims are establishing their own mosques in white communities like Orange County, CA and refusing for some reason to voluntarily convert to the teachings of the Eternal Prince of Peace; that fewer and fewer people believe the Earth was created in seven days a little over five thousands years ago by a gargantuan Semite with a beard; and the fact that University professors are having their students read Toni Morrison instead of William Shakespeare.

Yes, *these* are the evil parasites eating away at the intestines of America. We must do something about it. But what?

What shall we do?

Shall we steal a Presidential election?

Shall we take advantage of a terrorist act and use it as an excuse to implement a war plan we already had waiting in the wings?

Shall we save America by destroying it?

Shall we?

Shall we?

Shall we?

As I write these words a whole slew of authoritarian bills are being pushed through the U.S. Congress. One such bill—the perfect manifestation of what appears to be a growing trend in jurisprudence these days—is called The Violent Radicalization and Homegrown Terrorism Prevention Act (Senate Bill 1959). It has already passed the House of Representatives (as House Bill 1955). Only six people in the House voted against it, despite the fact that it's the most repressive piece of legislation ever to be proposed to Congress, despite the fact that it bans the right for the people to dissent in any form whatsoever.

Let me be clear: This is not my personal interpretation of the language of the bill. This *is* the bill.

The Violent Radicalization and Homegrown Terrorism Prevention Act empowers the U.S. government to arrest and detain any citizen or group of citizens, not because they're being violent or even advocating violence, but because their language or actions may seem to be *heading toward violence* at some point in the future.

Does it matter if it's the *near* future, the *distant* future?

No, for the wording of the bill is so broad and polymorphous that it can be interpreted in any way that best suits the government at any particular moment. American citizens can literally be rounded up and thrown into prison, or some subterranean cubicle far worse, because of their *future* crimes. If you ever doubted the word of a prophet, no matter how divinely inspired, you should definitely be concerned about this bill... even if you're not American. Particularly if you're not American. After all, what's uniquely American one day is uniquely *global* the next. The same type of person who stands on the corner of Hollywood and Cahuenga Blvd. preaching about rivers of wormwood and the imminent worldquake is the same type of person who will be in charge of predicting whether or not you're potentially violent enough to deserve a protracted stay in Guantanomo Bay—people like Tony Alamo, only with government funding and the majority of the U.S. Congress behind him.

> "Prepare your heart for sorrows. The people of the world need to immediately prepare their minds, their spirits, their hearts, and their souls for these catastrophes, which will surely come to pass within this very generation."
> –Tony Alamo

Let's turn back to the good Pastor's fire-and-brimstone pamphlet for a second, shall we?

"Any time now, a worldquake and a series of prophesied catastrophes will shockingly awaken the entire global population to a horrible, God-sent, unparalleled nightmare."

I believe I now know what that "horrible, God-sent, unparalleled nightmare" really is. Need I spell it out? It's written in the clouds, in the stars, in the broken lines on the palms of your hands. Peer closely into my crystal ball....

It's the dark legacy of the Dubya administration and the Clash of Civilizations and Senate Bill 1959.

It's The Violent Radicalization and Homegrown Terrorism Prevention Act and its mutant progenies being hatched in dozens of Congressional offices even as I write this.

Sweet Jesus, could it be that Tony Alamo was right?

If this bill (or any similar one) passes in the Senate, my confidence in his prognosticative abilities will be unshakeable. At that point, and that point alone, I will throw my support to Pastor Tony Alamo and help him secure the Republican nomination to be the next President of the United States.

Or, better yet, why waste time with the Executive Office? Let's appoint Alamo to be the guy who sits behind a mahogany desk in a cramped office at Harvard and writes a voluminous new Bible worshipped by the President's most trusted acolytes.

Dubya, as I'm sure you know, has mentioned on several occasions that God gives him good advice on a semi-regular basis. I suspect, however, that if we could eavesdrop on these conversations, we'd be surprised by the fact that God's voice sounds suspiciously like that of Samuel P. Huntington.

Or maybe even Tony Alamo.

Study closely the death-wish-laden prognostications of both and ask yourself: What's the difference?

Update

On September 25, 2008, Tony Alamo was arrested in Arizona for allegedly having sex with underage girls. As I write this, Alamo is awaiting trial in jail. I guess Alamo got the apocalypse he deserved. Oh, if only that were the case with all such prophets....

Senate Bill 1959 failed to become law during the 110th congress, which means The Violent Radicalization and Homegrown Terrorism Prevention Act is dead... until, that is, some wily congressman decides to reintroduce the bill under a different (and no doubt far more innocuous) title.

In fact, I suspect the worst aspects of the bill found their way into the National Defense Authorization Act (NDAA) for Fiscal Year 2012, signed into law by President Obama in the dead of night on New Year's Eve of 2011. The "Counter-Terrorism" provisions of the NDAA are even more nightmarish than the Orwellian provisions included in Senate Bill 1959. If you've never heard of the Act in question, I highly suggest you learn as much as you can about it. Before it's too late.

Works Cited

Alamo, Tony. "Brace Yourselves." *Tony Alamo Christian Ministries World Newsletter*. Vol. 06200 (Nov. 2006): 1-3, 5-9.

Brzezinski, Zbigniew. *Out of Control: Global Turmoil on the Eve of the 21ˢᵗ Century.* New York: Collier, 1993.

Fukuyama, Francis. *The End of History and the Last Man.* New York: The Free Press, 1992.

Huntington, Samuel P. *The Clash of Civilizations and the Remaking of World Order.* New York: Simon & Schuster, 1996.

Sheehan, Daniel. "'New Paradigm Politics' or the Old 'New World Order'? Lecture. Southern Oregon University. Ashland, Oregon, 9 Jan. 2003.

Part Six

Conspiracies and the Paranormal

André Breton at a Dada festival in Paris, March 27, 1920, wearing a slogan: "In order to love something you need to have seen and heard it for a long time you bunch of idiots."

– photo by Francis Picabia

CHAPTER TWENTY-ONE

CRYPTOSCATOLOGY: ANDRÉ BRETON & FORTEAN PHENOMENA

In 1919 a "meaningful coincidence" occurred: Charles Fort published *The Book of the Damned* and the surrealist André Breton founded an anti-literary review titled *Littérature*. The work of both men would eventually inspire large groups of artists, philosophers, and other strange people to follow in their respective footsteps, even long after each had exhaled his last gasp of air. In Breton's case, this is exactly the result he had been striving toward. Fort, on the other hand, couldn't have cared less. Nevertheless, it is interesting to note that both men—one in Europe, the other in America—were eagerly exploring the hidden realm of dreams, unexplained phenomena, and what the Swiss psychology Carl Jung would call "meaningful coincidences."

It is well known that the surrealists were heavily influenced by psychology, particularly the work of Sigmund Freud. Later, they would also draw upon the findings of Freud's student Carl Jung, whose theories concerning synchronicity dovetailed with their own mystical outlook on life. Jung developed the term "synchronicity" after noticing that both he and his patients had experienced an uncanny number of coincidences that clearly went beyond the mere forces of chance. For example, Jung once related the eerie incident of having suddenly woken up in the middle of the night convinced that someone had just entered his hotel room, only to find himself alone in the dark. He was certain he had been roused forth by "a feeling of dull pain as if something had struck his forehead and the back of his skull" (Holroyd 11), and yet there was no evidence of physical harm anywhere on his body. The mystery deepened the very next day when he discovered that not only had a patient of his shot himself through the forehead, but that the bullet had "lodged at the back wall of the skull" (Holroyd 14). Inevitably, the time of the tragedy coincided with Jung's fearful experience from the night before.

André Breton recorded similar experiences in his book *Nadja*. One night, while speaking to Picasso during the intermission of Apollinaire's *Couleur du Temps*, he was approached by a young man who:

> ...stammers a few words, and finally manages to explain that he had mistaken me for one of his friends supposedly killed in the war. Naturally, nothing more was said. A few days later, through a mutual friend, I begin corresponding with [the French poet] Paul Éluard, whom I did not know by sight. On furlough, he comes to see me: I am in the presence of the same person as at *Couleur du Temps*. (24, 27)

This striking example of synchronicity is preceded by a monologue that would not be at all out of place in Charles Fort's *The Book of the Damned*. Not only is the intellectual content similar, but the paradoxically convoluted and poetic style of the prose is also reminiscent of Fort's. Breton speaks about being interested in relating the events of his life only insofar as they are:

> ...at the mercy of chance... temporarily escaping my control, admitting me to an almost forbidden world of sudden parallels, petrifying coincidences, and reflexes peculiar to each individual, of harmonies struck as though on the piano, flashes of light that would make you see, really *see*, if only they were not so much quicker than all the rest. (19)

The facts that most interest Breton, he says, are of an "absolutely unexpected, violently fortuitous character." Furthermore, they are "of quite unverifiable intrinsic value."

Such "worthless" facts and "petrifying coincidences" were the core of both Charles Fort's private and professional life. He swam in an endless river of dreams and damned things, all of which he preserved in four iconoclastic books (*The Book of the Damned, New Lands, LO!*, and *Wild Talents*) currently available in a single volume titled *The Books of Charles Fort*. Over the course of 1062 pages Fort drops his bait into this forbidden river and invariably raises strangeness after strangeness, performing exploratory surgery upon each after he's captured them on the page. Many of them contain echoes of the experiences related by Jung and Breton. Like the latter gentleman, Fort would cringe from calling them mere coincidences.

"In the explanation of *coincidence* there is much of laziness, and helplessness, and response to an instinctive fear that a scientific dogma will be endangered. It is a tag, or a label..." (847). Fort follows this passage by relating the story of a glass-eyed man named Jackson who was wanted by the police. The police managed to arrest a glass-eyed Jackson in Boston. To their dismay, however, he wasn't the correct glass-eyed Jackson. They eventually found *their* Jackson in Philadelphia. For a moment, in a typically sarcastic tone, Fort ruminates over the possibility of universal symmetry: that if there's a Murphy with a hare lip in Chicago, there must be another hare-lipped Murphy somewhere else. As usual with Fort, just as soon as he proposes an idea, he rejects it as being too tidy.

He spends the next two pages listing a series of incidents clipped out of American and British newspapers from the years 1911, 1929, 1930, 1910, 1924, 1931, 1888, and 1892. (Fort was nothing if not a pack rat, at least where strange news articles were concerned.) Each story describes similar scenarios—scenarios that only a man with Fort's unique sense of pattern recognition could latch onto. In one story two dead men were found in the desert only 100 yards from each other, and yet the authorities claimed "there was no connection between the two deaths" (848). A separate story reported the discovery of a man, dead of heart failure, sitting on a park bench in the Bronx. Soon afterwards, another dead man was found sitting on a bench nearby. A separate story told of two women found dead in the River Dee in London. They had no relation to each other, lived on opposite parts of the town, and both left their respective houses at ten o'clock in the morning exactly two days before their bodies were found. Still another story describes the execution of three men "for the murder of Sir Edmund Berry Godfrey, on Greenberry Hill, London." This wouldn't be unusual except for the fact that the murderers were named Green, Berry, and Hill. With fastidious documentation Fort continues to relate proto-synchronicities like these until he comes to the following Breton-like conclusion:

> There is a view by which it can be shown, or more or less demonstrated, that there never has been a coincidence. That is, in anything like a final sense. By a coincidence is meant a false appearance, or suggestion, of relations among circumstances. But anybody who accepts that there is an underlying oneness of all things, accepts that there are no utter absences of relations among circumstances—
>
> Or that there are no coincidences, in the sense that there are no real discords in either colors or musical notes—
>
> That any two colors, or sounds, can be harmonized, by intermediately relating them to other colors, or sounds. (849-50)

James Joyce, author of what is arguably the ultimate Fortean novel *Finnegans Wake*, created his own term to describe these events: "coincidance" (49). Indeed, such pattern recognition as exhibited by Fort often involves an unconscious dance between the observer and the phenomenon observed. Perhaps these synchronicities grow out of a human desire to fill in the blank spaces of life, to find connections where there are none, to reconstruct reality to our own satisfaction. After all, is this not the ultimate goal of any surrealist? "This landscape is not good enough for me," the surrealist declares. "I think I shall include a giant fried egg with a horde of burning midgets on top just to liven it up a bit!" And impetuously, without thinking of the consequences, he does just that, for to do otherwise would be a living death.

While a surrealist consciously transforms the world, perhaps Charles Fort performed the same act unconsciously. Wanting a stranger world than the one in which he was forced to live, he went out and found just that between the dusty covers of bound newspapers yellowing with age and neglect. He found wild co-incidences; frogs that fell out of the skies; reports going back to 1779 of "vast wheel-like super-constructions" that "enter this earth's atmosphere" long before such reports became the subject of weekly tabloids (272); battalions of phantom soldiers; vanishing planets; blue, ancient Britons; gravesites the size of marbles belonging to a race of tiny beings who crucified cockroaches; two gigantic crows who perched upon the moon on the evening of July 3, 1882; a mouse who, in the year 1930, was heard to say, "I was along this way, and thought I'd drop in," then vanished along a trail of purple sparkles (863); mysterious beings who collect Ambroses; periwinkles that teleport from one side of the earth to the other; suns that briefly turn green; the unwavering certainty that the moon is not only thirty-five miles away, but also easily accessible by balloon; and cobwebs that threaten to cover the earth. This, of course, is only a sample of Fort's *oeuvre*. Like an alchemist, he was able to take base materials—turgid volumes of recent and not-so-recent history—and reshape them into pure strangeness, or gold by any other name. Max Ernst exhibited the same talent in his surrealist collages, in which he connected unrelated elements into what were often familiar landscapes, populating them with unexpected hybrids and alien creatures. If Ernst did this consciously and Fort unconsciously, in the end it doesn't matter. Any self-respecting alchemist would be proud of either result.

Tony "Doc" Shiels, a surrealist magician, painter, Punch and Judy professor, and all around roustabout of some note, has applied the term "surrealchemy" to his Fortean investigations in Cornwall County in the southwest of England, where he claims to have invoked a suspiciously Ernstian entity named Owlman. Sightings of the fine-feathered *daemon* were reported by numerous residents of Cornwall, all of them independently of each other. In 1976 one witness was reported as saying, "It was like a big owl with pointed ears, as big as a man. The eyes were red and glowing. At first I thought it was someone dressed up, playing a joke, trying to scare us. I laughed at it, we both did, then it went up in the air and we both screamed. When it went up you could see its feet were like pincers" (Shiels, *Monstrum!* 58).

Strangely, Max Ernst visited the Hellford River area of Cornwall—the exact location where Owlman was seen—back in the 1930s. At the time he was "accompanied by a… Celtic witchwoman, Leonora Carrington" (Shiels, "Surrealchemy" 13).[1] Of course, anyone familiar with his work will know that Ernst had a penchant for drawing entities with avian features, such as in his 1939 oil painting *The Robing of the Bride* (Gatt 83). In fact, his androgynous alter-ego Loplop has a decidedly bird-like head. Furthermore, the year during which the Owlman sightings occurred also happened to be the year of Ernst's death. One might say that the preceding tidbits are merely examples of the infamous "coincidences" we've already heard so much about. However, a more surreal-minded person might propose that the intense creative energy given off by Ernst's mind during his stay in Cornwall manifested a thought form into the physical world, and that it took the added energy released upon the artist's death to make this "psychic marionette" fully visible to normal human beings. The Tibetans call such phantoms *tulpas* (Keel 6).

Though this may sound like pseudo-scientific mumbo-jumbo, Carl Jung had a similar theory concerning flying saucers. In

---

1   Until recently, Leonora Carrington was the last living surrealist. She was a prolific painter and novelist who spent most of her days in Mexico City. She died of pneumonia on May 25, 2011 at the age of 94.

his book *Flying Saucers: A Modern Myth of Things Seen in the Sky*, he set forth the proposition that flying saucers are actually physical manifestations of the collective unconscious, symbols that "reflect our anxiety in a nuclear age and hope for a superhuman source of salvation," given life simply by our overwhelming need for them (Wilson 82). If that's not surrealism, then nothing is.

To the literal-minded, this may *still* sound like pseudo-scientific mumbo-jumbo, but Carl Jung is a psychiatrist and can get away with saying crazy things like that without being accused of having gone hi-diddle-diddle over the deep end. Crazy or not, the point is that surrealism and Fortean phenomena have been intimately related ever since that first "meaningful coincidence" in 1919. Breton's similarities to Charles Fort, Ernst's strange intersection with Tony "Doc" Shiels, and Jung's flirtation with flying saucers all prove there's a definite relationship between the planks of Breton and Fort. Each explore the invisible zones of everyday existence via ostensibly worthless techniques, i.e., dreams, fantasies, paranormal phenomena—everything that Western Man considers to be mere detritus. Both Breton and Fort practice what could be called "cryptoscatology" (translation from the Latin: "the study of secret shit"). Both wish to dig beneath the outer edges of consensus reality; to sift through the loam that no one else will touch; to rub the noses of the bourgeoisie into this forbidden soil; to shock "the dead sot, the slow of perception, the dignified, all sourpusses, the cursory or unobservant, some pedagogues, the timid, the gullible, and almost without exception—all persons who have their Science and Scientists from the daily newspapers," to paraphrase Tiffany Thayer's list of all those with whom *The Books of Charles Fort* would be unpopular (Fort xiv).

Finally, when both men died—Fort in 1932, Breton in 1966—the squares from the above list immediately declared Bastille Day and decided that Forteanism and surrealism were at last dead and buried along with their founders. Such premature forecasting proved thoroughly incorrect—to the great conster-

CRYPTOSCATOLOGY: CONSPIRACY THEORY AS ART FORM

nation of the dead sots and sourpusses. The proof that neither movement is dead lies in the fact that their core principles and ideas are still being written about and discussed decades after the original founders have long been devoured by the larvae of dipterous flies and other wonderfully ravenous creatures.

Works Cited

Breton, André. *Nadja*. New York: Grove Weidenfeld, 1960.

Fort, Charles. *The Books of Charles Fort*. New York: Henry Holt, 1957.

Gatt, Giuseppe. *Max Ernst*. New York: Hamlyn, 1970.

Holroyd, Stuart. *Magic, Words, and Numbers*. London: The Danbury Press, 1975.

Joyce, James. *Finnegans Wake*. New York: The Viking Press, 1968.

Keel, John A. *The Mothman Prophecies*. Lilburn: IllumiNet Press, 1991.

Sheils, Tony "Doc." *Monstrum!: A Wizard's Tale*. London: Fortean Tomes, 1990.

---. "Surrealchemy Versus Cryptozoology." *Strange Magazine* 8 Fall 1991: 13.

Wilson, Colin. *Enigmas and Mysteries*. London: The Danbury Press, 1976.

CHAPTER TWENTY-TWO

COLLABORATING WITH THE DEAD

Conspiracy research, like everything else, is an art form. It's an art form as valid, in its own way, as writing investigative articles for the *Los Angeles Times* or designing advertisements for Nokia or dancing for the Joffrey Ballet or performing the role of Hamlet in a park in New York. All of these art forms have something in common: None can survive without an audience. Just as plays can't exist without people to appreciate the performance, conspiracy researchers can't exist without people engaging in conspiracies. Conversely, people who engage in these conspiracies would often be less celebrated without conspiracy researchers acting on their behalf as unpaid public relations experts. Even an anonymous forger of classic paintings wants to get credit for his hard work from time to time; the same perverse impulse for recognition exists even in those who engage in conspiracies. After all, they're only human (or shape-shifting reptilians, as others would have you believe, but that's a different story). My PR quota for the year should be satisfied by this chapter, an investigative piece concerning the mysterious death of a man I went to high school with about seventeen years ago.

Conspiracy research, like everything else, is a figure-ground relationship. Before one can uncover the hidden ground, one must first become intimate with the figure (i.e., the official story). The official story of the death of Steve Semon, culled from a series of articles in both the *Los Angeles Times* and the *Daily Breeze*, goes something like this:

On Nov. 30, 1997, at 5:25 in the evening, FBI agent Steve Semon shoots himself to death in front of El Segundo policemen. The tragedy occurs at the beach near the Southern California Edison power plant in El Segundo. The case begins early Sunday at 2:30 A.M. when Semon is out on the town driving around with "two friends," one of whom he had met in 1989 while in Japan as an exchange student. For no apparent reason Semon pulls a gun on one of his "friends" and begins riffling through his car. He does not steal the car, allows the friend to flee, and waits for the police to come and arrest him. According to the police, Semon "behaved wildly, talking incoherently." After being released twelve hours later on $145,000 bail, the agent decides to head toward the beach. His roommate (an LAPD officer) happens to come upon a note, described by police as "a handwritten 'will,'" which causes him to call the police. When the police locate Semon at the beach, the FBI agent presses a handgun to his temple and pulls the trigger. Many of his friends describe this erratic behavior as "totally out of character." The autopsy finds no evidence of drugs or alcohol in his system. At the time of his death, Semon was the head of the FBI squad investigating the Democratic National Committee's fund-raising scandal, a story of political intrigue quite prominent in the headlines at that time.

I went to school with Steve Semon at Torrance High in suburban Torrance, California. When I was a Freshman, Semon was a Senior. We never knew one another, but we had a mutual friend named Eric. Eric had been Semon's best friend since Elementary School. On the morning of December 1, 1997, Eric called and insisted I pick up a newspaper. Because of Semon's prominent position in the FBI, his death had made the front page of the *Los Angeles Times'* Metro section as well as the front page of the *Daily Breeze* (the local Torrance newspaper). Somehow, both the *Los Angeles Times* and the *Daily Breeze* had neglected to mention the fact that Semon had been the lead investigator of the Democratic National Committee fundraising scandal. Though I would not discover this significant detail until months later, through a Freedom of Information Act request, this was definitely one of the first indications that a media blackout was descending upon the Semon story.

According to news reports, Semon graduated from USC in 1992 "with honors in both of his majors, accounting and international relations." ("International relations," for your information, is a clever buzzword for "psychological warfare."[1]) After working as an accountant for a few years, Semon decided to join the FBI. In November of 1996 he was assigned to "the bureau's Los Angeles office and to a white collar crime detail...." Unmentioned, of course, is his meteoric rise in the agency. Imagine being named the head of the FBI's most high-profile case after a single year, having worked on only *one* white collar

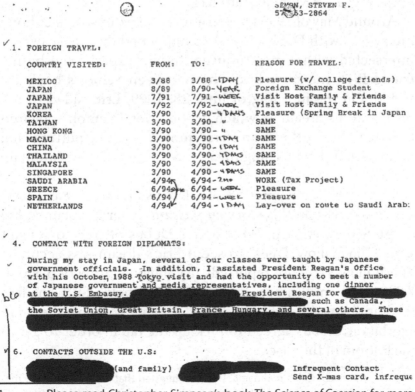

SEMON, STEVEN F.
57-53-2864

1. FOREIGN TRAVEL:

COUNTRY VISITED:	FROM:	TO:	REASON FOR TRAVEL:
MEXICO	3/88	3/88 -1DAY	Pleasure (w/ college friends)
JAPAN	8/89	8/90-YEAR	Foreign Exchange Student
JAPAN	7/91	7/91 -WEEK	Visit Host Family & Friends
JAPAN	7/92	7/92-WEEK	Visit Host Family & Friends
KOREA	3/90	3/90-4DAYS	Pleasure (Spring Break in Japan
TAIWAN	3/90	3/90- "	SAME
HONG KONG	3/90	3/90- "	SAME
MACAU	3/90	3/90-1DAY	SAME
CHINA	3/90	3/90- 1DAY	SAME
THAILAND	3/90	3/90- 7DAYS	SAME
MALAYSIA	3/90	3/90- 4DAYS	SAME
SINGAPORE	3/90	4/90 - 4DAYS	SAME
SAUDI ARABIA	4/94	6/94-2mo	WORK (Tax Project)
GREECE	6/94	6/94- WEEK	Pleasure
SPAIN	6/94	6/94- WEEK	Pleasure
NETHERLANDS	4/94	4/94 - 1DAY	Lay-over on route to Saudi Arab:

4. CONTACT WITH FOREIGN DIPLOMATS:

During my stay in Japan, several of our classes were taught by Japanese government officials. In addition, I assisted President Reagan's Office with his October, 1988 Tokyo visit and had the opportunity to meet a number of Japanese government and media representatives, including one dinner at the U.S. Embassy. ▇▇▇▇▇▇▇▇▇President Reagan for ▇▇▇▇▇▇▇▇▇▇▇▇ such as Canada, the Soviet Union, Great Britain, France, Hungary, and several others. These

6. CONTACTS OUTSIDE THE U.S.:

▇▇▇▇▇▇(and family) ▇▇▇▇▇▇▇▇ Infrequent Contact
Send X-mas card, infreque

1   Please read Christopher Simpson's book *The Science of Coercion* for more on that particular subject

337

crime investigation. At the time of his premature death, Semon was only twenty-eight years old. (Sources: *Los Angeles Times* 12/2/97; *Daily Breeze* 12/2/97, 1/8/98.)

Those are the facts. And there the case would stand, unsolved, until mid-1999 when I met a 77-year-old man named Robert Dobbs. It was Dobbs who showed me how to solve the mystery of Steve Semon's death.

* * *

I met Robert Dobbs through an article I published in the pages of *Paranoia* magazine #22. Back in the 1970s Dobbs was the official archivist of Marshall McLuhan, the author of such classic books as *Understanding Media* and *The Gutenberg Galaxy*. As I write this (in the Spring of 2003), Dobbs hosts a weekly two-hour radio show called *Cloak and Dagger* on one of the biggest AM radio stations in Canada.

Around May of 1999 I began a series of extensive telephone interviews with Dobbs. It just so happened that these events intersected with a most unusual dream experienced by my friend Eric, the same Eric who had been Semon's boyhood friend. On the morning of June 28, 1999, Eric called to tell me about his dream, in which his old friend Semon appeared to him and said (this is an exact quote): "They're putting Hell on hold and they're using microwave weaponry to reanimate the dead."

That night, while interviewing Dobbs on the phone, I happened to mention this story *en passant*. After I explained the entire Semon affair in great detail, Dobbs offered to consult with "The Willow Trees" to see if Eric's dream was accurate. The Willow Trees are reportedly a conglomeration of 6,500 to 7,000 dead entities accessible through a powerful Canadian medium named Gordon W. Cole.[2] Though Mr. Cole's fees are exorbitant, Dobbs agreed to pick up the tab in order to get to the bottom of the case.

---

2   This is not Cole's real name. Dobbs requested that I not identify the medium's actual name in this report so as to avoid putting his personal safety at risk from either the FBI or Japanese Intelligence.

Meanwhile, I decided to utilize more mundane research tools in order to extract as much information as I could from the material plane. I filed a Freedom of Information Act Request through the FBI. In fact, I wrote *two* separate requests—one in my name, the other in Eric's. The first inquiry (Eric's) was fairly straight-forward. It read as follows:

Federal Bureau of Investigation
U.S. Justice Department.
10th and Pennsylvania
Washington, D.C. 20535

July 7, 1999
To Whom It May Concern:

I grew up with a man named Steve Semon, who went on to become an FBI agent in July of 1996. In November of that year he was assigned to a white-collar crime detail at the bureau's Los Angeles office. He maintained that position for exactly a year before committing suicide in November of 1997. Having known him quite well, I've always found this behavior rather anomalous. Now that an appropriate period of time has passed, I'd like to know what conclusions the FBI has reached concerning Steve's death.

The newspapers reported that there were no drugs or alcohol in his system when he committed suicide. The bizarre behavior he exhibited a few hours prior to his death, reported in the enclosed article from the *Los Angeles Times*, is as anomalous as his suicide. Since the coroner ruled out drugs or alcohol as a cause, I'd like to know what the FBI's investigation ultimately uncovered. I'd also like access to any and all files the FBI may have in connection to Steve's brief career in the Agency. My intense bewilderment over Steve's suicide has led me to file this FOIA request. Please respond as soon as possible.

Sincerely,
Eric Williams

Eric mailed the preceding letter on the morning of July 7, 1999. Three weeks later, on the morning of August 1, I mailed a second request, this one under my name. It read as follows:

Federal Bureau of Investigation
U.S. Justice Dept.
10th and Pennsylvania
Washington, DC 20535

August 1, 1999

Dear Madame/Sir:

On the night of 6-27-99 a man who identified himself as Steven Semon appeared to me in a dream and told me that the government was using microwave weaponry (i.e., cellular phone towers) to reanimate the dead. "Hell is being put on hold," were his exact words. He then asked me to initiate a FOIPA search for any records pertaining to his life, death, and career. Imagine my shock when I checked the records of my local newspaper and discovered more than one article about the mysterious suicide of an FBI agent named Steven Semon who grew up in Torrance, CA.

Under the provisions of the Freedom of Information Act, I request access to all records pertaining to the Bureau's investigations into the life, death, and career of Steven Semon from 1969 to 1997. Mr. Semon was born January 7, 1969 and died on November 30 (St. Andrew's Eve), 1997. Semon was on the FBI squad investigating the Democratic National fundraising scandal when he ostensibly decided to take his own life on a beach in El Segundo, CA. First and foremost I'd like to see any documents pertaining to the investigation of Mr. Semon's death. I'd also like to see any documents pertaining to Mr. Semon's connection to the DNC investigation, microwave weaponry, cellular phone towers, and/or the reanimation of the dead.

I am willing to pay for copying expenses that do not exceed $35.

If any part of this request is refused, please explain the specific exemption justifying the refusal and direct me to the legal appeals procedure.

I have included three articles (dated 12-2-97, 12-3-97 and 1-8-98, respectively) from the *Daily Breeze* reporting Steven Semon's death in order to prove that the subject of this FOIPA request is indeed deceased, at least to some degree.

Thank you very much for your attention. I look forward to hearing from you.

Sincerely yours,
Robert Guffey

All we could do now was wait. Finally, early in October, Dobbs flew from his home in New York to White Rock, British Columbia and met with The Willow Trees. According to Dobbs, his discussion with Semon's spirit lasted for about fifteen minutes. As soon as Dobbs returned from New York, he sent me an audio tape[3] of that discussion through the mail. Space does not permit me to include the entire transcript of that discussion here.

In short, what Semon said was this: His temporary mental imbalance was chemically induced by a drug so sophisticated it was undetectable even during the autopsy. The drug was slipped into Semon's drink by his two colleagues from Japan while they dined at California Beach Sushi, a sushi bar in Hermosa Beach rumored to be owned by the Yakuza (the Japanese Mafia).[4] The two gentlemen with whom Semon dined that evening were Koji Kaneshiro and Jumpei Tomonaga. Kaneshiro and Tomonaga were working for a Japanese intelligence agency that wanted to pump Semon for information. Their mission was to dig up dirt on specific politicians involved in the Democratic National Committee fundraising scandal. Their intent was to use this information to blackmail the "weak sisters" involved in the scandal. They merely wanted to unbalance him, to get

3   Copy available upon request.
4   This particular restaurant, by the way, played a major role in the O.J. Simpson trial. It was alleged that Simpson often bought illegal narcotics from the restaurant. Nicole Brown Simpson visited the establishment the same day she was murdered.

him to talk. The drug was to act as a truth serum only. Instead, it caused Semon to become temporarily insane. When he was released from jail the next morning, the drug had worn off only slightly, just enough for him to be aware of the dire situation he was now in. He had violated his security oaths, betrayed the agency for whom he worked. His mind was still so unbalanced from the drug, suicide seemed the only viable option.

According to Semon, as of 1999 Kaneshiro and Tomonaga were still under surveillance by the FBI. Because of this (and other reasons), Dobbs strongly suggested I not publish an article about these experiences, on the basis that it might interfere with an on-going investigation. But as one might imagine, the material was too intriguing to let go. As a result, I began taking notes on what would later evolve into a surreal detective novel titled *A Thousand Kisses in Hell*, much of which is based on truth. (The bulk of Dobbs' conversation with Semon, for example, is the centerpiece of Chapter Eight.)

Meanwhile, my investigation into Semon's death was not over. On February 2, 2000, I received a hefty package from the FBI. It was almost Semon's entire file: 232 of 254 pages, each of them marred by frequent redactions. Twenty-two pages were withheld entirely for reasons of national security. The files confirmed some of the details uncovered by The Willow Trees. In one document sub-titled "Contact With Foreign Diplomats" Semon states, "During my stay in Japan, several of our classes were taught by Japanese government officials. In addition, I assisted President Reagan's Office with his October, 1988 Tokyo visit and had the opportunity to meet a number of Japanese government and media representatives, including one dinner at the U.S. Embassy. [20 spaces redacted] President Reagan for [68 spaces redacted] such as Canada, the Soviet Union, Great Britain, France, Hungary, and several others. These [128 spaces redacted]."

This document clearly demonstrates that Semon, an American nineteen-year-old, was working for the Reagan administration in Japan in 1988, at a time when my friend Eric was in close contact with him. Though Eric knew Semon had left the country for a year as an exchange student, he never heard even the slightest hint from Semon that he might be assisting the Reagan administration in any capacity at all (surely an event worthy of discussion). Semon's position must have been fairly sensitive—sensitive enough to be redacted from an official government document twelve years later. This could indicate that Semon's connection to certain United States law enforcement agencies began far earlier than his involvement with the FBI in the late 1990s. In fact, this might explain how Semon rose so quickly through the ranks of the agency in such a short period of time.

The weird revelations were not over. About a month later, Eric received a response from the FBI regarding his own FOIA request: a single page, signed by James M. Kelso Jr., claiming that the FBI possessed not even one document regarding the life and career of Special Agent Steve Semon.

This, despite the fact that I had a pile of them sitting in my bedroom! Allow me to restate my point. Pay close attention, now, these are your tax dollars at work: The nutty letter, the one that should have been round-filed the second it entered the FBI offices, received a thorough response in the form of 232 official government documents, whereas the rational, level-headed inquiry received nothing at all. If viewed from a logical perspective, this result is the exact opposite of what most people would expect. From a conspiratorial perspective, however, the result is in keeping with past policies of certain U.S. intelligence agencies, such as the CIA's penchant to fund tabloid newspapers like the *National Enquirer* in order to discredit legitimate UFO research.[5]

As of May 2005, the Semon investigation is officially CLOSED. But according to other sources, many of them now dead, the investigation behind the scenes is on-going.

Eric hasn't had any further Semon-related dreams since that first one seven years ago. To this day he's not entirely certain

---

5   For evidence of the prior statement, I refer the interested reader to Richard Dolan's book *UFOs and the National Security State* (Keyhole Publishing, 2000).

about the validity of that dream, whether it was a genuine paranormal phenomenon or the result of his slumbering imagination. But it wouldn't surprise me if Semon's ghost is still wandering around to this day, slipping into people's heads while they're asleep, begging for help. Given the tendency of spirits to haunt the earth until important issues from their lifetime have been resolved, I fear Semon might not get an opportunity to catch a few well-deserved winks until the distant future.

Try for a moment to imagine the colossal shock endured by Semon's psyche on the day of his death. Imagine leading your whole life convinced you're living in an über-patriotic Tom Clancy novel, only to awaken one morning to discover the world has gone all akilter and you're now trapped in a jail cell at the bad end of an early Oliver Stone movie. That would be enough to drive anybody's sanity skittering over the edge. The sudden shock nudged Our Hero out of one reality and dragged him biting and scratching into another. This experience drove him stark raving *sane*. His brain didn't know how to handle it. So it did the only thing it could do: It snuffed itself out.

Now I'm sitting here six years after Semon's funeral, sifting through files that don't exist, reading about jobs he never had, blacked-out facts about his life that never happened because no one will ever be allowed to read about them. They're protected under national security—and without *that*, where would this great nation be? Evidence is only worthwhile if there are enough people willing to pay attention to it.

Every art form symbiotically feeds off its audience. Without an audience, a play is not a play; it's just a rehearsal. The value of a book unread is less than nothing. A football game that lacks a crowd to watch it is just a practice. The art of conspiracy research is no different.

The larger the audience, the more the art form grows. Most conspiracy researchers live under the delusion that if they could only get their message out to the widest group of people possible, they couldn't help but save the world. They're fighting for *Truth, Justice* and the *American Way*. The eyes of the world will soon be opened wide, the future of the planet altered by their valiant actions. "A Pulitzer Prize has been reserved for you, Mr. Guffey...."

Alas, I've often suspected that the true fans of the art form, the ones most dedicated to seeing it continue to flourish and grow, are the wingnuts committing the crimes the articles are ostensibly exposing. As Edgar Allan Poe demonstrated over a hundred years ago in "The Purloined Letter," the best way to hide anything is to leave it out in the open. But it never hurts to add a thin coat of white-out and black ink over every other syllable just in case....

A few decades ago, gonzo journalist Raoul Duke wrote, "When the going gets weird, the weird turn pro" (Thompson 8). In the intelligence world, this statement takes on a whole new meaning. When the going gets weird, the weird get preferential treatment by the Pickle Factory. "Here're your documents, kid. Eat 'em up. No one'll ever believe you anyway."

Perhaps Marshall McLuhan summed up the situation best when he wrote, "Only puny secrets need protection. Big discoveries are protected by public incredulity" (*Take Today* 92).

Of course, McLuhan could be wrong.

Please send my Pulitzer in care of the publisher.[6]

Works Cited

McLuhan, Marshall and Barrington Nevitt. *Take Today: The Executive as Dropout*. New York: Harcourt Brace, 1972.

Thompson, Hunter S. *The Great Shark Hunt*. New York: Popular Library, 1979.

---

6   Anyone who receives a visit from Steve Semon in their dreams can feel free to contact me via my email address: rguffey@hotmail.com

STOP FOR TEA IN THE LABYRINTH, PLEASE: A WORD (OR TWO) ABOUT ARCHETYPES, METAPHORS, AND MYTHS

In the introduction to this book, dear reader, you may recall that I compared the field of conspiracy theory to classical mythology; just as myths were employed by ancient man to explain the mysteries of the elements, conspiracy theories are often employed for the same purpose today. To those emotionally or professionally invested in legitimizing various conspiracy theories, this might sound as if I'm implying that the quixotic act of studying conspiracies could be considered ephemeral, transitory, or a fruitless lark. That's true, of course... but only if one considers mythology to be ephemeral, transitory, or a fruitless lark.

I don't. I never have.

Mythology, in all its forms, has guided human history since the beginning of human civilization, in both good ways and bad. When myths take the place of critical thinking and science (i.e., "The sun revolves around the Earth because Yahweh says so") this can be bad. When myths illuminate our existence and reveal aspects of our inner selves not previously explored (as in any of the great myth cycles from *Gilgamesh* to *Beowulf* to *Alice in Wonderland* to the *Oz* books to *Harry Potter*), this can be very, very good.

To the potential reader who picks up this tome on a whim and casually flips through its pages, *Cryptoscatology* might at first seem like a mad, scattershot dash through a mine field of random and chimerical theories with few logical connections between them. But nothing could be further from the truth. And we're all interested in truth, aren't we?

Of course we are.

This book is by no means random. In a way, I see *Cryptoscatology* as an epic novel populated by a cast of classic mythological characters who just so happen to be as real as you or I. All the traditional archetypes—so lovingly delineated by Carl Jung, Joseph Campbell, and other notable scholars of myth over the decades—are embedded in this narrative. You don't have to scratch too far below the metaphorical surface to identify the true personas assembled at the rickety, cluttered table upon which this Mad Tea Party is being held.

At one end of the table sits The Teacher, John Taylor Gatto, while at the exact opposite end sits The Trickster (à la the Coyote from Native American mythology), Robert Dobbs. They're chatting with each other, but neither can understand what the other is saying over the din. A few seats away, sipping some warm black tea, sits The Sage, Manly P. Hall. Nearby sits The Scientist, Charles Fort, as well as The Painter, Max Ernst. Muttering to each other conspiratorially between their hysterical fits of laughter are The Poets, William Shakespeare and André Breton. Over there are The Martyrs, William Morgan and Bishop James Pike. There, surreptitiously poisoning the teapot with some debased form of Lysergic Acid Diethylamide, are The Monsters: José Delgado, Sidney Gottlieb, and Louis Jolyon West. Over there, ignoring the rest of the partygoers as they kiss each other with great passion, are The Young Lovers (à la Harlequin and Columbine): Stephanie Hart, 16, and Nicholas Kunselman, 15. Pouting in the shadows, too aloof for the rest of the crew, stands The Devil wearing his Darth Vader costume purchased on sale for $5.99 through Amazon.com: Lieutenant Colonel Michael Aquino. In the center sits The Great Mother, Mae Brussell, quietly reading the newspaper—in fact, she's reading five of them at the same time. And there's The Innocent, Steve Semon, jotting down detailed notes on Michael Aquino's suspicious appearance. And there's The Double (à la Dr. Jekyll and Mr. Hyde), Sovereign Grand Commander Albert Pike himself, greedily consuming every foodstuff in sight. Right next to him sits The Journalist, Walter Bowart, eyeing the Monsters' poisoned tea and wondering if he shouldn't try a sip—just for research purposes, of course. And there's The Shaman, Philip K. Dick, trapped in the paralyzing grip of yet another mystical vision. Sheepishly ignoring the noise swirling around her is Our Familiar, Gordon W. Cole, half-wishing he was back on The Other Side with his Willow Trees; for some reason he can't fathom, however, he's sitting here at this table with a bunch of horrid freaks he's never seen before. And over there is The False Prophet, Tony Alamo, handcuffed to Samuel P. Huntington (who doesn't even understand how he got here in the first place). Sharing the same small chair: those amorphous Shapeshifters, L. Ron Hubbard and Cordwainer Smith, their eyes locked on the unreachable stars overhead. And in the very last seat: The Magician, Jack Whiteside Parsons, mixing ancient alchemical potions in a steaming beaker, secretly hoping he sets the whole damn table on fire.

Almost none of these archetypes interact with each other, not willingly at least. That's why I had to throw this tea party in the first place. If not for me, these unique eccentrics would never have sat down at the same table together. There's an excellent reason why it took me fourteen years to complete *Cryptoscatology*. Myths don't just sprout from the earth fully grown, and neither do proper archetypes. Myths evolve over time, slowly. I knew I couldn't even begin working on the task until I had assembled all the appropriate guests for this post-postmodern bacchanal; the second the ideal cast was complete, however, it didn't take me long to put all the pieces of the puzzle together. The result you now hold in your hands, along with a cup of curious tasting tea.

What's that, dear reader? You have one last question? Who am *I*, you ask? What archetypal role have I, the author, appropriated for this journey? Well, perhaps, in the end, I must identify myself with The Guide. In the introduction I announced my intention to take you by the hand and lead you through the strange, confusing labyrinth of myths someone (somewhere) decided to christen "Conspiracy Theory." Around one corner you encountered wise men; around another you came face-to-face with minotaurs. Sometimes you were unable to tell the difference between the two. The secret of the labyrinth is that it's not *necessary* to distinguish between them, at least not while you're still trapped inside the maze. Trust me, don't dwell on your bemusement for long. Sort it all out after you've left the light and the darkness of the labyrinth behind. Which, if I'm not mistaken, will be very soon now.

The exit, dear reader, awaits… along with the entrance to yet another labyrinth….

Feel free to take your tea with you.

It's on me.

−Virgil, 9/22/11

Index